Urban Politics

URBAN STUDIES INFORMATION GUIDE SERIES

Series Editor: Thomas P. Murphy, Director, Institute For Urban Studies at the University of Maryland, College Park (on leave) and Director of the Federal Executive Institute, Charlottesville, Virginia

Other books in this series:

SUBURBS—*Edited by Joseph Zikmund II and Deborah Ellis Dennis**

URBAN COMMUNITY—*Edited by Earl J. Reeves and Anthony J. Filipovitch**

URBAN DECISION MAKING: THE BASIS FOR ANALYSIS—*Edited by Mark Drucker**

URBAN EDUCATION—*Edited by George E. Spear and Donald W. Mocker**

URBAN FISCAL POLICY AND ADMINISTRATION—*Edited by John L. Mikesell and Jerry L. McCaffery**

URBAN HOUSING: PUBLIC AND PRIVATE—*Edited by John E. Rouse, Jr.**

URBAN INDICATORS—*Edited by Thomas P. Murphy**

URBAN LAW—*Edited by Robert D. Kline and Thomas P. Murphy**

URBAN MANAGEMENT—*Edited by Bernard Ross**

URBAN PLANNING—*Edited by Ernest R. Alexander, David S. Sawicki, and Anthony J. Catanese**

URBAN POLICY—*Edited by George Taylor and Dennis J. Palumbo**

WOMEN AND URBAN SOCIETY—*Edited by Hasia R. Diner**

*in preparation

The above series is part of the

GALE INFORMATION GUIDE LIBRARY

The Library consists of a number of separate series of guides covering major areas in the social sciences, humanities, and current affairs.

General Editor: Paul Wasserman, Professor and former Dean, School of Library and Information Services, University of Maryland

Managing Editor: Denise Allard Adzigian, Gale Research Company

Urban Politics

A GUIDE TO INFORMATION SOURCES

Volume 1 in the Urban Studies Information Guide Series

Thomas P. Murphy

Director, Institute for Urban Studies
University of Maryland, College Park
(on leave)

and

Director, Federal Executive Institute
Charlottesville, Virginia

Gale Research Company
Book Tower, Detroit, Michigan 48226

Library of Congress Cataloging in Publication Data

Murphy, Thomas P   , 1931-
    Urban politics.

    (Urban studies information guide series; v.1)
    Includes indexes.
    1. Municipal government--United States--Bibliography.
I. Title. II. Series.
Z7165.U5M85   [JS331]   016.352'008'0973   78-54117
ISBN 0-8103-1395-2

VITA

Thomas P. Murphy received degrees in political science from Queen's College (1952), Georgetown University (1960), and St. John's University (1963). He is on leave as the director of the Institute for Urban Studies and a professor of government and politics of the University of Maryland at College Park, and is currently the director of the Federal Executive Institute, Charlottesville, Virginia.

He has published articles in numerous journals including ADMINISTRATIVE SCIENCE QUARTERLY, AMERICAN JOURNAL OF ECONOMICS AND SOCIOL-OGY, CONTEMPORARY REVIEW, THE ECONOMIST, ETHICS, NATURAL RESOURCES JOURNAL, NEW LEADER, PERFORMING ARTS REVIEW, POLITY, PUBLIC ADMINISTRATION REVIEW, REVIEW OF POLITICS, and WESTERN POLITICAL QUARTERLY. His prior book length manuscripts include the following: THE POLITICS OF CONGRESSIONAL COMMITTEES (1977); URBAN POLITICS IN THE SUBURBAN ERA (1976), coauthor; NEW POLITICS CONGRESS (1975); UNIVERSITIES IN THE URBAN CRISIS (1975); ORGANIZING PUBLIC SERVICES IN METROPOLITAN AMERICA (1974), coeditor; GOVERN-MENT MANAGEMENT INTERNSHIPS AND EXECUTIVE DEVELOPMENT (1973); PRESSURES UPON CONGRESS (1972); SCIENCE, GEOPOLITICS, AND FED-ERAL SPENDING (1971); EMERGING PATTERNS IN URBAN ADMINISTRATION (1970), coeditor; and METROPOLITICS AND THE URBAN COUNTY (1970).

A member of the National Academy of Public Administration, he is also past president of the National Association of Schools of Public Affairs and Adminis-tration and current president of the National Center for Public Service Intern-ships.

CONTENTS

PREFACE

This volume represents an attempt to reduce the diverse field of urban politics to manageable proportions. Since substantial citations were deliberately used at the cost of eliminating peripheral items, much selectivity has been required. This is especially true with regard to macro aspects of urban politics, such as the federal and state relationship to urban issues and organization. Since significant oversights may be corrected in a subsequent edition or a related volume in the series, comments are seriously solicited regarding items omitted or not effectively characterized.

In establishing selection priorities, preference has been given to publications since 1970, with some older classics also included. Likewise, preference has been given to the more widely used journals which are readily available in most libraries. For this reason, almost no theses, dissertations, or papers delivered at professional meetings have been included.

Research and editorial assistance was provided at various times by Patricia Atkins, Judy Baer, Arthur Bernstein, Karen Bonner, Vincent Bonventre, David Felzenberg, and Lynn Kaplan. The typing and production work was handled by Joyce Carter, Nancy Dalton, Susan Houchens, Virginia Karas, Nancy Raines, Jan Reed, Barbara Rexrode, and Peggy Williams.

Charlottesville, Virginia

ABBREVIATIONS LIST

ACIR   Advisory Commission on Intergovernmental Relations
ASPA   American Society for Public Administration
CDOs   community decision organizations
COG   council of government
CZMA   Coastal Zone Management Act
EIS   Environmental Impact Statement
FCC   Federal Communications Commission
FHA   Federal Housing Authority
HEW   Department of Health, Education, and Welfare
HUD   Department of Housing and Urban Development
ICMA   International City Management Association
MBO   Management by Objectives
NACO   National Association of Counties
NEPA   National Environmental Policy Act
OD   Organizational Development
OEO   Office of Economic Opportunity
PPB   planning-programming-budgeting
PPBS   planning-programming-budgeting system
PUD   planned unit development
SBA   Small Business Administration
SMSAs   Standard Metropolitan Statistical Areas
UDC   Urban Development Corporation
WSO   West Side Organization

INTRODUCTION

Urban politics is an inherently complex field. This is attributable to its internal dynamics, the shifting populations, the diversity of citizens, the economic disparities (between individuals as well as between governments) that exist within a city and within its metropolitan area, the political party differences, and the different systems that have developed under disparate state governmental frameworks. Since the 1960s even the federal government has become a regular participant in competitive urban politics.

These disparities are reflected in every aspect of urban life in the various metropolitan areas, making it extremely difficult to compare metropolitan areas or cities or suburbs in the various states. Even if it were possible to hold constant the different socioeconomic and political conditions in the various areas of the country, there would still be substantial contrasts generated by the differential impact of the federal system and the unique styles of urban leadership employed.

URBAN POLITICAL LEADERSHIP AND DECISION MAKING

How can one compare New York City's Mayor Abraham Beame with Los Angeles's Thomas Bradley or with Chicago's late mayor, Richard Daley? Each of these mayors demonstrated urban leadership under different circumstances and times, in diverse geographic areas which vary in their heritage, with unequal levels of resources, different structural and organizational arrangements, and under unique state governmental systems. Their constituencies had varying expectations subjecting them to different pressures from the local newspapers and television stations. Even a factor such as the age of the city influenced the options available to these mayors and the ways in which they responded to the urban challenges they faced. Ultimately, for whatever combination of reasons, some experienced greater degrees of success in their leadership roles.

Leadership approaches and the potential decision options depend to a large extent upon the degree of home rule that these cities receive from their respective state governments. New York City and Chicago also have to cope with the impact of being part of an interstate metropolitan area, so that the policies and decisions of other state governments influence what they can and must do. Chicago and Los Angeles each are located in a major county of which they are the predominant component. New York City, on the other hand, has five counties within its borders. All three are surrounded by suburbs that are equally diverse. These three cities and metropolitan areas are the dominant forces in the politics of their states, yet often they are unable to control the policies adopted by the state government because their very size and perceived power often serves to unite the rest of the state against them and their interests.

Contrast this situation with the condition of small but significant cities such as Phoenix, San Antonio, Tulsa, Omaha, Spokane, Wichita, Fort Wayne, Harrisburg, Binghamton, Providence, and St. Petersburg, which dominate their metropolitan areas and are not forced to interact with other state governments. The studies of community power structure have shown that there is no single community power structure for all issues in any one community in any one urban area. However, this tends to be the case, to some degree, in the smaller cities. On the other hand, the mayor of New York, Chicago, or Los Angeles has a greater need to juggle the competing interests of the various influence centers engaged in city politics.

Organizing is much more intense in the major cities because the very magnitude of the area and the difficulty of making one's position known and respected requires the establishment of organizations and even interorganizational alliances to gain a hearing. For example, in the major cities in the 1970s, some of the most critical decisions a mayor has to make deal with public employee unions and their demands. Often the mayor is in a no-win situation. If he yields to the requests of one union, he will trigger more demands from all the other unions. He runs the risk of politically embarrassing strikes and even of creating the political forces his opposition will need to defeat him. However, in many of the smaller cities named, the entire scale of operation is such that municipal employees are not organized in unions, have a deeper community awareness, and therefore take less of an adversary position toward city leadership.

STRUCTURAL AND METROPOLITAN FACTORS

Similarly, the smaller cities are likely to constitute a greater percentage of the metropolitan population so that there is less competition with the suburbs and more opportunity to work out what in effect are metropolitan-wide decisions. For example, New York, Chicago, and Los Angeles contain 48.7, 50.1, and 33.7 percent respectively of the populations of their metropolitan areas. By contrast, San Antonio, Wichita, and Tulsa contain 84.7, 91.5, and 88.9 percent respectively of their metropolitan area's population.

Still another kind of situation exists with regard to the medium-sized cities which have become involved in some of the new city-consolidated governments such as Indianapolis-Marion County, Nashville-Davidson County, Miami-Dade County, and Savannah-Chatham County. These new governments essentially have established a metropolitan governmental system which is coextensive with the political system, so that leadership for the metropolitan area is determined in the city-county elections. Further, the leadership has all the powers of the city as well as of the county in carrying out electoral mandates.

This political system differs substantially from that of major cities which do not control the leadership of their counties. This is the situation in St. Louis, Baltimore, and San Francisco, all of which are city-counties. These cities are all land-locked so that they cannot expand and adapt their geographic borders through annexation. As a consequence, they face the problem of dealing with socioeconomic disparities between central city and suburban areas without one of the mechanisms available to many other central cities.

St. Louis is traditionally dominated by the Democratic party, however predominately Republican St. Louis County now surpasses the city in population as well as in per capita income. In such situations, the city and county often find themselves in competition for new business, federal grant money, and as a place of residence for affluent citizens. The impact of the competition may be detrimental to the metropolitan area as a whole, yet there may be no metropolitan decision-making mechanism which can take account of this factor. Governmental policy is the sum of the decisions of the individual cities and counties constituting the metropolitan area rather than the result of a coordinated and comprehensive approach.

In other words, urban politics does not necessarily mean partisan politics. It can be the competition for "who gets what, when, and how" in terms of competition among central cities, counties, and suburban cities which are becoming increasingly powerful forces in metropolitan politics. On a regional basis, urban politics can involve interregional competition among areas competing for the location of a federal district office, a new industry, a state university, or a federal laboratory.

Because large cities are so much more complex and diverse, they are less likely to have been subjected to reform movements resulting in the establishment of nonpartisan governments and the adoption of city manager forms of government. Not one of the largest cities, for example, has adopted the council-manager plan of government. In this form of government, a professional city manager receives policy guidance from the city council but is responsible for administering the government, subject only to the pleasure of the council. The council is elected on a nonpartisan basis and elects one of its members as the mayor, often on a rotating term basis.

This situation differs drastically from New York or Chicago where a mayor is elected on a partisan basis to be the full-time executive. The big city mayor selects his own professional staff--often including a chief administrative officer (C.A.O.) or deputy mayor who serves as a quasi city manager--to support him in dealing with the city council, which also is elected on a partisan basis. Further, in most large cities there is even a strange twist to the partisan political system. For example, the forty-three-member New York City Council contains five Republicans, one Liberal, and thirty-seven Democrats while the Chicago City Council contains one Republican and forty-nine Democrats. Los Angeles has a fifteen member nonpartisan city council. In circumstances such as this, urban politics often amounts to jockeying among members of the same dominant party or nonpartisan association to see who will emerge as the next candidate for mayor. John Lindsay profited from the competition among Democrats in winning his elections but eventually left the Republican party to become a Democrat.

BLACK AND ETHNIC POLITICS

Urban political leadership in the major cities in the nineteenth and twentieth centuries often was built upon the great numbers of immigrants and the large groups of ethnic voters among them. Energetic local politicians were able to organize these people who needed certain services from the urban government in return for political support. This formed the backbone of machine politics and bossism. Political leaders such as James Michael Curley of Boston, Frank Hague of Jersey City, Carmine DeSapio of New York, Tom Pendergast of Kansas City, Edward Crump of Memphis, Bill Green of Philadelphia, and finally Richard Daley of Chicago in themselves represented a rather comprehensive study of urban politics in its many manifestations. Boss Platt of Rhode Island reversed this process by building a machine on the basis of anti-immigrant sentiment.

Another important aspect of urban politics is the impact of substantial migrations of black citizens from rural to urban areas following World War II. By the 1960s this meant that some cities formerly having a white majority had evolved to the point that they now had a black majority. Gary, Newark, Cleveland, Detroit, Washington, and Atlanta have all elected black mayors. Even in cities not predominantly black, political fortunes improved as the black vote became so large that it could no longer be ignored. Yet Los Angeles showed its distinctiveness in 1974 by having a large white majority and electing a black mayor.

The changing demographic situation caused a political crisis in many cities. In Richmond, Virginia, for example, the obvious trend toward a black majority was strongly resisted by white political forces who arranged an annexation to bring 50,000 additional white citizens from a suburban county into the city in order to thwart the emerging black majority. Without the annexation, Richmond would have been 52 percent black in 1970, whereas with the annexation, the black population dropped to 42 percent of the total.

This case was so blatant that black citizens groups undertook legal action which extended over six years, several times reached the Supreme Court, and finally ended with a Court decision that there was sufficient economic and administrative benefit to the city of Richmond to justify the annexation. However, the Court concluded that the primary motivation had been to prevent black political domination of the city in violation of the 1965 Voting Rights Act. The Court, therefore, ordered Richmond to replace its at-large election system with a district system which would give blacks fair representation on the city council. Clearly, changing demographic situations have provided both challenges and opportunities to urban political leaders.

Most of the cities which have experienced heavy black in-migration and have become subject to black political control are also cities with a large number of white ethnic groups. One reason for the intensity of political competition in such cities is that the ethnic blue collar population and the blacks often are in competition for the same kinds of jobs both in the private sector and in the city and county governments.

THE POLITICS OF PUBLIC POLICY ISSUES

Another extremely sensitive political issue in urban areas relates to control over land, its use, and the zoning regulations. Land owners having friends in the government planning business are often able to secure favorable rezoning of their land which results in substantial profits. The financial implications of zoning decisions are so extreme that land owners and real estate operators are heavily involved in financing the campaigns of urban candidates and bribery has often been used to influence governmental decisions on land use. Community planning has always been controversial, but has become more so in recent years as the planning issues have been sharpened by concern for other values such as environmental quality. Often planning issues find environmentalists and existing neighborhoods pitted against land owners and their politician friends with the newspapers having a field day over the controversy.

Additional policy areas which have generated urban political disputes in recent years have involved the planning and construction of mass transit systems, the location and operation of neighborhood health centers, the creation or abolition of citizen review committees for police departments, the construction of highways, urban renewal projects, and the location of low income housing in or near middle and upper income areas.

URBAN GOVERNMENT AND THE POLITICS OF
THE FEDERAL SYSTEM

The size of the city can affect the need for some form of community decentralization as well as for metropolitan decision making. One of the impacts of the federal poverty program, as well as other Great Society federal programs such as Model Cities, was to reinforce community power bases within the large cities. Through federal programs, these groups were able to secure money which could be used to deal with governmental and community priorities unlikely to be accorded a priority position by the city, county, or state government. These programs not only created new governmental mechanisms in the form of neighborhood city halls in New York City and community service centers in Dayton, but also helped to train a new generation of potential political competitors for the traditional politicians in those cities.

Having attained a seat at the bargaining table, such groups, which in the past had been ignored by urban political power structures, sought to perpetuate their involvement and solidify their ability to negotiate with the other political forces and interest groups in the city. These experiences changed the nature of the demands that were raised by neighborhoods and moreover, the likelihood of their receiving a favorable response.

The fact that cities and counties are creatures of the state government affects their powers and behavior. Frequently state laws and constitutions control such matters as whether elections shall be partisan or nonpartisan, at large or by district, and how often they will occur. States also control many of the financial policies which affect urban politics. For example, in some states, cities and counties are limited to use of the property tax as a source of revenue and in some states there is a statutory limit as to the rate that might be charged. Cities and counties reaching the statutory limitation and still needing additional financing to provide services have been forced to create special districts, which have taxing authority independent of the state, to handle certain functions such as hospitals, sanitary sewers, and recreation areas. Although a means around the financial limitations on the city or county, this usually serves to further fragment governmental decision making in the metropolitan area.

Most states allow their cities to apply for charters which enable them to engage in certain functions under certain special conditions. This provides a measure of home rule which relieves the city of detailed control by the state in most matters. Increasingly, major urban counties also are securing the same kinds of delegated authority from the state, and in many cases are performing the same functions as major cities.

Disputes over these home rule issues, as well as over requests for state aid for various urban functions such as welfare, health, and education, have been factors in disputes over representation in the state legislature. Originally, few states operated on a one man-one vote principle and malapportionment of legislative seats was the rule rather than the exception. This favored the rural areas, for example, in states where the representation scheme in the state senate was to provide each county with one senator, regardless of its population. The Supreme Court ruling in Baker v. Carr in 1962, and in subsequent cases, established the one man-one vote principle and removed much of the rural domination of urban areas. Nevertheless, the spending and policy issues remain and form much of the content of urban politics at the state level.

In summary, urban politics consists of urban conflict, tensions, competitiveness, and intergovernmental decision making based on a wide variety of social, political, and economic differences. The outcomes of these competitions and decisions influences the structure of the governmental systems, the ability of cities, counties, and suburbs to take positive steps in the interest of their constituencies, the approach to metropolitan problems, the functioning of state legislatures, who controls city hall, and what level of citizen participation is encouraged. The whole process is influenced by the governmental environment within any particular metropolitan area. Finally, a strong movement in any one direction is always likely to trigger a countermove in the opposite direction, as some groups find their interests negatively affected by the success of groups with different interests.

Chapter 1

URBAN GOVERNMENTAL STRUCTURE

This chapter includes entries relating to forms and reforms of city government, and mayors, commissioners, and city managers.

1-1   Alford, Robert R. "The Comparative Study of Urban Politics." In UR-
       BAN RESEARCH AND POLICY PLANNING, edited by L.F. Schnore and
       H. Fagin, pp. 263-302. Beverly Hills, Calif.: Sage Publications, 1967.

       See 5-3.

1-2   Almy, Timothy A. "Local-Cosmopolitanism and U.S. City Managers."
       URBAN AFFAIRS QUARTERLY 10 (March 1975): 243-72.

       Attempts to determine the values and beliefs of city managers.
       Almy illustrates that local versus cosmopolitan-oriented city
       managers differ with respect to education, childhood experi-
       ences, and tenure in office. It is noted that the communities
       they manage differ in size and complexity and in the degree
       of public consensus. He concludes that local-cosmopolitan
       orientations have a real influence on managerial role defini-
       tions, a factor largely ignored by earlier studies.

1-3   Baker, John H. URBAN POLITICS IN AMERICA. New York: Charles
       Scribner's Sons, 1971.

       Proposes that the study of urban politics must be both inter-
       disciplinary and intergovernmental. This book deals with the
       politics and structure of urban government and presents an
       overview of the main issues faced in urban politics.

1-4   Banfield, Edward C. BIG CITY POLITICS. New York: Random House,
       1965.

       Compares the political systems of Atlanta, Boston, Detroit, El
       Paso, Los Angeles, Miami, Philadelphia, St. Louis, and Se-
       attle. Bearing in mind that most of the obstacles which block

1

solutions to urban problems are political, Banfield defines the political system of a city as the set of formal and informal arrangements through which officials make decisions. He concludes that while political systems of many large cities are similar, no two are identical.

1-5   _____, ed. URBAN GOVERNMENT: A READER. New York: Free Press, 1969.

A revision of an earlier work; comprises seven essays devoted to urban politics. This volume provides a discussion of different yet interrelated subjects, attempting to explain what actually happens in urban government in terms most widely used by political and other social scientists. Focuses on the processes rather than the techniques of government.

1-6   Banfield, Edward [C.], and Wilson, James Q. CITY POLITICS. Cambridge, Mass.: Harvard University Press, 1963.

Describes the make-up of urban politics in terms of decentralization, local power, interest-group conflict, the electorate, the press, organized labor, and the status of blacks in the city. The authors contend that the middle-class electorate and the federal government will increasingly guide the future trends in city politics and changes in local government.

1-7   Banovetz, James M., ed. MANAGING THE MODERN CITY. Municipal Management Series, vol. 1. Washington, D.C.: International City Management Association, 1971.

Discusses issues involving the management of cities. The city is viewed as a political, social, and economic institution, and as a crucial aspect of society. The book deals with cities as agents of urban government and examines urban management within the context of metropolitan and nonmetropolitan areas.

1-8   Berman, David R., and Merrill, Bruce D. "Citizen Attitudes Towards Municipal Reform Institutions: A Testing of Some Assumptions." WESTERN POLITICAL QUARTERLY 29 (June 1976): 274-83.

A study of citizen evaluation of municipal reforms. The municipal reform model supports the council-manager plan and nonpartisan elections conducted on a city-wide basis. The authors use attitudinal data from Phoenix to examine citizen attitudes toward components of the reform model. Earlier research indicates that low socioeconomic groups favor ward elections. In Phoenix, however, the opposite was found to be true.

1-9   Black, Guy. "The Decentralization of Urban Government: A Systems Approach." In EMERGING PATTERNS IN URBAN ADMINISTRATION, edited by F. Gerald Brown and Thomas P. Murphy, pp. 222-47. Lexington, Mass.: Lexington Books, 1970.

See 6-18a.

1-10 Bollens, John C., and Ries, John C. THE CITY MANAGER PROFESSION: MYTHS AND REALITIES. International City Management Profession Series, no. 1. Washington, D.C.: Public Administration Service, 1969.

Highlights the urban political environment of city manager government and discusses the role of the city manager as administrator and politician.

1-11 BOOK OF THE STATES. Chicago: Council of State Governments, 1935-- . Biennial.

Provides a source of information on the structures, working procedures, financing, and functional activities of state governments. It deals with the legislative, executive, and judicial branches of state governments and their intergovernmental relations including constitutions and elections, legislatures and legislation, administrative organization, finance, major state services, and the judiciary.

1-12 Booth, David A. "Council-Manager Government in Small Cities." PUBLIC MANAGEMENT 55 (November 1973): 7-9.

A study of the council-manager form of government in small cities. Booth observes that managers in small cities are often understaffed, required to hold multiple positions and frequently overworked. He concludes that the main problems existing in small city management include a lack of professionalism, inefficiency resulting from managers' multiple roles, and excessive limitations on managers.

1-13 Boynton, Robert Paul, and Wright, Deil S. "Mayor-Manager Relationships in Large Council-Manager Cities: A Reinterpretation." PUBLIC ADMINISTRATION REVIEW 31 (January-February 1971): 28-36.

Refutes studies presenting stereotyped and erroneous pictures of the role of city managers. The authors administered a questionnaire to forty-five council-manager cities with populations over 100,000 to determine the interrelationships of mayors and managers and some perceptions of the role of the manager in local government. The questionnaire focused on the electoral process, roles and characteristics of the council, budget processes, the use of boards and commissions, intergovernmental relations and the administration of public policies. They conclude that managers have become increasingly more involved in policy initiation and policy making, as a result of changing

community needs more than manager preferences. Managers
in large cities appear to be performing more like strong mayors
than the traditional stereotype of a city manager.

1-14   Bresnick, David. "Decentralizing the City: Who Gets Control?" NA-
TIONAL CIVIC REVIEW 62 (October 1973): 486-90.

Examines decentralization in New York City discussing the
major political actors and the competing plans. Those evaluated are former Mayor Lindsay, the borough presidents, former
Governor Nelson A. Rockefeller, the Scott Commission, and
New York City's ethnic groups. The author concludes that
in the forseeable future, New York and other cities will be
incorporated more fully into the state political systems.

1-15   Bromage, Arthur W. URBAN POLICY MAKING: THE COUNCIL-
MANAGER PARTNERSHIP. Chicago: Public Administration Service,
1970.

Discusses the various roles that a city manager plays, including
policy-making duties, relations with the city council, and the
manager's role in budget making. The stereotypical image of
a city manager who resides above political in-fighting and ad-
ministers the affairs of the city is shown to be unrealistic.
Powers that can be exercised by the manager, as well as
limitations to his power, are discussed.

1-16   Brown, F. Gerald, and Murphy, Thomas P., eds. EMERGING PAT-
TERNS IN URBAN ADMINISTRATION. Lexington, Mass.: Lexington
Books, 1970.

See 6-18a.

1-17   Cole, Richard L. "The Urban Policy Process: A Note on Structural and
Regional Influences." SOCIAL SCIENCE QUARTERLY 52 (December
1971): 646-55.

An analysis of the effect of local political structure and region on the policy process of cities with a population greater
than 50,000. The conclusions are: (1) political structure is
a very weak predictor of the three selected policy outputs;
(2) region is a more significant predictor of urban policy than
political structure, but its total impact is slight, and additional factors must be considered to construct a complete model of
the urban policy process; and (3) a model of the urban policy
process will need to be as intricate as the process it attempts
to depict.

1-18   Costello, Timothy. "The Change Process in Municipal Government."
In EMERGING PATTERNS IN URBAN ADMINISTRATION, edited by F.

Gerald Brown and Thomas P. Murphy, pp. 13-33. Lexington, Mass.: Lexington Books, 1970.

See 6-18a.

1-19 Costikyan, Edward N., and Lehman, Maxwell. RESTRUCTURING THE GOVERNMENT OF NEW YORK CITY: REPORT OF THE SCOTT COMMISSION TASK FORCE ON JURISDICTION AND STRUCTURE. New York: Praeger Publishers, 1972.

See 6-25.

1-20 Cunningham, James V., et al. "The Pittsburgh Atlas Program: Test Project for Neighborhoods." NATIONAL CIVIC REVIEW 65 (June 1976): 284-89.

Examines Pittsburgh's progress toward establishing a formal role for neighborhood groups. Citizens, planners, and researchers in Pittsburgh are developing improved community organizational techniques and a computerized neighborhood information center. Community advisory boards will be established to advise the council and the mayor and neighborhood boundaries will be determined by residents' perception.

1-21 Dean, John. THE MAKING OF A BLACK MAYOR. Washington, D.C.: Joint Center for Political Studies, 1973.

A detailed account of the successful mayoral campaign of Algernon (Jay) Cooper, Jr., a black man, of Pritchard, Alabama, by his campaign manager. Includes general campaign planning information such as demographics, registration and voting data, and strategies for the run-off, which was necessary in this case.

1-22 East, John Porter. COUNCIL-MANAGER GOVERNMENT: THE POLITICAL THOUGHT OF ITS FOUNDER, RICHARD S. CHILDS. Chapel Hill: University of North Carolina Press, 1965.

A consideration of the council-manager form of government and its father, reformer and a good government advocate, Richard S. Childs. Childs's philosophy sprang from pragmatism, in general, and progressivism, in particular, and reached the apex of its effect on urban governmental structure and politics in the 1890-1900 decade. Influential in the reforms in New York, he led valiant battles against the Tammany Hall machine.

1-23 Eddy, William B., and Murphy, Thomas P. "Applied Behavioral Science in Local Governments." In THE HUMAN RESOURCES OF CITY GOVERNMENTS, edited by Charles H. Levine. Vol. 13, Urban Affairs Annual Review. Beverly Hills, Calif.: Sage Publications, 1977.

Covers attempts by urban managers to solve the problems of
communities. They have been thwarted by a variety of con-
textual factors--including shortages of resources, political
forces, and the sheer complexity and multiplicity of the problems. Over the past decade, however, there has been a
growing consensus that traditional managerial approaches may
not be adequate for effective problem solving.

OD is catching on in urban management but will not reach
full bloom until urban managers have a clearer understanding
of how OD can help meet strongly felt needs. The kinds of
behavioral science approaches present in the OD movement,
as well as those in the PPBS and MBO experiments, should
equip urban managers with tools for making effective use of
such strategies. The forces that make OD and the applied
sciences work or fail are not unique to urban governance.

1-24 Eddy, W[illiam].B., and Saunders, R.J. "Applied Behavior Science in
Urban Administrative/Political Systems." PUBLIC ADMINISTRATION RE-
VIEW 32 (January-February 1972): 11-16.

Argues that the traditional bureaucratic model for governmental
organization is too rigid, closed, hierarchial, and controlled
to deal effectively with urban problems. The authors discuss
applying behavior science to urban agencies where the realities
of political/administrative problems are encountered.

1-25 Elazar, Daniel J. THE POLITICS OF BELLEVILLE: A PROFILE OF THE
CIVIL COMMUNITY. Philadelphia: Temple University, 1971.

An account of the political and governmental structure of
Belleville, Missouri. Elazar presents a "political map" which
addresses urban politics and a broad spectrum of geographic,
historical, cultural, and socioeconomic factors. The concept
of a "civil community" describes how an urban area may ex-
tend beyond its political and geographical boundaries. (See
also 7-45.)

1-26 Eldredge, H. Wentworth, ed. WORLD CAPITALS: TOWARD GUIDED
URBANIZATION. Garden City, N.Y.: Anchor Press-Doubleday, 1975.

See 4-43a.

1-27 Elkin, Stephen L. "Comparative Urban Politics and Interorganizational
Behavior." POLICY AND POLITICS 2 (Spring 1974): 289-308.

Examines some problems of comparative urban political inquiry
and argues for the application of organization theory based
upon the analysis of interorganizational behavior. The conceptual tools for this analysis permit a consideration of the most
important features of comparative urban politics: (1) variation
in patterns of governance, and (2) openness of local arenas.

1-28   Fainstein, Susan S., and Fainstein, Norman I. "Local Control as So-
       cial Reform: Planning for Big Cities in the Seventies." JOURNAL OF
       THE AMERICAN INSTITUTE OF PLANNERS 42 (July 1976): 275-85.

       See 6-36.

1-29   Fox, Douglas M. THE POLITICS OF CITY AND STATE BUREAUCRACY.
       Pacific Palisades, Calif.: Goodyear, 1974.

       A study of bureaucratic machinery, including the growing power
       of workers, definition of bureaucracy, methods to increase citi-
       zen control of the bureaucracy, administrative agencies, legis-
       latures and courts, political parties, interest groups and unions,
       the media, intergovernmental relations, and budgeting.

1-30   Francois, Francis B. "The Dilemma of Regionalism for Local Elected Of-
       ficials." PUBLIC MANAGEMENT 56 (January 1974): 8-10.

       See 6-42.

1-31   Greenstone, J. David, and Peterson, Paul E. RACE AND AUTHORITY
       IN URBAN POLITICS: COMMUNITY PARTICIPATION AND THE WAR
       ON POVERTY. New York: Russell Sage Foundation, 1973.

       See 4-65.

1-32   Greer, Ann L. THE MAYOR'S MANDATE: MUNICIPAL STATECRAFT
       AND POLITICAL TRUST. Cambridge, Mass.: Schenkman Publishing
       Co., 1974.

       A study of the role of mayor. According to the author, the
       mayor views his role as a coordinator who sees potential for
       mutually profitable cooperation, and for multiple payoffs. He
       may facilitate that cooperation without making political choices
       which benefit one party at the expense of others. The bene-
       fits of unrealized cooperation may increase the productivity of
       available resources, thus creating political power in the pro-
       cess.

1-33   Hahn, Harlan. "Reassessing and Revitalizing Urban Politics: Some
       Goals and Proposals." In his PEOPLE AND POLITICS IN URBAN SO-
       CIETY, pp. 11-37. Beverly Hills, Calif.: Sage Publications, 1972.

       Argues that since the game of urban politics may be played
       by a disparate set of contestants within a sharply confined
       arena, it ought to be a lively sport, engaging the time and
       energy of a large number of participants and perhaps even
       outrivaling other political contests as a source of interest and
       attention. Unfortunately, many communities do not realize
       such a description of urban politics. A need for increased
       experimentation, both in the design of political institutions

and in the study of urban politics is apparent. Also, political structures are needed that would enhance the participation of the local citizenry.

1-34   Haider, Donald. "The Political Economy of Decentralization." AMERI-CAN BEHAVIORAL SCIENTIST 15 (September/October 1971): 108-29.

Discussion of political power as an illusive and often fleeting phenomenon. It is often assumed that modern urban systems are centralized, however, Haider sees decentralization occurring gradually in some major cities; not solely or even mainly in terms of formal transfers of authority and power from higher levels to lower ones, but more in terms of flexibility, "informative" decentralization, negotiated arrangements, bargaining, and accommodations by bureaucracies to pressures from the mayor and from organized community groups. No single factor, he concludes, seems more important at this time in influencing the direction and extent of municipal decentralization than budgetary exigencies. The cost of decentralization is a major issue, given the state of the economy.

1-35   Hays, Samuel P. "The Changing Political Structure of the City in Industrial America." JOURNAL OF URBAN HISTORY 1 (November 1974): 6-38.

Develops a specific conceptual framework for comprehending the evolution of the city since the mid-nineteenth century. Influenced heavily by works in geography and sociology, this essay describes urban development as a constant tension between contrifugal and centripetal tendencies, between social differentiation and social integration. The city attempts to establish smaller contexts for domestic, religious, academic, and recreational activities, and to discipline and link the productive and occupational activities of man into more highly organized systems.

1-36   Hentoff, Nat. A POLITICAL LIFE: THE EDUCATION OF JOHN V. LINDSAY. New York: Alfred A. Knopf, 1969.

A biography of the former mayor of New York City, John Lindsay, and a study of a city administration in process. Hentoff discusses the development of Lindsay the man as well as Lindsay the politician. Both Lindsay and the author believe that U.S. cities are governable and that progress can be made; the real issue being whether cities will get the funds they need to radically attack the decay of their institutions and the myriad urban ills. Accordingly, the book emphasizes the disparity between the needs of cities and their resources.

1-37 "Improving County Government." PUBLIC MANAGEMENT 53 (April 1971): entire issue.

See 6-61.

1-38 Jones, Victor. "New Local Strategies." NATIONAL CIVIC REVIEW 59 (March 1970): 127-34.

Discusses the fear that city government and the associated local political system will be converted into an "engine to stifle dissent and manage conformity." Jones maintains that we cannot put the disquietude of the past decade to rest and return to the status quo. He believes that unless we have a revolution in the old-fashioned sense, institutional changes will occur slowly.

1-39 Kammerer, Gladys M., et al. THE URBAN POLITICAL COMMUNITY. Boston: Houghton Mifflin, 1963.

Presents the political profiles of eight communities in Florida ranging in population from 5,000 to 6,000 in order to examine council-manager tenure and turnover in relation to community political stability. The conclusions of the authors are as follows: (1) manager tenure and turnover are positively related to power exchanges; (2) manager tenure tends to be longer in communities that have a monopolistic style of politics than in communities that have a competitive style of politics; (3) local-amateur city managers have a longer average tenure than outside professional managers; (4) although a high rate of population growth is related to a shortening of manager tenure, population growth is not a sufficient explanation of manager tenure; and (5) separately elected mayors are a political hazard to managers.

1-40 Kaufman, Nathan B. "The Mayor in Suburbia." PUBLIC MANAGEMENT 55 (June 1973): 20-21.

A discussion of a mayor's responsibilities and relationship with the city manager by the mayor of University City, Missouri. The mayor defines his responsibilities as including the following: the maintenance of a high level of municipal services, the identification of local problems, and the promotion of efforts to apply new technology to community needs. The mayor must be able to analyze issues and must be sensitive to the impact of issues on different segments of the city. He must be able to locate the power centers and to get legislation passed in the city council.

1-41 Kneier, Charles M. CITY GOVERNMENT IN THE U.S. 3d ed. New York: Harper and Row, 1957.

A comprehensive textbook providing a broad overview of the

varieties of political and governmental structures in U.S. cities. Although dated, this book does provide basic information which focuses upon the ways in which urban administrators and politicians have met, or have failed to meet, the challenges resulting from urbanism.

1-42   Kotter, John P., and Lawrence, Paul R. MAYORS IN ACTION. New York: John Wiley & Sons, 1974.

The result of an exploratory, interdisciplinary, and comparative examination of the behavior of twenty mayors and their administrations during the 1960s. The purpose of the study was to improve current understanding of twentieth-century mayors in large- and moderate-sized U.S. cities and to expand the knowledge of the processes by which they attempt to govern our urban areas. The six cities and mayors interviewed and studied were Ivan Allen, Jr., of Atlanta; Ralph Locher of Cleveland; Erik Jonsson of Dallas; H. Roe Bartle of Kansas City, Missouri; Richard Lee of New Haven; and Victor H. Schiro of New Orleans.

1-43   League of Women Voters Education Fund. SUPER CITY/HOMETOWN, U.S.A.: PROPSECTS FOR TWO-TIER GOVERNMENT. New York: Praeger Publishers, 1974.

An assessment of a reform concept combing a metropolitan area-wide government with a return to grass roots control, popularly known as "two-tier government." The project had four major goals: (1) to provide citizens with suggestions of what they can do to change the policy-making process; (2) to review the structural and administrative responses of urban governments to cope with regional and neighborhood problems; (3) to compile opinions from a cross-section of citizen organization leaders and public officials about how cities and counties respond to contemporary problems, and to get their reactions to proposals for changing the system; and (4) to review the way metropolitan areas are separated into cities and counties to facilitate predictions about the possibility of balancing regional and local needs.

1-44   Levine, Charles H. RACIAL CONFLICT AND THE AMERICAN MAYOR. Lexington, Mass.: Lexington Books, 1974.

See 4-89b.

1-45   Lewis, Eugene. THE URBAN POLITICAL SYSTEM. Hinsdale, Colo.: Dryden Press, 1973.

Examines significant aspects of the urban political system. The author argues that a fundamental shift has occurred in the locus of power within the system, particularly in terms of the allocation of scarce public resources which has become an attribute of functionally defined bureaucracies and of the constituency and clientele groups with which they are related. Part 3, "The Structure of Political Power in Urban Systems," is of particular interest to students of urban politics.

1-46   LOCAL CHIEF EXECUTIVES' PERCEPTIONS OF POLICY-MAKING AND MANAGEMENT NEEDS. Vol. 1. Washington, D.C.: Department of Housing and Urban Development, Office of Policy Development and Research, February 1975.

Focuses on mayors, councilmen, county executives and county commissioners and how they perceive their policy-making and management needs. Over 400 documents were reviewed and excerpted in order to determine the views of local chief executives. Their major problem is the need to deal with many problems simultaneously. Policy-making and management priorities are not ranked but several areas of concern are delineated: intergovernmental relations, citizen participation, reorganization, policy-making processes, management techniques, personnel and technical assistance. A series of recommended actions is proposed.

1-47   Loveridge, Ronald O. CITY MANAGERS IN LEGISLATIVE POLITICS. Indianapolis: Bobbs-Merrill, 1971.

Examines the city manager's relation to the process of policy making and his role in conflict management. The author argues that the policy views and activities of the city manager largely determine who benefits in a community.

1-48   Mardis, Walter E., and Heisel, W. Donald. "When the Manager Plan Comes to Town." NATION'S CITIES 9 (May 1971): 20-23.

Presents the results of a survey, conducted by the authors in cities having populations over 5,000, indicating that the council-manager plan can yield favorable results in small- and medium-sized cities. Changes in administrative structure and procedures are almost inevitable. Further, the fact that most cities retained the council-manager plan once they adopted it indicates public satisfaction with it.

1-49   Martin, Roscoe C. METROPOLIS IN TRANSITION: LOCAL GOVERNMENT ADAPTATION TO CHANGING URBAN NEEDS. Washington, D.C.: Government Printing Office, 1963.

See 6-71a.

1-50   Mayer, A. "A New Level of Local Government is Struggling to Be Born." CITY 5 (March-April 1971): 60-64.

Argues that there must be an administrative and political decentralization of certain kinds of decisions and operations. Those that are purely local in character or impact must devolve from the city-hall level to subcity level. Also, there must be decentralization of activities and expertise into the localities.

1-51 Miles, C.R. "The Working Relationship Between Mayors and Administrators." PUBLIC MANAGEMENT 55 (June 1973): 13-19.

A discussion of the need for cooperation between mayor and city administrator by the city administrator of Adrian, Michigan. It is relatively easy for a mayor to replace an ineffective administrator, but the problem is more complex when the mayor is not doing a quality job. In that case, the city council, the administrator, and a variety of community interest groups must try to fill the void.

1-52 Morgan, David R., and Kirkpatrick, Samuel A., eds. URBAN POLITICAL ANALYSIS: A SYSTEMS APPROACH. New York: Free Press, 1972.

See 3-64.

1-53 Nordlinger, Eric A. "The Manager, the Community, and the Mayor." In his DECENTRALIZING THE CITY: A STUDY OF BOSTON'S LITTLE CITY HALLS, pp. 239-81. Cambridge: M.I.T. Press, 1972.

Examines the many roles of the city manager, four of which are organizational catalyst, communicational catalyst, facilitator of community participation, and issues advocate.

1-54 O'Dell, Doyal. "The Structure of Metropolitan Political Systems: A Conceptual Model." THE WESTERN POLITICAL QUARTERLY 26 (March 1973): 64-82.

Presents a model for classifying individual metropolitan political systems according to significant structural features. The model is founded upon the assumption that political structures have an effect on the performance of political functions.

1-55 Pope, H.G. "What's Ahead for Local Government Structure?" PUBLIC MANAGEMENT, July 1971, pp. 28-30.

Argues that future local government structure will not merely be an extension of past and present structures, but will be increasingly determined by the decisions and actions of federal and state establishments and by patterns of financing.

1-56 Pressman, Jeffrey L. "Federal Programs and Political Development in Cities." In IMPROVING THE QUALITY OF URBAN MANAGEMENT, edited by Willis D. Hawley and David Rogers, pp. 583-605. Beverly Hills, Calif.: Sage Publications, 1974.

See 7-89.

1-57 _____. "Preconditions of Mayoral Leadership." THE AMERICAN POLITICAL SCIENCE REVIEW 66 (June 1972): 511-24.

See 2-41.

1-58 Reuss, Henry S. REVENUE-SHARING: CRUTCH OR CATALYST FOR STATE AND LOCAL GOVERNMENTS. New York: Praeger Publishers, 1970.

See 7-92.

1-59 Robson, William A., and Regan, D.E., eds. GREAT CITIES OF THE WORLD. Vols. 1 and 2, 3d ed. London: George Allen and Unwin; Beverly Hills, Calif.: Sage Publications, 1972.

A monumental analysis of local governments around the world. It includes Chicago, Los Angeles, New York, and twenty-four cities outside the United States, including Amsterdam, Belgrade, Birmingham, Buenos Aires, Cairo, Calcutta, Copenhagen, Delhi, Ibadan, Johannesburg, London, Manila, Mexico City, Montreal, Osaka, Paris, Pretoria, Rio de Janeiro, Rome, Stockholm, Sydney, Tokyo, Toronto, and Warsaw.

1-60 Rogers, David. THE MANAGEMENT OF BIG CITIES: INTEREST GROUPS AND SOCIAL CHANGE STRATEGIES. Beverly Hills, Calif.: Sage Publications, 1971.

Demonstrates how the political and organizational ecology of cities affects their capacity to absorb the impact of rapid change. The author examines urban power structures, the organization and functioning of city government, the relations of major interest groups and coalitions within cities, inter-cities' relations and cities' relations with state and federal agencies. Rogers argues that cities lack the power to implement programs or policies.

1-61 Ruchelman, Leonard I., ed. BIG CITY MAYORS: THE CRISIS IN UR-BAN POLITICS. Bloomington: Indiana University Press, 1969.

Examines the various roles played by the mayors of large American cities and argues that a mayor cannot afford to emphasize any one role to the point of ignoring another. In addition to his ceremonial roles, the mayor functions as chief executive of the city, chief legislator, and chief of the city's political party.

1-62 Savitch, H.V., and Adler, Madeline. "Decentralization at the Grass Roots: Political Innovation in New York City and London." SAGE PROFESSIONAL PAPERS IN ADMINISTRATIVE AND POLICY STUDIES 2, 03-018. Beverly Hills, Calif. and London: Sage Publications, 1974.

See 3-83.

1-63 Sayre, Wallace S. "The Mayor." In AGENDA FOR A CITY: ISSUES CONFRONTING NEW YORK, edited by Lyle C. Fitch and Annamarie H. Walsh, pp. 563-601. Beverly Hills, Calif.: Sage Publications, 1970.

Part of a volume including in-depth surveys of policy problems confronting New York City. The author examines the various roles played by a mayor of the nation's largest city. The chapter is divided into two main parts: "The Mayor and His Constituencies," considering parties and the city electorates, the bureaucracies, the interest groups, the communication media, the state government, and the national government; "Strengthening the Mayor," investigating ways in which the political system can be reformed to provide more resources for dealing with the multiple and varied constituencies in New York City.

1-64 Schmandt, Henry J. "Decentralization: A Structural Imperative." In NEIGHBORHOOD CONTROL IN THE 1970S, edited by H. George Frederickson, pp. 17-35. New York: Chandler Publishing Co., 1973.

See 3-85.

1-65 Shalala, Donna E. NEIGHBORHOOD GOVERNANCE: PROPOSALS AND ISSUES. New York: American Jewish Committee, 1971.

A justification of the formal neighborhood government and a description of the assignment of power and responsibility and the roles of all levels of government.

1-66 _____. "Neighborhood Government: Has the Time Come?" NATION-AL CIVIC REVIEW 61 (April 1972): 185-89.

Examines various alternatives to the present structure of governments in metropolitan areas. Shalala discusses decentralization, centralization, and neighborhood government and believes that neighborhood government can be useful only when resources have been redirected and reallocated, when the state government is socially conscious, when the regional governmental system is well planned, and when the federal government is willing and eager to help bring about changes.

1-67 Shalala, Donna [E.], and Merget, Astrid. "The Decentralization Approach." In ORGANIZING PUBLIC SERVICES IN METROPOLITAN

AMERICA, edited by Thomas P. Murphy and Charles Warren, pp. 139-88. Lexington, Mass.: Lexington Books, 1974.

A detailed consideration of the opportunities and difficulties presented by various decentralization approaches. See 6-74f.

1-68 Stenberg, Carl W. "Decentralization and the City." In MUNICIPAL YEARBOOK 1972, pp. 88-96. Washington, D.C.: International City Management Association, 1972.

See 3-91.

1-69 Stillman, Richard J. THE RISE OF THE CITY MANAGER: A PUBLIC PROFESSIONAL IN LOCAL GOVERNMENT. Albuquerque: University of New Mexico Press, 1974.

Examines the role of the city manager in policy making. Chapter 1 traces the development of the city manager and chapters 2 and 3 examine the changes in the ideologies and leadership styles of its managers. Chapter 4 looks at some of today's city managers and compares them with managers before World War II. Chapter 5 compares the city manager with career diplomats and public school superintendents. The book concludes with an overall evaluation of the professional city manager.

1-70 Teaford, Jon C. THE MUNICIPAL REVOLUTION IN AMERICA; ORIGINS OF MODERN URBAN GOVERNMENT, 1650-1825. Chicago: University of Chicago Press, 1975.

Studies the transformation in the political structure, function, and external relationships of the American municipality from 1650 to 1825. During those years Americans discarded the model of urban government inherited from medieval Europe. The study focuses upon the forces which molded the municipal corporation as an institution of Western life.

1-71 Turner, E. Robert. "Large Cities and Council-Manager Government." VIRGINIA TOWN AND CITY 9 (April 1974): 13, 15.

A discussion of the excitement and rewards of the professional city manager by the former city manager of Cincinnati and former president of ICMA. He believes that council-manager government survives in the big cities because city managers have been willing to face challenges with integrity. Rochester, New York, and San Diego, California, are cited as illustrations of the strength of council-manager government.

1-72 U.S. Bureau of the Census. CENSUS OF GOVERNMENTS: 1962. Washington, D.C.: Government Printing Office, every 5 years.

Conducted at five-year intervals, the census covers four major fields: governmental organization, taxable property values, public employment, and governmental finances. Individual state summaries are divided into five basic types of local government: counties, municipalities, townships, school districts, and special districts. Includes each of the fifty states plus the District of Columbia and Puerto Rico.

1-73   Walsh, Annamarie Hauck. THE URBAN CHALLENGE TO GOVERN-MENT. New York: Praeger Publishers, 1969.

The summary volume of a series of studies on thirteen urban areas outside the United States by a team of scholars under a Ford Foundation grant. Integrates the findings of volumes on Calcutta, Casablanca, Davao, Karachi, Lagos, Leningrad, Lima, Lodz, Paris, Stockholm, Toronto, Valencia, and Zagreb.

1-74   Washington, R.O. "The Politicization of School Decentralization in New York City." URBAN EDUCATION 8 (October 1973): 223-30.

See 5-158.

1-75   Wickwar, William H. POLITICAL THEORY OF LOCAL GOVERNMENT. Columbia: University of South Carolina Press, 1970.

Views local government as an essential link between the central government and the people. Since local government is essentially a creature of law, Wickwar concludes that its political theory has largely been identical with its legal philosophy.

1-76   Wolfinger, Raymond E., and Field, John O. "Political Ethos and the Structure of City Government." AMERICAN POLITICAL SCIENCE REVIEW 60 (June 1966): 306-26.

A case study correlating the two major ethos and the two types of city governments in existence today. The two types of ethics studies include the "public-regardingness" ethic, which was defined by Banfield and Wilson as the municipal reform movement which is popular because of efficiency, impartiality and planning and the "private-regardingness" ethic, which was defined as identifying with the ward or neighborhood rather than the city as a whole. The two ethos that are studied are called the "middle class" ethos, which leans toward an efficient, honest, and impartial government, and the "immigrant" ethos, which is more interested in the material benefits that the government can bestow. The authors studied the governments of 309 major incorporated cities in the United States. The major hypothesis is that the cities with a high percentage of immigrants have a tendency to select a government with a private-regardingness ethic, and vice versa. The result did not support the hypothesis. In most cases there was a negative correlation. The cities with a high immigrant percentage tended to have the characteristics of a public-regardingness ethic. The authors then attempt to explain the results.

1-77   Wright, Deil S. "Intergovernmental Relation in Large Council Managers Cities." AMERICAN POLITICS QUARTERLY 1 (April 1973): 151-87.

See 7-115.

1-78   Yates, Douglas. NEIGHBORHOOD DEMOCRACY. Lexington, Mass.: Heath and Co., 1973.

An examination of the impacts and politics of decentralization experiments in urban government. Yates discusses how neighborhood democracy could be used as a tool to fight the "urban crisis." He studies seven experiments performed in New York and New Haven and tests four hypotheses about decentralization. Yates examines the concepts of internal democracy, leadership styles, and policy efficacy. He then attempts to explain patterns of neighborhood democracy and discusses the political economy of decentralization and the future of neighborhood government.

1-79   _____. "Service Delivery and the Urban Political Order." In IMPROVING THE QUALITY OF URBAN MANAGEMENT, edited by Willis D. Hawley and David Rogers, pp. 213-40. Beverly Hills, Calif.: Sage Publications, 1974.

Examines the issue of fragmentation in intergovernmental policy making as it applies to the urban manager. The problem of intergovernmental fragmentation in service delivery will not diminish, the author contends, unless new programs, funding levels, and administrative standards and procedures are clearly articulated. He concludes that a structural solution to the urban service delivery problem is to establish an administrative system for coordinated decision making on urban issues in the Congress, in the executive branch, and in state government, and to build a new communications system from the top down.

1-80   Yin, Robert K., and Yates, Douglas. STREET-LEVEL GOVERNMENTS. Lexington, Mass.: Lexington Books, 1975.

Assesses decentralization innovations of the last ten years. The authors argue that urban services operate at the street level and deal with tangible problems and individual residents, and that urban decentralization is based on the notion that urban services are the product of policy making at its point of contact. They observe that the different urban services are indeed differently constituted and that the server-served relationship has somewhat different traditions and ground rules in such services as police protection, education, and health. Consequently, problems of service delivery at the street level are not the problems of a single government structure, but are those of different street-level governments.

1-81   Zimmerman, Joseph F.   THE FEDERATED CITY: COMMUNITY CONTROL IN LARGE CITIES.   New York: St. Martin's Press, 1973.

See 3-104.

Chapter 2
POLITICAL LEADERSHIP AND POLITICAL PARTIES

This chapter includes entries relating to bossism, machine politics, and reformers; leadership models and management of conflict; and political parties and campaigns.

2-1   Adrian, C[harles].R., and Williams, O.P. FOUR CITIES. Philadelphia: University of Pennsylvania Press, 1963.

      Compares and analyzes through statistical controls variations in public policy in four communities of similar size over time. The main conclusion is that the loci of leadership are directly related to the form of political structure.

2-2   Alford, Robert R. "The Comparative Study of Urban Politics." In URBAN RESEARCH AND POLICY PLANNING, edited by L.F. Schnore and H. Fagin, pp. 263–302. Beverly Hills, Calif.: Sage Publications, 1967.

      See 5-3.

2-2a   Allen, Ivan, Jr. MAYOR: NOTES ON THE SIXTIES. New York: Simon & Schuster, 1971.

      An analysis of the politics and administration of Atlanta in the 1960s as recounted by the two-term mayor of the city. The major programs discussed are school construction, freeways, urban renewal, rapid transit, and the new stadium. Candid views are presented of the problems involved in managing and governing a large city with emphasis on the racial issue. During his second term the mayor organizes the business community to cooperate in making Atlanta a better place to live. Many successful programs were instituted and completed in the second term by this coalition of business and political leaders.

2-3   Banfield, Edward C. POLITICAL INFLUENCE. New York: Free Press, 1961.

      Considers who has influence and who is subjected to it. Ban-

field also discusses how influence works and the terms upon
which it is expended. He gives particular emphasis to the
roles of individuals and the characteristics of those roles and
cautions against extrapolation of the results of his study to
all metropolitan areas, as it is solely an attempt to set a basis
for systematic comparative analysis.

2-3a   Banovetz, James M., et al. "Leadership Styles and Strategies." In
MANAGING THE MODERN CITY, edited by James M. Banovetz, pp. 108-
33. Washington, D.C.: International City Management Association, 1971.

Discusses city managers roles with respect to their subordinates,
the council, neighboring governments, interest groups and
friends and critics. The concept of leadership and its pre-
requisites are not clearly defined. The authors present a
definition of leadership and examine the leadership environment of the administration focusing on the nature of administrative leadership in both an organizational and political context. Asserting that some leadership styles can be learned,
the authors discuss the development of leadership capacities
by examining motivation, leadership styles, and the resources
of leadership. The strategies and tactics of leadership are
also discussed.

2-3b   Bean, Walter. BOSS RUEF'S SAN FRANCISCO, THE STORY OF THE
UNION LABOR PARTY, BIG BUSINESS, AND THE GRAFT PROSECU-
TION. Berkeley, and Los Angeles: University of California Press, 1952.

The story of how a San Francisco lawyer, at the turn of the
century, managed to control almost every office in the city
government through graft and corruption. Boss Ruef manipu-
lated the Union Labor party and his handpicked mayor for personal advantage in dealing with local industry and gaining
control over the local government. Ultimately Ruef was con-
victed and incarcerated for extortion and bribery.

2-4   Biddle, William W. THE CULTIVATION OF COMMUNITY LEADERS;
UP FROM THE GRASS ROOTS. New York: Harper and Row, 1953.

Addresses the problem of finding community leaders. Biddle
examines the role of universities and colleges in the search
for community leadership and discusses the training of participant leaders, future citizens, and community educators.

2-5   Bresnick, David. "Decentralizing the City: Who Gets Control?" NA-
TIONAL CIVIC REVIEW 62 (October 1973): 486-90.

See 1-14.

2-6   Brown, Andrew Theodore. THE POLITICS OF REFORM: KANSAS CITY

1925-1950. Boston: Houghton Mifflin, 1954.

A study of the history of municipal government in Kansas City, Missouri, from 1925 to 1950, during which the city was administered under the council-manager form of government. Brown discusses machine politics in Kansas City, the politics of nonpartisanship in local elections, and reform and the responsibilities of power. The author points out that the most striking aspect of reform government in Kansas City has been its longevity.

2-7   Caro, Robert A. POWER BROKER: ROBERT MOSES AND THE FALL OF NEW YORK. New York: Alfred A. Knopf, 1974.

A lengthy but startling insight to urban power politics which documents how Robert Moses forced highway, public housing, and parks development on New York City and State. He controlled a series of independent authorities which enabled him to by-pass the traditional city bureaucracy and pressure the city's elected leaders and bankers.

2-8   Dahl, Robert A. WHO GOVERNS? New Haven, Conn.: Yale University Press, 1961.

Explores questions such as: Are there great inequalities in the influence of different citizens upon government decisions? Who does, in fact, govern? How does a "democratic" system work amid inequal distribution of resources? New Haven, Connecticut, is the subject of the study. Dahl emphasizes pluralism--that different factors are influential in different decisions.

2-9   D'Antonio, William, and Form, William H. INFLUENTIALS IN TWO BORDER CITIES--A STUDY IN COMMUNITY DECISION-MAKING. Notre Dame, Ind.: University of Notre Dame Press, 1965.

See 3-26.

2-10   Davy, Thomas J. "Education of Urban Administrators: Considerations in Planning and Organizing Graduate Degree Programs." PUBLIC MANAGEMENT 54 (February 1972): 5-9.

Examines the roles of urban administrators, the possible changes in the political system of which the students will be a part, the characteristics of students likely to enroll in such courses, and the pedagogical methods by which students can acquire their skills.

2-10a   Dorsett, Lyle W. THE PENDERGAST MACHINE. New York: Oxford University Press, 1968.

A study of one of the most powerful urban political machines in history. The Pendergasts controlled Kansas City for five decades and launched Harry Truman as a national politician.

2-11   Dye, Thomas R., and Hawkings, Brett W., eds. POLITICS IN THE METROPOLIS. 2d ed. Columbus, Ohio: Charles E. Merrill, 1971.

See 6-32.

2-11a Eddy, William B., and Murphy, Thomas P. "Applied Behavioral Science in Local Governments." In THE HUMAN RESOURCES OF CITY GOV-ERNMENTS, edited by Charles H. Levine. Vol. 13, Urban Affairs Annual Review. Beverly Hills, Calif.: Sage Publications, 1977.

See 1-23.

2-12   Field, Arthur. URBAN POWER STRUCTURES. Cambridge, Mass.: Schenkman Publishing Co., 1970.

An attempt to clarify some of the more complex and puzzling questions concerning the study of distribution, creation, and use of the active and potential power in the city. The author identifies three problems of the theory and research of power: how much to describe and explain, and why; who has the power and how much is being used; and what are the relative weights of different kinds of power. Includes four critiques of Field's essay to achieve a rigorous treatment of the concept of power.

2-13   Flinn, Thomas A. LOCAL GOVERNMENT AND POLITICS. Glenview, Ill.: Scott, Foresman and Co., 1969.

Provides a conceptual framework within which to study the problems of local politics. The author analyzes local governmental authority, accountability, influence, and elites. He also discusses subsystems, such as education, welfare, planning, and urban renewal.

2-14   Freeman, L.C. PATTERNS OF COMMUNITY LEADERSHIP. Indiana-polis: Bobbs-Merrill, 1968.

The final report of a study on community leadership in Syra-cuse, New York, from 1959-61 examines the relationship be-tween individuals' social characteristics and their participation in community decision making. The following questions were raised: What is a community leader? To what degree is leadership concentrated? What factors affect differential rates of leadership by various segments of the population?

2-14a Gleason, Bill. DALEY OF CHICAGO. New York: Simon & Schuster, 1970.

Daley is pictured as a politician who served his apprenticeship in Illinois politics during the 1940s and 1950s. In each political office he held Daley learned a little more about the operation and management of a political organization. Daley had guided the political life of Chicago since 1955. The book discusses Daley's strategy and techniques for getting things done in the city. It examines Daley policy in the area of civil rights and civil disturbances. The 1968 Democratic Convention provides an interesting background for understanding the Daley organization and its administration of the city. Daley's relationship to state and federal officials is also discussed.

2-14b Gluck, P.R. "Incentives and the Maintenance of Political Styles in Different Locales." WESTERN POLITICAL QUARTERLY 25 (December 1972): 753-60.

Analyzes amateur and professional styles of politics by using data on the structure of incentives for urban, suburban, and rural party activists to examine the extent to which political styles are supported in different locales. A conclusion of the study is that in urban party organization, the structure of recruitment incentives support the amateur style.

2-15 Goodall, Leonard E., ed. URBAN POLITICS IN THE SOUTHWEST. Tempe: Arizona State University, 1967.

See 4-61.

2-16 Hawley, Willis D. "The Extent and Direction of the Non-partisan Bias of Elections." In his NONPARTISAN ELECTIONS AND THE CASE FOR PARTY POLITICS, pp. 22-43. New York: John Wiley & Sons, 1973.

Focuses on the question of how nonpartisan elections affect Democratic and Republican candidates for local office. The data analyzed by Hawley tends to validate the common assumption that there is an overall Republican bias to nonpartisanship, but that its magnitude, measured solely by the number of councilmanic and mayoral positions affected, is less substantial than one might have expected, based on previous studies. The Republican benefit thesis appears to explain the model impact of nonpartisanship, but Hawley contends that it is too crude and proposes an alternative theory.

2-17 _____. "Party and Class Differences in Political Resources and Behavior." In his NONPARTISAN ELECTIONS AND THE CASE FOR PARTY POLITICS, pp. 44-76. New York: John Wiley & Sons, 1973.

Focuses on the way that variations in community characteristics might explain variations in the partisan bias of nonpartisanship among cities. Nearly all of the available evidence shows that Democrats, and persons of lower socioeconomic status, tend to have fewer resources with which to make the linkages discussed than do Republicans. Nonpartisanship, Hawley concludes, tends to enhance the "electability" of Republican candidates, because removing party labels from the ballot and discouraging party activity reduces the institutional mechanisms through which individuals organize their political decision making, thus placing greater demands on their ideology, cognitive capacity, experience, and nonparty sources of political communication and mobilization.

2-18 _____. "Some Policy Consequences of Nonpartisanship." In his NON-PARTISAN ELECTIONS AND THE CASE FOR PARTY POLITICS, pp. 107-42. New York: John Wiley & Sons, 1973.

Deals with the question of how nonpartisan elections in a city affect public policy outcomes. Conclusions indicate that policies in cities with partisan elections come closer to manifesting the dispositions attributed to partisan Democrats than those of Republicans and that partisanship encourages more liberal policies because it (1) facilitates political action in the face of conflict, (2) reduces the voters' vulnerability to demagoguery and enhances the political opportunities of ethnic minorities, and (3) encourages the resolution of community issues in the political arena by elected public officials.

2-19 _____. "Toward an Explanation of the Variability in the Partisan Bias of Nonpartisanship." In his NONPARTISAN ELECTIONS AND THE CASE FOR PARTY POLITICS, pp. 77-106. New York: John Wiley & Sons, 1973.

Explores the extent to which demographic and political characteristics of communities account for differences in the extent and direction of the partisan bias of nonpartisanship. The characteristics of a community affect the nature of election campaigns. For example, in some cities, Democratic strength is so strong that it is in the best interests of Republican candidates to run without party affiliation. In eighty-eight cities studied, Republicans were, on the average, somewhat more likely to win in nonpartisan elections than in partisan elections.

2-20 Hulcher, Wendell E. "Elected Local Leadership in Municipal Government." ANNALS OF THE AMERICAN ACADEMY OF POLITICAL AND SOCIAL SCIENCE 405 (January 1973): 137-44.

Argues that the complexities of our technological age have resulted in unprecedented responsibilities and challenges for local elective officials. It is not at all clear, Hulcher concludes, that local leadership is responding fast enough to either the traditional functions of local government or the newer complexities of our technological age.

2-21   Hunt, A. Lee, Jr., and Pendley, Robert E. "Community Gatekeepers: An Examination of Political Recruiters." MIDWEST JOURNAL OF POLITICAL SCIENCE 16 (August 1972): 411-38.

   Discusses the role which recruiting agents play in defining the pool of eligibles for political office candidacies. The study indicates the existence of an independent structure of political actors in the community who, through their choice of whom to promote for candidacy, translate implicit and vague community norms and values into concrete responses to the recurrent question of who should govern. The study also indicates a difference between individually operating recruiting agents and recruitment groups.

2-22   Jacob, Philip. "Autonomy and Political Responsibility: The Enigmatic Verdict of a Cross-National Comparative Study of Community Dynamics." URBAN AFFAIRS QUARTERLY 11 (September 1975): 36-57.

   See 3-49.

2-23   Janowitz, Morris, ed. COMMUNITY POLITICAL SYSTEMS. Glencoe, III.: Free Press, 1961.

   See 3-50.

2-24   Karnig, Albert K. "Black Representation on City Councils: The Impact of District Elections and Socio-Economic Factors." URBAN AFFAIRS QUARTERLY 12 (December 1976): 223-56.

   See 4-86.

2-24a   _____. "Private-Regarding Policy, Civil Rights Groups, and the Mediating Impact of Municipal Reforms." AMERICAN JOURNAL OF POLITICAL SCIENCE 19 (February 1975): 91-106.

   Examines the proposition that municipal reforms tend to make less effective the impact of private-oriented demands for public policy. The study uses data from 1960 of 417 American cities with a population of over 25,000, containing at least 1,000 nonwhites.

2-24b   Kaufman, Herbert. "Administrative Decentralization and Political Power." PUBLIC ADMINISTRATION REVIEW 29 (January-February 1969): 3-15.

   Discusses three major values as components of the administrative system: executive leadership, representation, and neutrally competent bureaucrats. These values fluctuate in their importance to different groups at different times. Minority groups have attacked the system because it appears to reward only the powerful groups and impedes changes needed by other groups. The result of this growing minority dissatisfaction has been a

demand for administrative decentralization. The author suggests that the three major values follow a cycle. Decentralization being a manifestation of inept bureaucratic implementation. This in turn will lead to stronger executives with centralized power. At some point there will be a cry for greater
representation within the elected body and councils will be
strengthened. In attempting to remove politics from administration there will be more responsibility invested in the bureaucracy.

2-24c Kirlin, John J. "Electoral Conflict and Democracy in Cities." JOUR-
NAL OF POLITICS 37 (February 1975): 262-69.

Attempts to measure electoral conflict in city politics. The
author compares an analysis of electoral conflict in Los Angeles suburbs with the analysis of Prewitt and Eulau of the San
Francisco Bay metropolitan area. The measure of electoral
conflict used by Prewitt and Eulau was the average rate of
incumbent defeat where the Los Angeles study used the rate
of groups of incumbents. The Los Angeles study resulted in
different conclusions from those suggested by the Prewitt and
Eulau study. (See also 2-43.)

2-25 Kotler, Milton. NEIGHBORHOOD GOVERNMENT: THE LOCAL
FOUNDATIONS OF POLITICAL LIFE. Indianapolis: Bobbs-Merrill,
1969.

Addresses the issue of power politics as it affects neighborhoods. The author maintains that the source of political conflict in a city is the competition for power among downtown
interests or between downtown and the neighborhoods. It is
misleading to view the neighborhood as anything other than
the basic unit of political life. Accordingly, political education based on the practice of local control is the only way
that neighborhoods can overcome the oppressive domination
by big-city political interests.

2-26 Leach, Richard H., and O'Rourke, Timothy G., eds. DIMENSIONS
OF STATE AND URBAN POLICY MAKING. New York: Macmillan,
1974.

See 5-101.

2-27 Levine, Charles H. RACIAL CONFLICT AND THE AMERICAN MAYOR.
Lexington, Mass.: Lexington Books, 1974.

See 4-89b.

2-28 Levine, Charles [H.], and Kaufman, G. "Urban Conflict as a Constraint
on Mayoral Leadership: Lessons from Gary and Cleveland." AMERICAN

POLITICS QUARTERLY 2 (January 1974): 78-104.

Presents an alternative to the pluralist-based models of mayoral leadership. The authors use case studies of black mayoral leadership style in Gary and Cleveland and conclude that style is more effective when related to the community situation.

2-29 Lineberry, Robert L., and Fowler, Edmund P. "Reformism and Public Policies in American Cities." AMERICAN POLITICAL SCIENCE REVIEW 61 (September 1967): 701-16.

Suggests that socioeconomic cleavages help to determine political forms--type of ballot, methods of electing councilmen, and so on. The authors expand this causal relationship by arguing that political form is one factor that impacts upon political output. Reformed and unreformed governments impact differently on policy making in American cities. They demonstrate this by using two policy outputs, taxation and expenditure levels of cities, as dependent variables. The independent variables are several socioeconomic characteristics. The findings show that reformed cities spend and tax less than unreformed cities with some exceptions. Responsiveness of political systems to class, racial, and religious cleavages depends very much on the local government political structure.

2-30 LOCAL CHIEF EXECUTIVES' PERCEPTIONS OF POLICY-MAKING AND MANAGEMENT NEEDS. Vol. 1. Washington, D.C.: Department of Housing and Urban Development, Office of Policy Development and Research, February 1975.

See 1-46.

2-31 Lowi, Theodore J. AT THE PLEASURE OF THE MAYOR. New York: Free Press of Glencoe, 1964.

An attempt to explain the politics of New York City. The first part of the book describes the role of the mayor, the powers of the county organization and county leader, and the dominance of the Democratic party. The second section examines the ethnic, religious, and social factors that influence the politics of the city. Lowi discusses the political machine and the political role of various interest groups. The third part explores the theoretical aspects of the city's political arena. He examines the loss of the machine and the gain of the stronger interest groups and concludes that community power is weak in scope as well as depth, and suggests that some restoration of the machine should be made.

2-32 _____. "Machine Politics--Old and New." PUBLIC INTEREST 9 (Fall 1967): 83-92.

Deals with the demise of political machines which can now be put in perspective. The author briefly reviews the reasons for the divergent political structures in New York and Chicago such as population, efficiency, reform, and merit systems. He feels the new machines are really the city bureaucracies which instead of becoming neutral have become independent. New machines are similar in organization to old machines but different in that they are more numerous, they are functional rather than geographic, and rely upon formal authority instead of popular vote. Several examples are cited to show how centralized authority is thwarted in light of the existing fragmentation. The 1961 mayoral election is shown to be similar to past elections where bosses put their tickets together carefully. In the end the old machines are seen to be not as bad as once depicted.

2-33 _____. "Why Mayors Go Nowhere." WASHINGTON MONTHLY 3 (January 1972): 55-61.

Contends that the great political resources of New York are available to politicians on the state level, but not to New York City mayors. New York governors are often considered presidential possibilities because they have governed such a large and diverse northeastern industrial state, but mayors of the biggest city in the United States have gained little national power. The author reasons that since mayors have increasingly tried to gain more local autonomy for the city, they have alienated state officials who could be influential in helping them attain higher office.

2-34 Lupsha, Peter A. "Constraints on Urban Leadership, or Why Cities Cannot be Creatively Governed." In IMPROVING THE QUALITY OF URBAN MANAGEMENT, edited by Willis D. Hawley and David Rogers, pp. 607-23. Beverly Hills, Calif.: Sage Publications, 1974.

Develops a set of testable propositions about the limits of urban leadership. The author argues that political scientists and the public at large are being unreasonable when they expect mayors, managers, and other elected city officials to be leaders. The constraints are such that leadership is nearly impossible; management and incremental reaction are the only viable possibilities. He concludes that reactive politics and crisis policy will probably continue to be the usual means to creative change.

2-35 Miller, Richard G. PHILADELPHIA--THE FEDERALIST CITY: A STUDY OF URBAN POLITICS, 1789-1801. Port Washington, N.Y.: Kennikat, 1976

An examination of the politics of Philadelphia from 1789-1801, during which it was the nation's capital. Two political parties, the Federalists and the Republicans, competed for control of of the city. This distinguished Philadelphia from other areas of the country where the rural environments impeded party organization. The keen competition between the two parties in Philadelphia led to increased party identification and voter participation.

2-36   Miller, Zane L.   BOSS COX'S CINCINNATI.   New York: Oxford University Press, 1968.

An attempt to relate an understanding of how American cities coped with the problems of urbanization through a study of Cincinnati. He looks at the history of Cincinnati from the 1850s to 1913. The physical aspects of the city are described. Miller then discusses the problems the city faced between 1884 and 1894 and the struggles of the local government in dealing with these problems. The history of the reform movements in Cincinnati from the early 1890s to the early 1910s is traced. The use of community action groups and the various religious coalitions, along with the rise of George B. Cox and his political movement brought a change in local politics. In the final section, Miller details the fall of Cox from power through the combined efforts of the Democratic party and a perjury trial.

2-37   Morgan, David R., and Kirkpatrick, Samuel A., eds.   URBAN POLITI-CAL ANALYSIS: A SYSTEMS APPROACH.   New York: Free Press, 1972.

See 3-64.

2-38   Murphy, Thomas P.   "From Pendergast to Truman."   In his METROPOLI-TICS AND THE URBAN COUNTY, pp. 66-85.   Washington, D.C.: Washington National Press, 1970.

A summary of the political background of Kansas City and its impact on the metropolitan area with emphasis on James Pen-dergast, Harry Truman, and then (pp. 101-80) on a reform movement which terminated boss rule of Jackson County.

2-39   O'Conner, Edwin.   THE LAST HURRAH.   Boston: Little, Brown and Co., 1956.

The story of Boston's James Michael Curley, who in a fifty-year career was elected to Congress three times, elected mayor four times and governor once. Yet he was defeated three times for mayor and twice for governor and twice was sent to jail.

2-40   Perrucci, Robert, and Pelesuk, Marc.   "Leaders as Ruling Elites: The Interorganizational Bases of Community Power."   AMERICAN SOCIO-

LOGICAL REVIEW 35 (December 1970): 1040-57.

See 3-76.

2-41 Pressman, Jeffrey [L.]. "Preconditions of Mayoral Leadership." THE
      AMERICAN POLITICAL SCIENCE REVIEW 66 (June 1972): 511-24.

      A study of Oakland, California, proposing seven environmental
      requirements for effective mayoral leadership: (1) sufficient
      financial and staff resources for the city government, (2) city
      jurisdiction in social program areas, (3) mayoral jurisdiction
      within the city government in these policy fields, (4) a salary
      large enough to enable the mayor to spend full time on the
      job, (5) sufficient staff support for the mayor, (6) ready vehi-
      cles for publicity, and (7) politically oriented groups, includ-
      ing a political party, which the mayor can mobilize.

2-42 Prewitt, Kenneth, and Eulau, Heinz. "Political Matrix and Political
      Representation: Prolegomenon to a New Departure From an Old Problem."
      AMERICAN POLITICAL SCIENCE REVIEW 63 (June 1969): 427-41.

      A case study on political representation. The authors attempt
      to devise a matrix that explains situations that make a govern-
      ment representative. Past theories of representation and the
      concept of pluralism are analyzed. The authors conclude that
      the political matrix components which determine how responsive
      a government is are the following: the complexity of the social
      environment, the impact of elections in forcing incumbents from
      office, the degree of public support perceived by the council,
      and the amount of sponsorship in political recruitment.

2-43 _____. "Social Bias in Leadership Selection, Political Recruitment, and
      Electoral Context." JOURNAL OF POLITICS 33 (May 1971): 293-315.

      A study of eighty-two city councils in the San Francisco Bay
      metropolitan region. The findings suggest that factors other
      than those of social status affect movement from the active
      stratum into leadership positions. The study indicates that the
      recruitment process varies with the type of electorate, and
      that political and social status characteristics help define the
      group of citizens from which leaders are usually drawn. (See
      also 2-24c.)

2-44 Rakove, Milton. DON'T MAKE NO WAVES--DON'T BACK NO
      LOSERS: AN INSIDERS ANALYSIS OF THE DALEY MACHINE. Bloom-
      ington: University of Indiana Press, 1974.

      Studies of the Daley political organization in Chicago which
      was written by a participant who over a period of years of
      watching, listening, and doing was able to analyze the politi-

cal and administrative system of Chicago. Discusses the demographics of Chicago and Daley the man, the mayor, and the politician. The majority of the book is devoted to understanding the structure and dynamics of the Cook County political organization, the ward organizations, and the relationship between the political machine and the Democratic party. The Republicans as the loyal opposition are examined as is the machine's relationship with politicians in the state capital and in Washington. A final analysis in the book analyzes the impact of both suburbs and minorities on the future of the machine. The author concludes with the belief that the machine will survive by making the minor adjustments necessary to contemporary change.

2-45 Remy, Ray. "The Professional Administrator in Regional Councils." PUBLIC MANAGEMENT 56 (January 1974): 11-13.

See 6-80.

2-46 Royko, Mike. BOSS RICHARD J. DALEY OF CHICAGO. New York: E.P. Dutton and Co., 1971.

A study of the late Mayor Daley and his emergence as a political and ethnic leader. Royko paints a picture of Daley as a partisan strongman who built a machine and wed his powers aggressively in governing Chicago and in influencing politics and policy making at the local, state, and national levels. He examines Daley's role in the 1968 Democratic Convention in Chicago, both inside and out of the convention hall.

2-47 Ruchelman, Leonard I., ed. BIG CITY MAYORS: THE CRISIS IN URBAN POLITICS. Bloomington: Indiana University Press, 1969.

See 1-61.

2-48 Sayre, Wallace S. "The Mayor." In AGENDA FOR A CITY: ISSUES CONFRONTING NEW YORK, edited by Lyle C. Fitch and Annamarie H. Walsh, pp. 563-601. Beverly Hills, Calif.: Sage Publications, 1970.

See 1-63.

2-49 Sayre, Wallace S., and Kaufman, Herbert. GOVERNING NEW YORK CITY: POLITICS IN THE METROPOLIS. New York: W.W. Norton, 1965.

A classic study of urban bureaucracy and the interplay of politics and administration in the context of New York City. So many interest groups compete with each other in New York that there is no single ruling elite to dominate the political and governmental system. The authors observe that the central organs of the government have failed to provide a high level of integration.

2-50 Schultze, William A. URBAN AND COMMUNITY POLITICS. North Scituate, Mass.: Duxbury Press, 1974.

Provides a synthesis of contemporary scholarship defining and explaining the politics of the American city. The book is divided into five main sections. Part 1, "Urban Environment and Politics," provides a physical, political, social, and intellectual view of cities. Part 2, "Urban Conflict," deals with the formal and informal actors who participate in conflict. Part 3, "Urban Conflict Management," deals with intergovernmental relations, policy formation, and policy adoption. Part 4, "Policy in the Urban Setting," includes case studies in urban politics. Part 5 concludes with an examination of life styles.

2-51 Shapiro, Walter. "One Who Lost." WASHINGTON MONTHLY 4 (December 1972): 7-15.

The author describes his experiences running for the congressional seat in Michigan's Second District. He claims that most congressional primaries "have all the glamour of a Fuller Brush route and are discreetly ignored by both the local media and the majority of the voters."

2-52 Stedman, Murray S., Jr. "Why Urban Parties Can't Govern." NATIONAL CIVIC REVIEW 61 (November 1972): 501-4.

Examines the relationship between urban political organizations and urban problems. The author contends that no amount of new resources, skill, or hard work can restore urban political organizations to their former power and effectiveness. The traditional political system has broken down because the conditions which formerly supported it have changed rapidly. Two key concepts, group theory and limited government, have become antiquated.

2-53 Stokes, Carl B. PROMISES OF POWER: A POLITICAL AUTOBIOGRAPHY. New York: Simon & Schuster, 1973.

Discusses the governing of a large American city by the first black man to be elected mayor of a large municipality touching upon many contemporary urban problems. The book follows the educational process that Stokes is exposed to as he deals with the problems of racism, violence, political patronage, and black voting strength. Even though Stokes became disillusioned with urban politics and decided not to run for re-election, he sees much hope for black politics in the future.

This future lies in working within the political process rather than establishing independent or quasi-sovereign political institutions for blacks.

2-54 Talbot, Allan R. THE MAYOR'S GAME: RICHARD LEE OF NEW HAVEN AND THE POLITICS OF CHANGE. New York: Praeger Publishers, 1967.

A political and administrative study of efforts to rebuild the city of New Haven, Connecticut. It outlines the program developed by Mayor Lee and analyzes how this program was organized and who were his major allies and opponents. A discussion is presented of how resources were mobilized to attack the physical problems of confronting the city. One section is devoted to an examination of improving the human resources of the city by trying to solve the problems of racial injustice and poverty. The focus of the book is on the mayor and his ability to use the political and administrative resources available to bring about change.

2-55 Wolfinger, Raymond E. "Why Political Machines Have Not Withered Away and Other Revisionist Thoughts." JOURNAL OF POLITICS 34 (May 1972): 365-98.

Suggests that machine politics still exists in America and presents a definition of machine politics linked to incentives for political participation. Explanations for the existence of machines and for their demise are analyzed. The author discusses the political machines in New Haven, Connecticut, and defines machine politics. Research discussing the difficulty of assessing patronage is presented. A typology of two-dimensional incentives is developed based upon tangible-intangible and routine-substantive characteristics. Many of the functions performed by political machines in the past for the poor and the needy are still required. In addition the machine performs services for many business and professional groups who seek to advance their causes.

2-56 Zink, Harold. CITY BOSSES IN THE UNITED STATES. New York: AMS Press, 1968.

Examines the lives and careers of twenty political bosses. A broad background of bossism is presented in the first section, and the bosses themselves are described in section 2. According to Zink, some bosses would switch from party to party, others would switch to being a reformer after having been a machine boss, while still others were the head of a long established and efficiently-run machine.

Chapter 3
PARTICIPATORY DECISION MAKING

This chapter includes entries relating to community power structure, citizen participation, interest groups (except ethnics), and the media.

3-1   Aberbach, J[oel].D., and Walker, J[ack].W. "Citizen Desires, Policy Outcomes & Community Control." URBAN AFFAIRS QUARTERLY 8 (September 1972): 55-76.

Examines reform via the movement for community control of schools in America's largest cities. This case study of school decentralization in Detroit from 1969 to 1971 includes a brief history of the movement, a report on recent basic attitudinal changes toward decentralization, reactions among both racial groups to efforts to recall several members of the Detroit Board of Education in August 1970, and implications.

3-2   Adrian, C[harles].R. "Leadership and Decision Making in Manager Cities: A Study of Three Communities." PUBLIC ADMINISTRATION REVIEW 18 (Summer 1958): 208-13.

Updates a continuing study of policy leadership in three middle-sized council-manager cities from 1953 to 1957. Tentative conclusions assert that the manager and his administration are the principal sources of policy innovation and leadership in council-manager cities even though they may seek to avoid a public posture of policy leadership, and that managers have resources that enable them to withstand even strong attempts by councilmembers to wrest away policy leadership. Concludes that nonofficial groups provide a greater amount of leadership in council-manager cities than generally practiced.

3-3   _____. PUBLIC ATTITUDES AND METROPOLITAN DECISION MAKING. Pittsburgh: University of Pittsburgh, Institute of Local Government, 1962.

Suggests that activists and scholars in the field of metropolitan area problems have been less successful because their assumptions about the nature of the political process and system have not mirrored reality. Conclusions are that the future metropolis will probably operate through the process of cooperative federalism, suburban governments will survive, and urban counties will expand their functions. Adrian indicates that the greatest future changes will be in the increased financial and administrative role of the state and federal governments.

3-4 _____. "Urban America: Social Science as Catharsis." POLITY 4 (Spring 1972): 385-93.

Notes that current mobility means that the metropolis cannot be governed by a single jurisdiction and therefore all traditional concepts about local government are not applicable to metropolitan areas. Adrian believes that the metropolis should be viewed as a decision system of limited scope and its operation studied through the use of decision theory and communication theory.

3-5 Alford, R[obert].R. "Bureaucracy and Participation in Four Wisconsin Cities." URBAN AFFAIRS QUARTERLY 5 (September 1969): 5-30.

Hypothesizes that a government's level of development is not necessarily related to the scope of citizen participation in the decision-making process. Voter turnout, the organization of civic groups with the goal of influencing government decisions, and the size and activity of political parties may be at high level with or without a high level of bureaucratization.

3-6 Aronowitz, Stanley. "Dialectics of Community Control." SOCIAL POLICY 1 (May-June 1970): 47-51.

Discusses the following objectives of community control: (1) achieving quality services under indigenous leadership within communities; (2) securing a more favorable allocation of resources by city, state, and federal governments to improve service delivery systems; (3) developing a cadre of political and social leadership within the community capable of reflecting the community's aspirations and helping to deliver quality services; and (4) gaining some measure of control of the ghetto economy.

3-7 Bachrach, P. "A Power Analysis: The Shaping of Anti-Poverty Policy in Baltimore." PUBLIC POLICY 18 (Winter 1970): 155-86.

Contrasts the power struggle in Baltimore in 1966-67 with the disparate 1968-69 power struggle. The first period was characterized primarily by a white power center that severly restricted the development of political issues involving the black community. In the second period, the system's elitist war against the power aspirations of blacks was less effective. New conflicts relating to ghetto problems arose, and black access to established decision-making centers was more open. The author analyzes how power has been utilized during a period of transformation in shaping and sustaining ideological and political institutions that in turn affect the distribution of power among persons and groups in a local community.

3-8   Bailey, Robert, Jr. RADICALS IN URBAN POLITICS: THE ALINSKY APPROACH. Chicago: University of Chicago Press, 1974.

Focuses on a single Alinsky organization to shed understanding on the political actions and theoretical significance of Alinsky groups. Several aspects examined include decision-making processes, leadership recruitment, and issue generation within the groups. The Organization for a Better Austin in Chicago was studied by a multiple-methods approach.

3-9   Bockman, Sheldon, and Hahn, Harlan. "Networks of Information and Influence in the Community." In PEOPLE AND POLITICS IN URBAN SOCIETY, edited by Harlan Hahn, pp. 71-94. Beverly Hills, Calif.: Sage Publications, 1972.

See 3-44.

3-10   Bolan, Richard S., and Nuttall, Ronald L. URBAN PLANNING AND POLITICS. Lexington, Mass.: D.C. Heath and Co., 1975.

See 5-21.

3-11   Bowman, Lewis; Ippolito, Dennis S.; and Levin, Martin L. "Self-Interest and Referendum Support: The Case of a Rapid Transit Vote in Atlanta." In PEOPLE AND POLITICS IN URBAN SOCIETY, edited by Harlan Hahn. Beverly Hills, Calif.: Sage Publications, 1972.

See 3-44.

3-12   Boyd, William L., and O'Shea, David. "Theoretical Perspectives on School District Decentralization." EDUCATION AND URBAN SOCIETY 7 (August 1975): 357-76.

See 5-24.

3-13   Browne, Edmond, Jr., and Rehfuss, John. "Policy Evaluation, Citizen Participation and Revenue Sharing in Aurora, Illinois." PUBLIC ADMINISTRATION REVIEW 35 (March/April 1975): 150-57.

See 7-21.

3-14   Browne, William P., and Salisbury, Robert H. "Organized Spokesmen for Cities: Urban Interest Groups." In PEOPLE AND POLITICS IN URBAN SOCIETY, edited by Harlan Hahn, pp. 255-78. Beverly Hills,

Calif.: Sage Publications, 1972.

See 3-44.

3-15   Clark, Terry N. "The Structure of Community Influence." In PEOPLE AND POLITICS IN URBAN SOCIETY, edited by Harlan Hahn, pp. 283-314. Beverly Hills, Calif.: Sage Publications, 1972.

See 3-44.

3-16   _____. "Urban Typologies and Political Outputs: Causal Models Using Discrete Variables and Orthogonal Factors, or Precise Distortion Versus Model Muddling." SOCIAL SCIENCE INFORMATION 9 (December 1970): 7-34.

Examines the comparative advantages of different types of causal models. The author studies community structure and decision-making patterns in a national sample of fifty-one American communities to compare the results of near orthogonal variates with discrete variables in various causal systems. He concludes that there are advantages to both--that precise distortion and model muddling should be used together as mutually complementary.

3-17   _____, ed. COMMUNITY STRUCTURE AND DECISION-MAKING: COMPARATIVE ANALYSES. San Francisco: Chandler Publishing Co., 1968.

This series of articles identifies the types of community structures which give rise to different patterns of decision making, and examines how these patterns influence the actual outcomes of community decisions. Variables include demographic, economic, legal-political, and cultural characteristics; leadership and decision-making patterns; and output differences.

3-18   Clark, Terry N.; Lineberry, Robert L.; and Bonjean, Charles M., eds. COMMUNITY POLITICS: A BEHAVIORAL APPROACH. New York: Free Press, 1971.

An interdisciplinary overview of community, politics, and power. The concept of power, the multiplicity of local governments, the effects of fragmented metropolitan areas, the structure of mass participation in community politics, elites and power structures, community politics and public policies, and the attitudes and values of community leaders and decision makers are examined. The book contains a bibliography of community politics and community power structure.

3-19   Clubb, Jerome M., and Traugott, Michael W. "National Patterns of Referenda Voting: The 1968 Election." In PEOPLE AND POLITICS IN

URBAN SOCIETY, edited by Harlan Hahn, pp. 137-70. Beverly Hills, Calif.: Sage Publications, 1972.

See 3-44.

3-20   Cole, Richard L. "Revenue Sharing: Citizen Participation and Social Service Aspects." ANNALS OF THE AMERICAN ACADEMY OF POLITICAL AND SOCIAL SCIENCE 419.(May 1975): 64-74.

See 7-31.

3-21   Crain, Robert L.; Katz, Elihu; and Rosenthal, Donald B. THE POLITICS OF COMMUNITY CONFLICT. Indianapolis: Bobbs-Merrill, 1969.

A study conducted by a sociologist, a social psychologist, and a political scientist of the politics of fluoridation using survey research methodology. The authors considered two hypotheses for the frequent failure of flouridation referenda: (1) voters in American cities are alienated and feel threatened by forces they do not comprehend, and (2) special characteristics of decision making in local governments which make fluoridation especially vulnerable to veto. The authors examined the relationships between the nature of the local government and the adoption or rejection of fluoridation by the community.

3-22   Crenson, Matthew. "Organizational Factors in Citizen Participation." JOURNAL OF POLITICS 36 (May 1974): 356-78.

An examination of the internal characteristics of community organizations, based on a comparative case study of seven neighborhood groups of Baltimore. Findings indicated that intraorganizational conflict resulted in an ill-defined agenda which instigated conflict in a community group. The author suggests that the nature of government programs for community organization makes it difficult for government-sponsored groups to arrive at an agenda of projects and proposals; therefore, they are counterproductive.

3-23   Cunningham, James V. "Drafting the Pittsburgh Charter: How Citizens Participated." NATIONAL CIVIC REVIEW 63 (September 1974): 410-15.

A look at the events surrounding the drafting of the Pittsburgh charter. A predominately citizen commission determined that a complete new home rule charter should be written, compiled lists of current local issues, and wrote a discussion draft. The Pittsburgh experience reveals movement toward greater roles for ordinary citizens in the governing of American cities.

3-24   Dahl, Robert A. "The City in the Future of Democracy." AMERICAN POLITICAL SCIENCE REVIEW 62 (December 1967): 953-70.

Raises and answers some basic political questions: What is the appropriate democratic political unit? What constitutes an appropriate citizenry for the purpose of self-rule? Have the ideals and institutions of democracy reached their culmination in the nation-state? The answers lie within the purview of the democratic city. But unlike their ancient Greek counter-parts, citizens will have no single loyalty and no single com-munity, and nowhere will they find the all-inclusive com-munity.

3-25 _____. WHO GOVERNS? New Haven, Conn.: Yale University Press, 1961.

See 2-8.

3-26 D'Antonio, William, and Form, William H. INFLUENTIALS IN TWO BORDER CITIES--A STUDY IN COMMUNITY DECISION-MAKING. Notre Dame, Ind.: University of Notre Dame Press, 1965.

A study of leadership, use of power, and decision making in the cities of El Paso, Texas, and Juarez, Chihuahua, Mexico. Having evaluated the problems of community leadership in a border setting, the authors relate their findings to the larger problems of democratic decision making in the two nations.

3-27 David, Stephen M., and Peterson, Paul E., eds. URBAN POLITICS AND PUBLIC POLICY: THE CITY IN CRISIS. New York: Praeger Publishers, 1973.

See 5-44.

3-28 Downes, Bryan T., and Friedman, Lewis A. "Local Level Decision-Making and Public Policy Outcomes: A Theoretical Perspective." In PEOPLE AND POLITICS IN URBAN SOCIETY, edited by Harlan Hahn, pp. 315-44. Beverly Hills, Calif.: Sage Publications, 1972.

See 3-44.

3-29 Downes, Bryan T., and Greene, Kenneth R. "The Politics of Open Housing in Three Cities: Decision Maker Responses to Black Demands for Policy Changes." AMERICAN POLITICS QUARTERLY 1 (April 2, 1973): 215-43.

The results of a study of the process through which local deci-sion makers, in this case city councilmen of three middle-sized Michigan cities, respond to problems in their communities. The authors examine the consideration of city open housing ordinances which the three cities ultimately did adopt. Re-search focused on how demands for open housing were trans-formed into public policy and how variations in this process affected the stringency of the ordinance finally adopted.

3-30   Eisinger, Peter K. "The Conditions of Protest Behavior in American
        Cities." AMERICAN POLITICAL SCIENCE REVIEW 67 (March 1973):
        11-28.

        Explores various environmental conditions associated with politi-
        cal protest activities in American cities. The author con-
        tends that formal political structure, the responsiveness of
        government, social structure, and social stability impost con-
        straints on political activity or provide opportunity for it.
        The political behavior of individuals and groups is a function
        of the opportunities, barriers, weaknesses and resources within
        the political system, not merely the resources they command
        themselves. There is thus a nexus between the environment,
        in terms of a structure of political opportunities, and politi-
        cal behavior.

3-31   _____. "The Pattern of Citizen Contacts with Urban Officials." In
        PEOPLE AND POLITICS IN URBAN SOCIETY, edited by Harlan Hahn,
        pp. 43-70. Beverly Hills, Calif.: Sage Publications, 1972.

        See 3-44.

3-32   _____. "Racial Differences in Protest Participation." AMERICAN
        POLITICAL SCIENCE REVIEW 68 (June 1974): 592-606.

        Challenges the view that protest is an extraordinary political
        tactic used only by those who lack the resources to employ
        more conventional methods. Eisinger contends that there are
        racial variations in role and nature of protest. Among blacks,
        protest is an integral and normal feature of adapting to urban
        politics. Among whites, it is an extraordinary form of politi-
        cal participation, limited predominantly to the upper middle
        class.

3-33   Fantini, Mario; Gittell, Marilyn; and Magat, Richard. COMMUNITY
        CONTROL AND THE URBAN SCHOOL. New York: Praeger Publishers,
        1970.

        An account of conflicts in urban education which covers the
        issues and priorities of the New York City teachers' strike,
        the New York demonstration districts, compensatory education,
        the Coleman Report, testing, alternative school systems, and
        black identity. The authors view community control as a
        demand for school accountability by parents ignored in the
        past, particularly those of low-status groups in northern cities.
        It requires a total city commitment, genuine delegation of
        power, and continued efforts to relate the community of the
        larger society. The study traces the developments of the
        theory of community participation and examines their impli-
        cations.

3-34   Fowler, E[dmund].P., and Lineberry, R[obert].L. "Patterns of Feedback in City Politics." In URBAN POLITICAL ANALYSIS: A FREE SYSTEMS APPROACH, edited by D.R. Morgan and S.A. Kirkpatrick, pp. 361-67. New York: Free Press, 1972.

Illustrates feedback in the political system with three theories: reform, group theory of politics, and structural-functional theory.

3-35   Fowler, Floyd J. CITIZEN ATTITUDES TOWARD LOCAL GOVERN-MENT, SERVICES AND TAXES. Urban Observatory Program Series, no. 1. Cambridge, Mass.: Ballinger, 1974.

Comparative studies based on the multi-city research projects. This ten city survey found that assumptions made about citizen attitudes were often proved wrong by the surveys. A total of 4,300 people were interviewed in Albuquerque, Atlanta, Baltimore, Boston, Denver, Kansas City, Missouri, Milwaukee, Nashville, San Diego, and Kansas City, Kansas.

3-36   Fox, Douglas M. THE POLITICS OF CITY AND STATE BUREAUCRACY. Pacific Palisades, Calif.: Goodyear, 1974.

See 1-29.

3-37   Francis, Mark. "Urban Impact Assessment and Community Involvement: The Case of the John Fitzgerald Kennedy Library." ENVIRONMENT AND BEHAVIOR 7 (September 1975): 373-404.

Explores the implications of one of the earliest and most cele-brated cases of a social impact assessment of an urban develop-ment project--the J.F.K. Library proposed for Cambridge, Mas-sachusetts. Covers the history, issues, and actors of the con-troversy, the preparation of the Environmental Impact State-ment (EIS), an overview of the draft EIS, and the impact of the document on the Cambridge community.

3-38   Fredericks, Steven J. "Curriculum and Decentralization: The New York City Public School System." URBAN EDUCATION 9 (October 1974): 247-56.

See 5-69.

3-39   Gilbert, Claire W. COMMUNITY POWER STRUCTURE: PROPOSITION-AL INVENTORY, TESTS, AND THEORY. Gainesville: Florida Univer-sity Press, 1972.

Based on the assumption that through a systematic inventory of existing knowledge of community power one can evaluate generalizations and hypotheses and test them with gathered data. Data quality control reasoning is applied to classify community power structures on the basis of seventy-three factors which might be sources of bias. The factors are summarized as follows: (1) characteristics of the researcher, (2) conceptual characteristics, (3) conditions of observations, (4) breadth of the study, (5) methods of reporting, and (6) work process.

3-40   Gittell, Marilyn. "Decentralization and Citizen Participation in Education." PUBLIC ADMINISTRATION REVIEW 32 (October 1972): 670-86.

Contends that restructuring the governance of American education offers the possibility of creating an environment in which priorities can be reordered and responsiveness to the various communities of interest assured. Citizens must participate in the educational process to insure quality education. Community control implies the redistribution of power and the establishment of an environment in which more meaningful educational policies can be developed and in which a wide variety of alternate solutions and techniques can be tested.

3-41   Gittell, Marilyn, et al. LOCAL CONTROL IN EDUCATION. New York: Praeger Publishers, 1969.

See 5-74.

3-42   Godschalk, David R. "Citizen Participation in New Communities." In his PARTICIPATION, PLANNING AND EXCHANGE IN OLD AND NEW COMMUNITIES: A COLLABORATIVE PARADIGM, pp. 193-255. Chapel Hill: University of North Carolina, Center for Urban and Regional Studies, 1972.

Describes an exploratory field study of citizen activists and authorities in the new communities of Reston, Virginia, and Columbia, Maryland. The essay attempts to discover the extent to which these communities conform to the ideal paradigm of collaborative planning. Results indicate that citizen involvement in Reston is characterized by open conflict, civic innovation, and much volunteer activity. In Columbia, however, there is a history of conflict avoidance, professionally accomplished innovation, more limited volunteer activism, and an ample professional staff.

3-42a Haar, Charles M. BETWEEN THE IDEA AND THE REALITY. A STUDY OF THE ORIGIN, FATE, AND LEGACY OF THE MODEL CITIES PROGRAM. Boston: Little, Brown and Co., 1975.

See 7-55b.

3-43   Hadden, Jeffrey K.; Masotti, Louis H.; and Larson, Calvin J., eds.

METROPOLIS IN CRISIS--SOCIAL AND POLITICAL PERSPECTIVES. 2d ed. Itasca, Ill.: Peacock, 1971.

See 5-75.

3-44 Hahn, Harlan, ed. PEOPLE AND POLITICS IN URBAN SOCIETY. Beverly Hills, Calif.: Sage Publications, 1972.

Twelve essays constituting a comprehensive treatment of participatory decision making. The major topics are the expression of public sentiments, influencing public officials, and local responses to public demands.

3-45 _____. "Reassessing and Revitalizing Urban Politics: Some Goals and Proposals." In his PEOPLE AND POLITICS IN URBAN SOCIETY, pp. 11-38. Beverly Hills, Calif.: Sage Publications, 1972.

See 3-44.

3-45a Hamilton, Randy H. "Bridging the Gap Between Citizens and City Government." In EMERGING PATTERNS IN URBAN ADMINISTRATION, edited by F. Gerald Brown and Thomas P. Murphy, pp. 64-80. Lexington, Mass.: Lexington Books, 1970.

See 6-18a.

3-46 Hunt, A. Lee, Jr., and Pendley, Robert E. "Community Gatekeepers: An Examination of Political Recruiters." MIDWEST JOURNAL OF POLITICAL SCIENCE 16 (August 1972): 411-38.

See 2-21.

3-47 Hunter, F. COMMUNITY POWER STRUCTURE. Chapel Hill: University of North Carolina Press, 1953.

The three categories of power assessed are: historical references; motivation and other psychological concepts; and values, morals, and ethical considerations.

3-48 Jackson, John S. III, and Shade, William L. "Citizen Participation, Democratic Representation, and Survey Research." URBAN AFFAIRS QUARTERLY 9 (September 1973): 57-89.

Demonstrates how survey research can be used as a form of citizen participation. The authors report a survey research application as a part of the "Goals for Carbondale" program conducted in Carbondale, Illinois, by the Citizens Advisory Committee. They compare the citizen participation activists of the city to the community at large and conclude that citizen participation units may enhance the quality of the opinion-policy linkage, and that they may lend some important symbolic legitimacy to the process.

3-49   Jacob, Philip. "Autonomy and Political Responsibility: The Enigmatic
        Verdict of a Cross-National Comparative Study of Community Dynam-
        ics." URBAN AFFAIRS QUARTERLY 11 (September 1975): 36-57.

        Examines the question of whether political autonomy engenders
        increased political responsibility at the local level and is
        based on studies conducted in India, Poland, United States,
        and Yugoslavia. Interviews with 3,930 local political leaders
        ascertained attitudes toward and perceptions of autonomy
        within a framework of personal value-commitments, role ex-
        pectations, and leadership behavior, as well as leaders' as-
        sessments of the political and social climate of their commu-
        nities. Includes data on resource mobilization and popular
        involvement in community action.

3-50   Janowitz, Morris, ed. COMMUNITY POLITICAL SYSTEMS. Glencoe,
        Ill.: Free Press, 1961.

        A collection of essays which view the urban community as the
        arena in which political power is exercised. Politics is a
        specialized form of behavior, requiring skill and long-term
        commitment and qualities different from those exercised in
        the rest of the group life of the community. The essays sug-
        gest that the major problem confronting community leadership
        is not the manipulation of the citizenry by a small elite, but
        the inability of elites to create the conditions necessary for
        making decisions.

3-51   Jansiewicz, Donald R. THE NEW ALEXANDRIA SIMULATION: A
        SERIOUS GAME OF STATE AND LOCAL POLITICS. San Francisco:
        Canfield Press, 1973.

        Examines state and local politics within a human context.
        Designed for an introductory course in state and local govern-
        ment, this book instructs players to assume a variety of criti-
        cal decision-making roles in a composite state of "New Alex-
        andria." Through participation in the game, students hope-
        fully will better understand the issues and patterns of com-
        petition and cooperation which are characteristic of the Ameri-
        can state and local political process.

3-52   Jennings, M. Kent, and Zeigler, Harmon. "Interest Representation in
        School Governance." In PEOPLE AND POLITICS IN URBAN SOCIETY,
        edited by Harlan Hahn, pp. 201-30. Beverly Hills, Calif.: Sage Pub-
        lications, 1972.

        See 3-44.

3-52a   Jones, E. Terrence. "Mass Media and the Urban Policy Process." In
        URBAN PROBLEMS AND PUBLIC POLICY, edited by Robert L. Lineberry
        and Louis H. Masotti, pp. 59-63. Lexington, Mass.: Lexington Books,
        1975.

See 5-103a.

3-53 Jones, Ruth S. "Changing Student Attitudes: The Impact of Community Participation." SOCIAL SCIENCE QUARTERLY 55 (September 1974): 439-50.

A report on the effectiveness of one formal program specifically designed to encourage student participation in the local
community. The program is assessed in terms of its ability to
inspire positive attitudes toward the actors and the processes
of the American political system, to develop increased political interest and awareness, and to promote student involvement
in current political issues within the local communities.

3-54 Kafogles, Madelyn L. "Equality of Opportunity in Decision Making."
AMERICAN JOURNAL OF ECONOMICS AND SOCIOLOGY 29 (January
1970): 1-17.

Argues that broader citizen participation in public affairs is
necessary because, in a democracy, consensus as well as efficient decisions are more likely to be achieved if the decision-making process reflects the freely expressed values of the
individuals affected. The author examines this premise in
terms of the various relationships that determine the amount
and type of participation that will develop, the individual
aspects of participation, the interrelationship of collective
and private aspects, and equality of opportunity.

3-55 Knox, Michael D.; Kolton, Marilyn S.; and Dwarshuis, Louis. "Community Development in Housing: Increased Tenant Participation." PUB-
LIC WELFARE 32 (Summer 1974): 48-53.

Analyzes local housing authorities' innovations to increase
tenant participation in public housing management and the
implications of these innovations for community development.
Discusses providing information about needs and concerns; providing goods and services; decision making, policy formulation,
and planning; and homeownership. The authors conclude that
not only can residents define their own needs and make decisions on programs affecting their lives, but they can supplement existing human resources and provide improved service
delivery.

3-55a Kotler, Milton. "Rise of Neighborhood Power." FOCUS 4 (December
1975): 4, 5, 8.

Discusses Community Development Block Grant programs which
have been used in several cities to permit grant funds to be
spent in ways which are useful to community groups. In Wash-

ington, D.C., voters passed a charter referendum establishing advisory neighborhood councils which will advise the government on public policy in areas such as planning, recreation, and social services. In Simi Valley, California, the council created five neighborhood council districts similar to town meetings. Similar programs have been developed in the Chinese community in New York City and in a black community in Greenville, Mississippi.

3-56 Krefetz, Sharon Perlman, and Goodman, Allan E. "Participation for What or for Whom?" JOURNAL OF COMPARATIVE ADMINISTRATION 5 (November 1973): 367-80.

A review and critique of both populist and elitist arguments concerning participation. Populists believe that participation is desirable because of its positive effects on the participants; elitists, on the other hand, view participation as undesirable because of its negative effects on administration and decision making. Popular participation not only makes program administration less efficient, but may actually lower the quality of the programs. The authors suggest that the conflict might be resolved if there were empirical data to test the conflicting assumptions underlying them.

3-57 Lewis, Eugene. THE URBAN POLITICAL SYSTEM. Hinsdale, Colo.: Dryden Press, 1973.

See 1-45.

3-58 Lipsky, Michael, and Levi, Margaret. "Community Organization as a Political Resource." In PEOPLE AND POLITICS IN URBAN SOCIETY, edited by Harlan Hahn. Beverly Hills, Calif.: Sage Publications, 1972.

See 3-44.

3-59 Lyons, W.E., and Engstrom, Richard. "Socio-Political Cross Pressures and Attitudes Toward Political Integration of Urban Government." JOURNAL OF POLITICS 35 (August 1973): 682-711.

Studies survey data in relation to the impact of social distance, tax benefit, and regime government orientations on voter attitudes toward two different types of integrative proposals in two separate urban communities. The study also examines the effects of these sociopolitical orientations upon individual attitudes toward integrative proposals. The authors isolate substantive considerations which would enhance further research.

3-60 Magill, Robert S., and Clark, Terry N. "Community Power and Decision Making: Recent Research and Its Policy Implications." SOCIAL SERVICE REVIEW 49 (March 1975): 33-45.

An assessment of factors that influence community power and decision making: revenue sharing, the conflict between pluralism and power elites, and the effects of centralization.

3-61 Mandelker, Daniel R. "Legal and Political Forums for Urban Change." ANNALS OF THE AMERICAN ACADEMY OF POLITICAL AND SOCIAL SCIENCE 405 (January 1973): 41-46.

Contends that the courts play only a limited role in bringing about major social reform. Effective judicial intervention in social controversy requires agreement upon the goals and objectives of social change. Mandelker argues that we have not achieved this agreement, and our failure to do so has limited the impact which courts can have on the underlying causes of social unrest. He believes that the policy conflicts created by social reform efforts can only be resolved in a political forum.

3-62 Manheim, Marvin L. "Reaching Decisions about Technological Projects with Social Consequences: A Normative Model." TRANSPORTATION 2 (April 1973): 1-24.

States that the public has lost confidence in technical professions and in their ability to make decisions about large scale projects in the public interest. Manheim outlines a model for the role of the technical professions. The objective is defined and then a process for achieving this objective is proposed. A key element of the process is a four-phase strategy of technical and community interaction activities to achieve the objective. This theoretical model has served as the basis for a procedural guide for use by highway and transportation agencies, and as the basis for the development of federal guidelines for assessing the social, economic, and environmental impacts in highway planning and decision making.

3-63 Mithun, Jacqueline S. "Cooperative Community Solidarity Against Urban Renewal." HUMAN ORGANIZATION 34 (Spring 1975): 79-86.

Examines the intrusion of an urban renewal program into a black Buffalo community. This case study describes the interaction between community representatives and urban renewal officials for a year and a half during the planning stages and examines why citizens fail to influence government decisions.

3-64 Morgan, David R., and Kirkpatrick, Samuel A., eds. URBAN POLITICAL ANALYSIS: A SYSTEMS APPROACH. New York: Free Press, 1972.

Systems analysis of urban politics. Section 2 discusses the urban environment and includes the classic article by Banfield and Wilson concerning public-regardingness as a value premise in voting behavior. Section 3 deals with various inputs of the urban political system, including public opinion, urban party politics, and the urban electoral system. Section 4 examines urban political decision makers and structures, including city councils, urban courts, and municipal executives and administrators. Section 5 examines such issues as reformism, public policies, governmental structure, urban environment, and educational policy. The sixth section consists of an essay by Fowler and Lineberry concerning patterns of feedback in city politics. In the postscript comparative community politics and public policy are analyzed.

3-65   Mott, George Fox. "Communicative Turbulence in Urban Dynamics-- Media, Education, and Planning." ANNALS OF THE AMERICAN ACADEMY OF POLITICAL AND SOCIAL SCIENCE 405 (January 1973): 114-30.

An examination of the three most pervasive mechanisms creating communicative turbulence and affecting decision making in our society: media, education, and planning. Although the author believes that they can effectively enable us to meet the critical problems of the day, they also can create enough turbulence to threaten constructive efforts toward meeting the challenges of urban change and reformation. He analyzes their impact and concludes that people are bad-weather animals, acting only when the climate becomes unbearable.

3-66   Mott, Paul E. "Configurations of Power." In THE STRUCTURE OF COMMUNITY POWER, edited by Michael Aiken et al., pp. 85-99. New York: Random House, 1970.

Attempts to delineate the manner in which community power groups are linked to form the core of the community influence process. The author develops a model which depicts communities as organizations that function for the exchange of influence.

3-67   _____. "Power, Authority and Influence." In THE STRUCTURE OF COMMUNITY POWER, edited by Michael Aiken et al., pp. 3-18. New York: Random House, 1970.

Attempts to define power, influence, and authority, and indicate how they are related to social control and to one another. These concepts are woven into a framework which is tested for its capacity to generate new hypotheses and fresh interpretations of existing research findings.

3-68   Mulder, Mark. "Power Equalization through Participation." ADMINISTRATIVE SCIENCE QUARTERLY 16 (March 1971): 31-38.

Criticizes the popular assumption that participation of the less

powerful in decision-making processes results in an equiliza-
tion of power between the otherwise more powerful and the
less powerful. Empirical data on European work councils and
three laboratory experiments indicate that participation actually
increases power differences.

3-69 Mulder, Mark, and Wilke, Henke. "Participation and Power Equalization." ORGANIZATIONAL BEHAVIOR AND HUMAN PERFORMANCE
5 (September 1970): 430-48.

Presents empirical evidence undermining the popular assumption that participation in decision making will result in power
equalization between the "haves" and "have nots." Evidence
indicates that when great differences exist in the expert power
of group members, the participation process provides the more
powerful persons with greater opportunities for using their expert power--resulting in an increase of their influence over
the less powerful.

3-70 Newton, Kenneth. "American Urban Politics: Social Class, Political
Structure and Public Goods." URBAN AFFAIRS QUARTERLY 11 (December 1975): 241-64.

Summarizes the effects of fragmentation as follows: (1) it
creates a large number of political arenas with control of access points; (2) it prevents solutions to problems; (3) it creates
powerless forms of government; (4) it obstructs conflict; (5) it
provides no strong base for political opposition; (6) it curtails
citizen access; and (7) it encourages feelings of powerlessness
and helplessness.

3-71 Nie, Norman H.; Verba, Sidney; and Gae-On, Kim. "Political Participation and the Life Cycle." COMPARATIVE POLITICS 6 (April 1974):
319-40.

Presents data to establish a relationship between age and political participation. If, however, a correction is made for the
differing educational attainments of the various age groups, it
is found that older groups participate as much as any average
citizen.

3-72 Nisbet, Robert. COMMUNITY AND POWER. New York: Oxford University Press, 1962.

Deals with the impact of certain conceptions of political power
upon social organization in modern Western society and traces
the political factors that explain the contemporary quest for
community. The author concludes that we are suspended between two worlds of allegiance and association. On the one
hand is the historic world which entails loyalties to family,
church, profession, and the local community. On the other

hand is the world of values associated with the absolute political community. In the Western democracies, we have begun
to move into the latter without completely abandoning the
former.

3-73 O'Brien, David J. NEIGHBORHOOD ORGANIZATION AND INTEREST-
GROUP PROCESSES. Princeton, N.J.: Princeton University Press, 1975.

A theoretical and empirical analysis of the problems involved
in efforts to organize the residents of a poor neighborhood to
pursue their common interests vis-a-vis other interest groups
and public authorities in the local decision-making process.
The approach is based upon the assumption that even though
persons in a poor neighborhood have interests in common,
they are all "self-interested individuals" who are trying to
cope rationally with their problems.

3-74 Orbell, J., and Uno, T. "A Theory of Neighborhood Problem Solving:
Political Action vs. Residential Mobility." AMERICAN POLITICAL
SCIENCE REVIEW 66 (June 1972): 471-89.

Examines how and why people respond to neighborhood problems, and the consequences of their responses for the neighborhood itself. This paper is based upon survey data of different parts of the San Francisco metropolitan area. Findings
indicate that higher-status whites are prone both to voice and
exit, but more to voice; lower status whites are more prone
to exit; blacks are more likely to voice in response to problems than are whites of similar status who live in similar urban areas.

3-75 Overly, Don H. "Decision-Making in City Government: A Proposal."
URBAN AFFAIRS QUARTERLY 3 (December 1967): 41-53.

Contends that many inadequacies of local government can be
overcome by the use of systems analysis, even though it may
prove disruptive to traditional forms of local government. It
would increase the visibility of the decision process; focus more
attention upon the question of optimum resources allocation;
and force officials to face directly the issue of administrative
feasibility.

3-76 Perrucci, Robert, and Pelesuk, Marc. "Leaders as Ruling Elites: The
Interorganizational Bases of Community Power." AMERICAN SOCIOLOG-
ICAL REVIEW 35 (December 1970): 1040-57.

Examines community power in terms of the phenomena of inter-
organization which results from the same people holding overlapping executive positions in different organizations. This

study, undertaken in a small midwestern community, tested the existence of ruling elites in the community power structure. It found that such a group existed with actual power, common interests, and definite social ties. Although not involved in every community decision, this elite had a power resource in the form of ties to the decision makers of community organizations.

3-77 Peterson, George E. "Voter Demand for Public School Expenditures." In PUBLIC NEEDS AND PRIVATE BEHAVIOR IN METROPOLITAN AREAS, edited by John E. Jackson, pp. 99-115. Cambridge, Mass.: Ballinger, 1975.

Examines specific hypotheses about the character of household demands for public services by analyzing a single issue referenda of local tax elections. The chapter is divided into three sections. The first compares citizen demands for public school spending to household demands for ordinary goods. The comparison reveals that a demand function can be derived which is analogous in every respect to the demand functions that economists ordinarily treat. Section 2 presents several empirical estimates of the demand for public school spending, employing individual household as well as aggregate school district data. The last section explores the policy implications of the strong "tax-price" term contained in the household demand function.

3-78 Pettigrew, Thomas F. "When a Black Candidate Runs for Mayor: Race and Voting Behavior." In PEOPLE AND POLITICS IN URBAN SOCIETY, edited by Harlan Hahn, pp. 95-118. Beverly Hills, Calif.: Sage Publications, 1972.

See 3-44.

3-79 Riker, William H. A THEORY OF POLITICAL COALITIONS. New Haven, Conn.: Yale University Press, 1962.

Uses the theory of n-person games to construct a theory of coalitions applicable to the study of politics. Riker's dynamic model is described in detail from a mathematical perspective. The last chapter assesses the relevance of the model to the world.

3-80 Rissman, Frank, and Gartner, Alan. "Community Control and Radical Social Change." SOCIAL POLICY 1 (May-June 1970): 52-55.

Argues that the community control movement is at a "decisive turning point" in its development, examines the basic aims of the movement, its preliminary accomplishments, and the special dilemmas it faces. The authors conclude that the demand for local community control must be connected to larger, na-

tional and international issues because the basic problems of
our society originate and the basic control of resources lies
at a national and centralized level.

3-81   Rogers, David. THE MANAGEMENT OF BIG CITIES: INTEREST
GROUPS AND SOCIAL CHANGE STRATEGIES. Beverly Hills, Calif.:
Sage Publications, 1971.

See 1-60.

3-82   Sanders, Marion K. THE PROFESSIONAL RADICAL: CONVERSATIONS
WITH SAUL ALINSKY. New York: Harper and Row, 1970.

A series of conversations between the author and community
organizer, Saul Alinsky, between 1965 and 1969. The first
part acquaints the reader with Alinsky--where he came from
and how he developed his radical ideology. In the second
part, Alinsky relates his ideas on community organization.
He maintains that an organizer must be highly trained, politically sophisticated, and creative. He must deal with issues
on a regional and national basis, not just a local level, due
to the severity and magnitude of the problems. He does not
believe people should be organized on the basis of altruism,
"the way white liberals tried to do something for the Blacks,"
because the right things get done for the wrong reasons. He
talks about his struggles with Eastman Kodak in Rochester,
New York, with the Woodlawn Organization, and with Mayor
Daley in Chicago.

3-83   Savitch, H.V., and Adler, Madeline. "Decentralization at the Grass
Roots: Political Innovation in New York City and London." SAGE PRO-
FESSIONAL PAPERS IN ADMINISTRATIVE AND POLICY STUDIES 2,
03-018. Beverly Hills, Calif. and London: Sage Publications, 1974.

A pamphlet studying the relationships between conditions surrounding decentralization and decision-making processes within
decentralized subsystems. The authors examine three conditions
that must be fulfilled if decentralization is to be successful:
(1) subsystem legitimacy, (2) leadership capability, and (3)
structural capability.

3-84   Schaffer, Albert, and Schaffer, Ruth C. WOODRUFF: A STUDY OF
COMMUNITY DECISION-MAKING. Chapel Hill: University of North
Carolina Press, 1970.

Studies decision making in the fictitious community of Woodruff,
located in the Midwest. Woodruff has both heavy industry and
farming, a metropolitan city, and old and new ethnic groups.
The metropolitan city's ecological structure and the town's
lack of taxing powers prevented both government units from
obtaining the revenues needed to accommodate a growing econ-

omy and population. As the gap between demands and services widened, the conflicts intensified. The authors examine this situation, and the reasons why efforts to change the social and ecological structure failed to ease the tensions.

3-85 Schmandt, Henry J. "Decentralization: A Structural Imperative." In NEIGHBORHOOD CONTROL IN THE 1970S, edited by H. George Frederickson, pp. 17-35. New York: Chandler Publishing Co., 1973.

Argues that there are no fixed factors in the decentralization process. It is time to move from abstractions to concrete plans for determining precise responsibilities that can be delegated to the neighborhood level and the machinery that can be used for administering them. Further, a set of coherent strategies for translating these plans into action must be formulated.

3-86 Schultze, William A. URBAN AND COMMUNITY POLITICS. North Scituate, Mass.: Duxbury Press, 1974.

See 2-50.

3-87 Skogan, Wesley G. "Groups in the Policy Process: The Police and Urban Crime." POLICY STUDIES JOURNAL 3 (Summer 1975): 354-58.

Contends that urban law enforcement bureaucracies now serve as interest groups in their own right. The author believes that their emergence as autonomous combatants in the policy-making process has exacerbated the management problems of public officials, leading many mayors simply to abdicate their responsibilities as policy implementers.

3-87a Spiegel, Hans B.C., ed. CITIZEN PARTICIPATION IN URBAN DEVELOPMENT. 2 vols. Washington, D.C.: Center for Community Affairs of the NTL Institute of Applied Behavioral Science, 1968.

Volume 1 discusses "Concepts and Issues" of public participation, and reviews the development and application of the concept. The second volume deals with "Cases and Programs" and presents examples of public participation (pre-1967).

3-88 _____. DECENTRALIZATION: CITIZEN PARTICIPATION IN URBAN DEVELOPMENT. Vol. 3. Fairfax, Va.: Learning Resources Corp. National Training Laboratories, 1974.

Deals with the concept of decentralization. The first chapter introduces the reader to the subject, and the second examines decentralization in terms of the Model Cities program. In chapter 3, "The New York City Experience," John Lindsay and others examine the city government in light of decentralization. Chapter 4 examines the delivery of municipal services and considers the fiscal implications of decentralization. The differences between community and decentralized control of schools are assessed in chapter 5, and chapter 6 investigates the effect of decentralization on jobs. In the final chapter, the neighborhood unit is reconsidered in light of decentralization.

3-89   Stedman, Murray S., Jr. URBAN POLITICS. 2d ed. Cambridge, Mass.: Winthrop Publishers, 1975.

Examines several aspects of urban politics. Part one, "The Urban Political Environment," deals largely with political institutions and processes in cities. Part two describes the official model of urban politics, in essence the pluralist model. Part three discusses old style politics and part four examines community power structures, i.e., who has power. Finally, part five examines politics in the delivery of urban services.

3-90   Steggert, Frank X. COMMUNITY ACTION GROUPS AND CITY GOVERNMENTS. Cambridge, Mass.: Ballinger, 1975.

Contains material from ten final reports of participating "urban observations." Steggert presents a summary of citizen participation organizations under the Urban Observatory program. He reports common findings with respect to the: (1) kinds of citizen groups engaged in contacts with city governments; (2) issues that initiated such involvements; and (3) estimates of group effectiveness. In Denver and Atlanta, for example, middle-class activism was triggered by proposed rezonings. Increased activism in the inner city of Milwaukee resulted from social changes, such as urban renewal and highway construction. Steggert concludes that when people move out of the cities the people left behind have voices but no resources, and even their voices ultimately lapse into passivity. How to develop viable forms of citizen participation will be the critical urban question of the future.

3-91   Stenberg, Carl W. "Decentralization and the City." In MUNICIPAL YEARBOOK 1972, pp. 88-96. Washington, D.C.: ICMA, 1972.

Discusses and differentiates three types of decentralization-- territorial, administrative, and political. The author describes the progress that has been made in decentralizing services and citizen decision making concerning their delivery. He cites factors that determine the degree of authority and discretion provided to citizen groups, including jurisdictional size, location, type, and form of government.

3-92   "Symposium on Neighborhoods and Citizen Involvement." PUBLIC ADMINISTRATION REVIEW 32 (May-June 1972): 189-223.

This symposium is an effort by the National Capital Area chap-

ter of the American Society for Public Administration to clarify
the issues and problems associated with citizen involvement
and participation. The topics presented are: "Citizens and
the Administrative State: From Participation to Power," "Citizen Participation in Metropolitan Planning," "Citizen Partici-
pation--An Exercise in Futility: An Action Program for ASPA,"
"Neighborhoods and Citizen Involvement," "Citizen Participation and Racism," "Citizen Participation: Myths and Realities,"
"Academic Advisors and Citizen Participation," and "Citizen
Participation Recommendations."

3-93   Taebel, Delbert A. "Citizen Groups, Public Policy, and Urban Trans-
        portation." TRAFFIC QUARTERLY 27 (October 1973): 503-15.

        Discusses the activity of citizen groups in highway programs.
        Taebel examines five basic factors which either contribute to
        or impede the efforts of citizen action groups: legitimacy,
        the scope of conflict, the span of attention, technocratism,
        and immobilization.

3-93a   Vanecko, James J., et al. COMMUNITY ORGANIZATION EFFORTS,
        POLITICAL AND INSTITUTIONAL CHANGE, AND THE DIFFUSION OF
        CHANGE PRODUCED BY COMMUNITY ACTION PROGRAMS. FINAL
        REPORT ON PHASE I. Chicago: National Opinion Research Center,
        1969.

        An evaluation of those characteristics of community action
        agencies which affect the responsiveness of other institutions
        to the poor. The authors examine the way community action
        agencies influence institutional and procedural changes in pub-
        lic schools, the private welfare sectors, employment practices,
        and neighborhood political structure. The paper includes fifty-
        seven tables.

3-94   Verba, Sidney, and Nie, Norman H. PARTICIPATION IN AMERICA:
        POLITICAL DEMOCRACY AND SOCIAL EQUALITY. New York: Harper
        and Row, 1972.

        Examines citizen participation in the political process and its
        effect on the responsiveness of government leaders. By assess-
        ing a number of variables, the authors construct a model of
        the causes and consequences of participation that is applicable
        to any nation. They describe the extent and type of partici-
        pation, the kinds of groups who participate, and some of the
        consequences of participation.

3-95   Warren, Roland L.; Rose, Stephen M.; and Bergunder, Ann F. "Com-
        munity Decision Organizations and Urban Reform." URBAN AND SO-
        CIAL CHANGE REVIEW 7 (Spring 1974): 42-47.

        Results of a study of six organizations in nine cities in the

United States. The study sheds light on how community decision organizations (CDOs) operate as individual organizations
in their interaction with each other and with other types of
organizations. The data and analysis focuses on the organizations' efforts to improve life-style of low-income residents of
the inner cities.

3-96   Washnis, George J. MUNICIPAL DECENTRALIZATION AND NEIGH-
       BORHOOD RESOURCES. New York: Praeger Publishers, 1972.

       Examines decentralization in twelve cities. In recent years
       advocates of decentralization have emphasized the need to
       seek out citizen attitudes and to give citizens greater author-
       ity. To determine the significance of this trend, the Center
       for Governmental Studies, in conjunction with International
       City Management Association, conducted a survey of the
       eight hundred largest cities and urban counties in the United
       States. Twelve cities were selected as a representative sample
       of different regions, city size, types of decentralization, and
       forms of municipal government. The cities include Atlanta,
       Baltimore, Boston, Chicago, Columbus, Houston, Kansas City,
       Missouri, Los Angeles, New York, Norfolk, San Francisco,
       and San Antonio.

3-97   Watterson, Wayt T., and Watterson, Roberta S. THE POLITICS OF
       NEW COMMUNITIES: A CASE STUDY OF SAN ANTONIO RANCH.
       New York: Praeger Publishers, 1975.

       Examines the impacts of new communities on local areas.
       After presenting a documentary history of San Antonio Ranch,
       Texas, from its inception through various trial procedures, the
       author relates the events and their causes to a framework of
       political and decision-making theory for each level of govern-
       ment involved, including local, state, regional, and federal.
       He emphasizes the pervasive federal influence on local events.
       Finally, he examines the San Antonio Ranch case in terms of
       new community development in general.

3-98   Weissman, H.H. COMMUNITY COUNCILS AND COMMUNITY CON-
       TROL. Pittsburgh: University of Pittsburgh Press, 1970.

       Develops a model to explain the operation of neighborhood
       councils and other voluntary civic organizations and to suggest
       how they might be more effective in achieving their ends.
       The focus of the study is the DuPont Neighborhood Council.

3-99   Whalen, Richard J. A CITY DESTROYING ITSELF; AN ANGRY VIEW
       OF NEW YORK. New York: Apollo Editions, 1965.

       Short essays describing the author's concern and frustration
       over New York City. Whalen suggests that New York has

received the type of government it deserves. Many leading citizens, as well as the middle class, turned their backs on the city in its time of need. The author laments the civic indifference and apathy of New Yorkers. Business and labor leaders have shunned the opportunity and the responsibility for making the city a much better place. New York, he says, has been abandoned physically and psychologically and requires a change of heart on the part of all its citizens.

3-100 Willeke, Gene E. "Citizen Participation: Here to Stay." CIVIL ENGINEERING 44 (January 1974): 78-82.

Advocates citizen participation in the planning process. Willeke believes citizen participation would result in a better plan, increase the probability of the plan's implementation, and increase the likelihood that potential beneficiaries will receive the benefits intended for them. Other benefits which he cites include conflict resolution among various segments of society, increased credibility and acceptance of the planning agency, and public education.

3-101 Wilson, James [Q.], and Banfield, Edward [C.]. "Political Ethos Revisited." THE AMERICAN POLITICAL SCIENCE REVIEW 65 (December 1971): 1048-62.

Study of a sample of predominantly male Boston homeowners discovering two distinctive political orientations towards the scope, goals, and principles of local governmental action. One ethos, the "unitarist," reflects holistic and community-serving conceptions of the public interest; the other one, the "individualist," is characterized by localistic and people-helping conceptions of the public good. The authors found that, although the unitarists comprised only a small part of the Boston electorate, their influence on the city's affairs was far out of proportion to their numbers.

3-102 Wirt, Frederick M., ed. FUTURE DIRECTIONS IN COMMUNITY POWER RESEARCH: A COLLOQUIUM. Berkeley and Los Angeles: University of California, Institute of Governmental Studies, 1971.

Collection of essays prepared for a colloquium on the study of community power. In the first essay, Charles Adrian develops a theory of community power. "Dimensions of Power Structure," by Charles Bonjean, discusses a power structure typology and some of the problems it presents. Terry N. Clark looks at community structure, decision making, budget expenditures and urban renewal in fifty-one American communities. The application of computers to community power study is examined by Floyd Hunter. Harry M. Scoble states his view of where the pluralists went wrong in "The Power Grid of the Metropolis." G. Ross Stephens discusses the dimensions of community power, and John Walton addresses the question, "Why Study Power Structures?"

3-103 Wofford, John G. "Participatory Planning for Boston Metro-Area Transportation." CIVIL ENGINEERING 43 (April 1973): 78-81.

Participation of private citizens, organized groups, and local officials in the transportation planning and decision-making process as a key ingredient in Boston's attempt to achieve a balanced transportation system. Each transportation technology was allotted a main area of responsibility in order to create a truly integrated transportation system. The author concludes that to insure this system, it is necessary to use reasoned analysis and an open forum to guarantee that public decisions are responsive to a wide spectrum of values and priorities.

3-103a Zimmerman, Joseph F. "Community Building in Large Cities." ADMINISTRATION (DUBLIN) 20 (Summer 1972): 71-87.

Argues that a community spirit is essential to a healthy local government. Four steps can be taken to promote this spirit in disadvantaged neighborhoods: (1) official recognition and support of neighborhood organizations, (2) improvement of neighborhood-municipal communications, (3) administrative decentralization, and (4) transfer of political powers to neighborhood governments.

3-104 _____. THE FEDERATED CITY: COMMUNITY CONTROL IN LARGE CITIES. New York: St. Martin's Press, 1973.

Examines the origins of the neighborhood government movement and discusses the politics of establishing a system of limited neighborhood control of schools in New York and Detroit. Zimmerman focuses upon the administrative response of large municipal governments to the growing pressures for neighborhood government, assesses arguments for and against the reform model, and analyzes the political support for the changes.

3-105 Zisk, Betty [H.]. LOCAL INTEREST POLITICS. Indianapolis: Bobbs-Merrill, 1973.

Examines interest group influence from data obtained from interviews with city councilmen in the cities of the San Francisco Bay area. The author presents a theory which links the economic environment, the quality of group life, council/group relations, and policies in these cities. She examines the attitudes of councilmen toward interest group activity and their awareness of group influence.

3-106 _____. "Local Interest Politics and Municipal Outputs." In PEOPLE

AND POLITICS IN URBAN SOCIETY, edited by Harlan Hahn, pp. 231-54. Beverly Hills, Calif.: Sage Publications, 1972.

Assesses the relevance of political activity to policy outputs. The author finds that policy outcomes are greatly circumscribed by the environment in which the political decisions are made. Nevertheless, the political conversion and translation process have an independent effect on some public choices. The author found that political potential, such as words, attitudes, or a paper organization, carries little weight in comparison to concrete activity such as group participation in elections and council reliance on group aid in selling their ideas to the community.

3-106a _____ . "The Study of Urban Politics." AMERICAN JOURNAL OF POLITICAL SCIENCE 17 (February 1973): 196-204.

Argues that urban specialists have failed to define their field, to agree on common concepts and strategies, and to cooperate among themselves. The study of urban politics should include more comparative and interdisciplinary work and more emphasis on decision-making processes rather than structure.

3-107 Zisk, Betty H.; Eulau, Heinz; and Prewitt, Kenneth. "City Councilmen and the Group Struggle: A Typology of Role Orientations." JOURNAL OF POLITICS 27 (August 1975): 618-46.

Analyzes the perceptions, attitudes, and behavior of city councilmen toward group spokesmen and toward interest group activity in general and examines the influence of interest groups on political decision makers. The authors conclude that most councilmen do not view interest group activities as indispensable to the political system, and that unless groups are both salient and valued, the political actor in the local community makes little effort to modify his behavior on their behalf.

Chapter 4
SOCIOETHNIC POLITICS

Included in this chapter are entries relating to black communities, white ethnic groups, and urban social systems.

4-1   Aberbach, J[oel].D., and Walker, J[ack].L. "The Attitudes of Blacks and Whites Toward City Services: Implications for Public Policy." In FINANCING THE METROPOLIS, edited by John P. Crecine, pp. 519-38. Beverly Hills, Calif.: Sage Publications, 1970.

Study of Detroit in 1967-68 reviewing the public's evaluations of services by analyzing the correlates of dissatisfaction among black and white citizens. The authors conclude that within the present delivery system and within the existing city service levels, public opinion is a crucial factor in public agency actions.

4-2   _____. RACE IN THE CITY: POLITICAL TRUST AND PUBLIC POLICY IN THE NEW URBAN SYSTEM. Boston: Little, Brown and Co., 1973.

Studies of race relations and politics in Detroit, in 1967 and 1971. Attitudes of black and white residents about city life--their complaints and fears, their likes and dislikes, and their evaluation of Detroit as a work place and residence--are described. The meaning of the new black militancy and the responses of white citizens were also investigated.

4-3   Altshuler, Alan A. COMMUNITY CONTROL: THE BLACK DEMAND FOR PARTICIPATION IN LARGE AMERICAN CITIES. New York: Pegasus, 1970.

Examines the black demand for community control and looks at areas in which the current power structure can meet the demands of the oppressed.

4-4   Ambrecht, Biliana C.S., and Pachon, Harry P. "Ethnic Political Mobilization in a Mexican American Community: An Exploratory Study of East Los Angeles 1965-1972." WESTERN POLITICAL SCIENCE QUAR-

TERLY 27 (September 1974): 500-519.

Examines the attitudinal and behavioral changes in a sample group of an east Los Angeles Mexican-American community. The authors explore the rise in ethnic consciousness, evaluate the political relevance of this progress and conclude that there is increased potential for ethnic political mobilization because of increased desire to engage in cooperative activity, increased awareness of the relevance of politics, and increased desire to favor ethnically-based political activity.

4-5   Aron, William S.; Alger, Norman; and Gonzales, Richard T. "Chicanoizing Drug Abuse Programs." HUMAN ORGANIZATION 33 (Winter 1974): 388-90.

Focuses on the problem of drug addiction and its underlying conditions of poverty, lack of education, and discrimination in the Mexican-American community of LaColonia in Oxnael, California. These conditions lead to a negative self-image and high unemployment. The authors conclude that drug programs must be open to anyone and the area itself must be rehabilitated in order to improve the community.

4-6   Bailey, Harry A., ed. NEGRO POLITICS IN AMERICA. Columbus, Ohio: Charles E. Merrill Books, 1967.

Selected articles presenting an empirical and systematic explanation of Negro politics in America. The readings cover the decades of 1950 and 1960 and include the Negro subcommunity and the political system, political leadership in the subcommunity, Negro politics in the South and North, government outputs to the subcommunity, and the future of Negro politics.

4-6a   Banfield, Edward [C.], and Wilson, James Q. CITY POLITICS. Cambridge, Mass.: Harvard University Press, 1963.

See 1-6.

4-7   Baron, Harold M. "Institutional Racism in the Modern Metropolis." In ON THE URBAN SCENE, edited by Morton Levitt and Ben Rubenstein, pp. 99-114. Detroit: Wayne State University Press, 1973.

Distinguishes between the ideology of racism and institutional racism. Baron believes that the Kerner Commission did not deal with the real problem of institutional racism. He develops a three-part model to handle urban racism in an institutional structure and observes that under the new institutional arrangements of metropolitan racial controls is a shift in the ideology of racism and its symbols.

4-8   Barrera, Mario; Munoz, Carlos; and Ornelas, Charles. "The Barrio as
       an Internal Colony." In PEOPLE AND POLITICS IN URBAN SOCIETY,
       edited by Harlan Hahn, pp. 465-98. Beverly Hills, Calif.: Sage Pub-
       lications, 1972.

       See 4-68.

4-9   Barth, E.C., and Abu-Labau, B. "Power Structure and the Negro Sub-
       Community." AMERICAN SOCIOLOGICAL REVIEW 24 (February 1959):
       69-76.

       Influence system in the Negro subcommunity of "Pacific City"
       related to other dimensions of the subcommunity of social
       structure. The influential Negroes and Negro organizations
       were identified using a research design similar to that em-
       ployed by Floyd Hunter in his study of "Regional City." This
       provided a basis for comparison of findings. The data indicate
       that the Negro leaders were primarily concerned with issues
       of an interracial nature. Their subcommunity lacked large
       scale business and industrial organizations and, consequently,
       no genuine power structure had developed. The investigation
       suggests that use of a typological approach is very effective
       when carried out within the framework of a comparative re-
       search design.

4-10   Bates, Timothy. "Trends in Government Promotion of Black Entrepreneur-
       ship." REVIEW OF BLACK POLITICAL ECONOMY 5 (Winter 1975):
       175-84.

       A study examining the Small Business Administration's (SBA)
       efforts to assist minority businessmen. It looks at the changes
       in the volume of dollars channeled to central city business-
       men under SBA loan programs. Bates divided loan recipients
       into white, black, and other minority groups. His evidence
       indicates that government loans to encourage black capitalism
       have been declining and government efforts to aid minority
       enterprise have stagnated.

4-11   Bellush, Jewel, and David, S.M., eds. RACE AND POLITICS IN
       NEW YORK CITY. New York: Praeger Publishers, 1971.

       Attacks the pluralist view that competing groups characterize
       the decision-making process in American cities. The emer-
       gence of conflicts in American cities involving their black
       citizenry has caused doubts about the pluralists' notion that
       our cities are governed in a democratic and responsive way.
       The book examines the policy areas of health, education,
       housing, welfare, and police, using New York City as its
       example. In each policy area the participants in the decision-
       making area were identified, the actors were traced during the
       time of conflict, and specific outcomes of the conflict were
       determined and analyzed.

4-12 Bergsman, Joel, and Jones, Melvin. "Modeling Minority Economic Development." REVIEW OF BLACK POLITICAL ECONOMY, Fall 1973, pp. 41-71.

Describes a model viewing minority development in the nation as a whole in terms of education, training, and capital. A second model looks at a single city and the early stages of a community development corporation whose first business venture is a cable TV company in terms of interaction of income, education, and political power.

4-13 Boggs, James. "Blacks in the Cities: Agenda for the 70s." THE BLACK SCHOLAR 4 (November-December 1972): 50-61.

An article taken from a speech at the Black Consciousness Conference at the University of Detroit in 1972. Boggs particularly emphasizes how blacks can change cities to be better places to live and work. He sees a need to develop a new outlook among blacks and he considers ways to accomplish this.

4-14 Booher, David E. POVERTY IN AN URBAN SOCIETY: A BIBLIOGRAPHY. Exchange Bibliography Series, no. 246. Monticello, Ill.: Council of Planning Librarians, 1971.

Available from the Council of Planning Librarians, Box 229, Monticello, Illinois 61856. $3.00.

4-15 Boyd, William L., and Seldin, Florence. "The Politics of School Reform in Rochester, New York." EDUCATION AND URBAN SOCIETY 7 (August 1975): 439-63.

Notes that the serious problems of urban education have produced countless calls for reform. Despite extensive efforts, especially in the area of community control and school desegration, little progress has been made and all hope of reform has been abandoned. The authors examine this issue through a study of the Rochester, New York, school system. The findings illustrate the general inability of minority groups to obtain social and political goals through protest or other more conventional forms of bargaining. The authors argue that the schools cater to white middle class values and that concessions made to minority groups, like community control, are only token measures and lack real power.

4-16 Browne, Robert S. "The Constellation of Politics and Economics." REVIEW OF BLACK POLITICAL ECONOMY 2 (Fall 1971): 44-55.

Contends that blacks have attained political power without first having economic power; this is a reversal of the normal process. Blacks must now secure increased capital investment in their neighborhoods, but their political power has not yet been sufficient to achieve this.

4-17   Calaldo, E.C.; Johnson, R.M.; and Kellstedt, L.A. "Political Atti-
tudes of Urban Blacks and Whites, Some Implications for Policy Makers."
In URBAN POLITICAL ANALYSIS: A SYSTEMS APPROACH, edited by
D.R. Morgan and S.A. Kirkpatrick, pp. 116-26. New York: Free
Press, 1972.

Draws on an ongoing study of agencies of social change and
political behavior in Buffalo. It deals with issues such as
black political efficacy and black-white perceptions of public
policy and governmental action. The study concludes that
blacks do not show a sense of despair and hopelessness and
have made considerable progress in the past few years in terms
of the nation and local community.

4-18   California State Advisory Committee to the United States Commission on
Civil Rights. POLITICAL PARTICIPATION OF MEXICAN AMERICANS
IN CALIFORNIA. Washington, D.C.: U.S. Commission on Civil
Rights, August 1971.

Presents the discussion and recommendations of the commission
on the political participation of Mexican Americans. Topics
discussed include reapportionment and its effect on the Mexican-American community, voter rights, influence on major
political parties, political use of police and the courts, political appointments, Mexican-American political problems in
rural and urban areas, and political racism in California.

4-19   Caplovitz, David. THE MERCHANTS OF HARLEM: A STUDY OF
SMALL BUSINESS IN A BLACK COMMUNITY. Beverly Hills, Calif.:
Sage Publications, 1973.

Discusses a survey of retail businesses in Harlem by the Harlem
Development Project in the spring and summer of 1968. Caplovitz compares black and white Harlem businessmen and attempts to show whether differences are due to race, experience,
size, or type of establishment.

4-20   Carmichael, Stokely, and Hamilton, Charles. BLACK POWER. New
York: Vintage, 1967.

Attempts to raise the consciousness of blacks in the United
States and to provide a framework by which the "politics of
liberation" can take place. Blacks in this country must unite,
recognize their heritage, and build a sense of community.
The authors call for a rejection of the racist values and institutions of our society. Blacks and other minorities must
gain solidarity before they can work effectively to overcome

oppression. The authors conclude that blacks must lead and run their own organizations before they can make progress in combating racism.

4-21   Chamberlayne, Prue. "Teachers Versus the Community." NEW SOCIETY 26 (November 1973): 398-400.

Discusses the teaching of children in minority communities by predominately white teachers. Minority groups charge the white teachers with cultural bias and the continued production of illiterates. This article reviews the violent and nonviolent reactions of various minority groups and fractions.

4-22   Chapin, F. Stuart, Jr. "Determinants of Activity Patterns." In his HUMAN ACTIVITY PATTERNS IN THE CITY, pp. 157-94. New York: John Wiley & Sons, 1974.

Assumes that free time activity choices can be considered an indicator of life-style. The conclusions in this chapter bring out several contrasts both within and between a nonblack low income neighborhood and a black low income community in the Washington, D.C. area. In the black community, passive activities account for up to 72.5 percent of the average subject's free time; in the white community, 45.8 percent. The study indicates that in the black community, passive activities are most strongly associated with unemployment, the male sex, and old age. In the white community passive activities are related to status, poor health, degree of alienation, and old age. The absence of opportunities in these two communities for choosing other alternatives may have some bearing on the heavy emphasis on passive activities.

4-23   _____. "Variations in Activity Patterns Among Different Population Segments." In his HUMAN ACTIVITY PATTERNS IN THE CITY, pp. 123-55. New York: John Wiley & Sons, 1974.

Explores ethnic and status differences in discretionary activity patterns and deals with the effects of role and personal characteristics on activity patterns. Chapin concludes that once a population is subaggregated along ethnic and status lines, the influence that role and personal characteristics have on activity choices becomes much more focused.

4-24   Chisholm, Shirley. "Ghetto Power in Action: The Value of Positive Political Action." In THE BLACK POLITICIAN: HIS STRUGGLE FOR POWER, edited by Mervyn M. Dymally, pp. 40-42, 123-31. Belmont, Calif.: Duxbury Press, 1971.

Text of Chisholm's speech to the National Urban League on July 27, 1969. She called for the end of two Americas--one white, the other black; attacked defense spending and the

Vietnam War, suggesting we spend the money at home to help alleviate hunger.

4-25   Cho, Yong Hyo. "City Politics and Racial Polarization: Bloc Voting in Cleveland Elections." JOURNAL OF BLACK STUDIES 4 (June 1974): 396-417.

Looks at nineteen elections over a period of years and studies bloc voting by blacks in an effort to measure the success of black political power. Cho concludes that bloc voting was significant in nearly every election since 1965 but its influence is decisively greater in local elections than in national and state elections. He also finds that blacks see greater benefits in local elections and find them more relevant to their interests than state or national elections.

4-26   Christmas, Walter, ed. NEGROES IN PUBLIC AFFAIRS AND GOVERN-MENT. Vol. 1. New York: M.W. Lads Co., 1966.

A Who's Who in black public affairs. It covers the United Nations, the Congress, the Judiciary, the Diplomatic Service, and the executive departments and agencies. A biographical sketch is given of each black official which includes date and place of birth and death, accomplishments, work experience, and education.

4-27   Christopher, Maurine. AMERICA'S BLACK CONGRESSMEN. New York: Thomas Y. Crowell Co., 1971.

Christopher gives a biographical sketch of each of twenty-seven black representatives in Congress and tells how each came to be elected, the problems faced, and individual accomplishments. The list of black officials includes both men and women dating from the post-Civil War years.

4-28   Clark, Dennis. "The Tradition Persists." In his THE IRISH IN PHILA-DELPHIA: TEN GENERATIONS OF URBAN EXPERIENCE, pp. 145-64. Philadelphia: Temple University Press, 1974.

Shows the Irish as leaders of the community through the organization of labor unions serving under President Kennedy. Clark gives a historical summary of men and their actions in Philadelphia to show the strong tradition of loyalty, leadership, and Catholic beliefs the Irish possessed. With the rise of the urban crisis, the Irish achievement of social advancement, based upon political and electoral persistence and personal diligence, was no longer an antidote for the ills of urban institutions. With the increase of the black population in the city and the changing forces in the Catholic Church, the Irish organization underwent great changes. By the 1960s, the Irish were no longer the powerful force they were for the previous fifty years.

4-29 _____. "The Urban Irishman." In his THE IRISH IN PHILADELPHIA: TEN GENERATIONS OF URBAN EXPERIENCE, pp. 165-83. Philadelphia: Temple University Press, 1974.

Clark traces the process and organization of the Irish from the 1800s to the present. Two significant trends were observed: (1) Industrialization and urbanization became the process through which the Irish moved from folk society into modern life, (2) Irish temperament, cultural outlook, and historical experiences equipped them to cope with the contradictions and turmoil of urban life. They used religion and ethnic ties to promote their own organization and advancement under city conditions, and proved extremely adaptable. Clark also makes comparisons between the Irish development in Philadelphia and in cities such as Boston and New York.

4-30 Clark, Kenneth. DARK GHETTO. New York: Harper Torchbooks, 1965.

Clark's interpretation of the facts of the ghetto; the truths behind the delinquency, narcotics addiction, infant mortality, homicide, and suicide statistics. He participated in Harlem Youth Opportunities Unlimited (HARYOU), a study on youth in the ghetto, between 1962 and 1964.

4-31 Cohen, David K. "Segregation, Desegregation, and Brown." SOCIETY 12 (November/December 1974): 34-40.

Contends that Brown v. Board of Education, the historic 1954 Supreme Court decision outlawing racial segregation, has been an enormous positive force in American history, but that it has generated enormous uncertainty concerning its ultimate consequences. Desegregation raised white consciousness and changed some white institutions; but the impact of the decision and its benefits have cost dearly, because the society is resistent to desegregation.

4-32 Cohen, Fay G. "The Indian Patrol in Minneapolis: Social Control and Social Change in an Urban Context." LAW AND SOCIETY REVIEW 7 (Summer 1973): 779-86.

A case study based on participant-observation between January 1969 and June 1970. The citizen patrols served two main functions: (1) observation of police squad car activity in the area, and (2) arrangements for intoxicants to be taken home. The patrols were only symbolic to show that Indians should police themselves. They had no formal authority and did not attempt to enforce the law.

4-33 Connolly, Harold X. "Black Movement into the Suburbs: Suburbs Doubling Their Black Populations During the 1970's." URBAN AFFAIRS QUARTERLY 9 (September 1973): 91-111.

See 6-23.

4-34 Cottingham, Phoebe H. "Black Income and Metropolitan Residential Dispersion." URBAN AFFAIRS QUARTERLY 10 (March 1975): 273-96.

Uses 1970 Census data for the Philadelphia metropolitan area to test assumptions about the residential dispersion of blacks into the suburbs. Cottingham finds that blacks are reluctant to move outside of the central city, even when they attain higher incomes. Indicators show that the residential patterns which exist in Philadelphia are similar to many metropolitan areas--whites live in the suburbs and blacks in the central city.

4-35 Davidson, Chandler. BIRACIAL POLITICS: CONFLICTS AND COALITION IN METROPOLITAN SOUTH. Baton Rouge: Louisiana State University Press, 1972.

A history of black political involvement since Reconstruction. The material compares current data with that of previous years to demonstrate certain political progress. Davidson develops a new southern strategy based on an economic coalition of blacks and whites and not electoral tokenism. A feasible coalition would contain a formal biracial alliance to work together for common goals, including income redistribution, redistribution of opportunity, and popular decision making. This coalition would be a radical departure from traditional practices, but Davidson argues that the cost of black separatism is higher.

4-36 Davis, Lenwood G., and Van Horne, Winston. "The City Renewed: White Dream-Black Nightmare?" BLACK SCHOLAR 7 (November 1975): 2-9.

Studies the city as a fulcrum of black power, white economic control of the city, attractiveness of the suburbs for blacks, and costs of the city's renewal to black people. The authors suggest that: (1) black leaders raise the consciousness of the black masses, (2) there be political education of the blacks by black leaders, (3) blacks sacrifice in order to achieve and sustain effective levels of socioeconomic mobilization, and (4) blacks show whites the potential of black destructive power.

4-37 Downes, B[ryan].T. "A Critical Reexamination of the Social and Political Characteristics of Riot Cities." SOCIAL SCIENCES QUARTERLY 51 (September 1970): 349-60.

Contends that agreement must first be reached on the meaning of "objective deprivation" before further analysis of the characteristics of riot cities can be undertaken. Nevertheless, the data does support the hypothesis that urban racial violence is likely when environmental conditions reach the "explosive point." These conditions generate hostile beliefs and attitudes

which may result in violence as a political resort when instigated by a precipitating factor. Violence should not be
viewed as pathological and exceptional when normal channels
for handling public complaints are inadequate.

4-38 Downs, Edward R., Jr. "The Impact of the Robinson-Patman Act on
Minority Business Development." REVIEW OF BLACK POLITICAL ECON-
OMY 4 (Fall 1973): 1-19.

Explores section 2(d) of the Robinson-Patman Act which pro-
hibits discrimination in payments afforded to one customer to
the exclusion of other competing customers. The major underlying purpose of this law has not been fulfilled. Two sections
of the act have actually hampered the development and staying
power of minority enterprises. Downs cites two reasons: (1)
the act does not take into account the differences in minority
businesses, and (2) government efforts to increase the number
of minority businesses have failed to recognize that these two
sections do in fact militate against minority enterprises. The
author proposes an antitrust solution.

4-39 Dye, Thomas R. THE POLITICS OF EQUALITY. New York: Bobbs-
Merrill Co., 1971.

Examines the history of the development of a racially stratified
society beginning with a slave policy, the pattern of political
and social forces that maintained that society, and the political role of blacks and whites in meeting persistent demands
for change in the relative status of the two races. The book
is an overview rather than a detailed account. Dye predicts
continued black social and economic equalization through
increased group awareness, black voting power, and the forces
of assimilation.

4-40 Dymally, Mervyn, ed. THE BLACK POLITICIAN: HIS STRUGGLE FOR
POWER. Belmont, Calif.: Duxbury Press, 1971.

A series of articles by successfully elected black politicians
placing the present struggle for racial justice in the United
States in the arena of political education, organization, and
action. Some of the areas covered include historical perspective, need for black power, strategies for black power, and
political power for participation and racial change.

4-41 Eisinger, Peter K. PATTERNS OF INTERRACIAL POLITICS. New York:
Academic Press, 1976.

Theoretically and empirically analyzes the effects of the increasing number of minority individuals who are participating
in politics. The author examines the effects of interracial

politics on such items as political progress, decision making, stability, and cooperation within the interracial structure.

4-42 _____. "Racial Differences in Protest Participation." AMERICAN POLITICAL SCIENCE REVIEW 68 (June 1974): 592-606.

See 3-32.

4-43 Ekstrom, Charles A., and Keil, Thomas J. "Political Attachment in Black Philadelphia: Does 'Public Regardingness' Apply?" URBAN AF-FAIRS QUARTERLY 8 (June 1973): 489-506.

A study comparing black and white political trends in the city between 1943 and 1969 by analyzing voting data. The authors evaluate the dimensions and significance of black political participation in Philadelphia politics and suggest that the relevance of the public-private continuum will decline and a trend of racial clevage as a basis for new significant orientations to the local polity will emerge. The study also tests hypotheses involving blacks and machine politics.

4-43a Eldredge, H. Wentworth, ed. WORLD CAPITALS: TOWARD GUIDED URBANIZATION. Garden City, N.Y.: Anchor Press-Doubleday, 1975.

Analysis by eleven urban planners of the urban growth of eleven capital cities. Nine cities (Brasilia, Caracas, Dakar, London, Moscow, Paris, Stockholm, Tokyo, and Washington) are national capitals. Two (Chandigarh and Toronto) are regional capitals considered by the authors to represent their nation in a more interesting way than its capital city. The book includes three analytic chapters by Eldredge on the urban crisis, national urban policy, and the delivery of urban services.

4-44 Elkin, Stephen L. "Comparative Urban Politics and Interorganizational Behavior." POLICY AND POLITICS 2 (Spring 1974): 289-308.

See 1-27.

4-45 Ellis, W. WHITE ETHICS AND BLACK POWER. Chicago: Aldine, 1969.

A book about the West Side Organization (WSO), an independent, black community-based organization near the West Side of Chicago. The book shows how the organization's leaders have lied, broken the law, and been mistreated in their efforts to achieve equality. WSO is not a political organization, thus the book does not discuss ward or precinct politics. The author contends that it is difficult to describe West Side politics because the details of how the area is ruled are relatively unknown.

4-46   Esslinger, Dean R. IMMIGRANTS AND THE CITY: ETHNICITY AND
MOBILITY IN A NINETEENTH CENTURY MIDWESTERN COMMUNITY.
Port Washington, N.Y.: Kennikat, 1975.

A study of South Bend, Indiana, attempting to relate urbanization and immigration. Over ten thousand of South Bend's
foreign-born and their descendants were examined concen-
trating on population movement, occupational mobility, and
social mobility. The author draws heavily upon federal census materials and discusses their shortcomings.

4-47   Fainstein, Norman I., and Fainstein, Susan S., eds. THE VIEW FROM
BELOW: URBAN POLITICS AND SOCIAL POLICY. Boston: Little,
Brown and Co., 1972.

An analysis of urban politics as it affects lower income people,
examining institutional forms, decision-making processes, and
governmental policy outcomes. Issues include poverty and
race, urban services and social welfare, and strategies for
change.

4-48   Farley, Reynolds. "The Changing Distribution of Negroes Within Metropolitan Areas--The Emergence of Black Suburbs." AMERICAN JOURNAL
OF SOCIOLOGY 75 (January 1970): 512-29.

See 6-37.

4-49   Fisher, Sethard. POWER AND THE BLACK COMMUNITY: A READER
ON RACIAL SUBORDINATION IN THE UNITED STATES. New York:
Alfred A. Knopf, 1970.

Reviews the rise of institutional racism in the modern world,
provides a theoretical framework for the rise and current use
of racism, covers gains and losses among black Americans,
shows that black subordination has been resisted, and discusses
tactics and strategy for racial equality within the United States.

4-50   Fleming, Harold C. "The Social Constraints." CENTER MAGAZINE 9
(January/February 1976): 16-22.

Contends that the United States is more racially and economi-
cally segregated today than ever before. The enemy of neighborhood stability is fear, not diversity. Politics of red-lining
and block-busting have encouraged white flight, and coordinated national, state, and community level growth strategies
are necessary to counter pre-set patterns of physical sprawl
and social stratification.

4-51   Forman, Robert E. BLACK GHETTOS, WHITE GHETTOS, AND SLUMS.
New York: Forman, 1959.

A study of black-white relations involving the problem of

housing and residential segregation in cities. Specific topics
include: local ordinances, institutional means, informal means,
and quasi-institutional means, family disorganization, vice,
alcohol and drugs, effects of slum housing, and children in
the slums. The author stresses that the basic practices of modern residential segregation were developed shortly before and
during the early 1920s. Even though racism has declined,
residential segregation has developed its own dynamics based
on property values which have fostered hostility.

4-52   Fox, Jeanne. REGIONALISM AND MINORITY PARTICIPATION. 2d
ed. Washington, D.C.: Joint Center for Political Studies, 1974.

See 6-41.

4-53   Fried, Marc. "Sources of Working-Class Attitudes and Values." In his
THE WORLD OF THE URBAN WORKING CLASS, pp. 177-79. Cam-
bridge, Mass.: Harvard University Press, 1973.

An analysis of the attitudes of the people living in the West
End of Boston including ethnocentrism, authoritarianism, alienation, and social conformity in relation to political power,
religion, and neighborhood structure. There appears to be
an ideological base for attitudes of people in higher status
positions, but working class people seem more specific in attitude more often determined by both reference group influences
and by situational variations. Nevertheless, attitudes may
serve similar purposes for people in different social classes.

4-54   _____. "Working-Class Life and the Structure of Social Class." In his
THE WORLD OF THE URBAN WORKING CLASS, pp. 224-58. Cam-
bridge, Mass.: Harvard University Press, 1973.

Deals with the working class life and social class structure in
the West End of Boston, the attitudes that influence the working life conditions, and the significance of social class structure research. The author argues that cultural patterns are the
result of economic, political, and social realities.

4-55   Gabriel, Richard A. THE ETHNIC FACTOR IN THE URBAN POLITY.
New York: MSS Information Corporation, 1973.

Tests existing theories of ethnic political behavior, including
assimilationist and mobilizationist theories, against data gathered
about two ethnic groups in a northeastern city and suburb.
Gabriel offers a new theory of how and why ethnicity continues
to affect political behavior. The data indicate that ethnic
identification is still very strong. Neither education, occupa-
tion, age, nor income have significant effects on reducing an
individual's identification with his ethnic group. Gabriel concludes that the urban political system of the future may well

be served by the old political machine due to ethnic identifi-
cations.

4-56   Gabriel, Richard A., and Savage, Paul L. THE ETHNICITY ATTRI-
BUTE: PERSISTENCE AND CHANGE IN AN URBAN AND SUBURBAN
ENVIRONMENT. Storrs: University of Connecticut, Institute of Urban
Research, 1973.

Notes that previous studies of ethnicity and assimilation have
used poor methodology by relying too heavily upon the ag-
gregative approach. The authors conducted a survey of re-
gistered voters in Warwick and Providence, Rhode Island,
considering factors that erode ethnic ties, factors that support
ethnic identification, and the role of ethnicity in the process
of assimilation.

4-57   Gelb, J. "Black Republicans in New York: A Minority Group in a
Minority Party." URBAN AFFAIRS QUARTERLY 5 (June 1970): 454-73.

A study of black Republicans in New York City between 1958
and 1960, based upon interviews with thirty-one black Republicans conducted during 1967-68. Gelb concludes that they
are faced with problems of ineffective leadership, limited
patronage, lack of funds, and lack of participation in club
activities and political campaigns.

4-58   Glasco, Lawrence A. "The Life Cycles and Household Structure of
American Ethnic Groups: Irish, German, and Native-born Whites in
Buffalo, New York." JOURNAL OF URBAN HISTORY 1 (May 1975):
339-64.

Employs the method of life cycle analysis. Glasco's study is
a contribution to the literature on ethnic stratification and
· acculturation because it assesses the impact of variables such
as age and sex. The study reveals that even though all three
groups had distinctive life cycles, the men's patterns differed
mainly in their economic cycles, while the women's patterns
differed in terms of both economic and household cycles.

4-59   Glazer, Nathan, and Moynihan, D. BEYOND THE MELTING POT.
Cambridge: M.I.T. Press and Harvard University Press, 1963.

Examines five minority groups in New York City: blacks,
Jews, Puerto Ricans, Italians, and Irish. The authors clarify
the political and cultural impact of ethnicity on the city and
include an analysis of the characteristics on specific problems
faced by each group.

4-60   Goldsmith, William W. "The Ghetto as a Resource for Black Americans."

JOURNAL OF THE AMERICAN INSTITUTE OF PLANNERS 40 (January 1974): 17-30.

Contends that all of the major proposals for improving conditions for black Americans including suburbanization, augmented
employment, ghetto capitalism, and separatism, ignore the
real issue which, according to Goldsmith, is the creation of
cohesive black political and economic power. Goldsmith advocates community power and control, noting that levels of
capability and competence have been rising within the ghettos
while interaction with outside areas has waned. He concludes
that the most desirable solution would be for whites and blacks
to mobilize their economic and political power and to pool
and organize resources in order to develop some independence
from the dominant society.

4-61   Goodall, Leonard E., ed.   URBAN POLITICS IN THE SOUTHWEST.
Tempe: Arizona State University, 1967.

Provides comparative data on urban political patterns in a
group of cities with similar characteristics. Most of the cities
studied are relatively young and rapidly growing and lack a
tradition of strong, well-organized political parties or machines. They have large Mexican-American populations and
a high proportion of middle-income families. The cities
studied include: Albuquerque, Austin, Fort Worth, Houston,
Oklahoma City, Phoenix, San Antonio, San Diego, Tucson,
Tulsa, and Wichita.

4-62   Goodlet, Carlton B.   "Mass Communications, U.S.A.: Its Feet of
Clay."   BLACK SCHOLAR 6 (November 1974): 2-6.

An abridged version of a 1974 speech delivered before the Association for Education in Journalism. Goodlet claims that in
our "racist society," the mass communications media remains
one of the cornerstones by which whites impose their will upon
their "domestic colonials." Noting that Congress and government agencies such as the FCC continually frustrate black efforts to operate media communications, Goodlet advises blacks
to stop patronizing white media productions and take aggressive measures, including the jamming of white-owned stations.
He concludes by calling for unity among blacks in the effort
to end white domination of the media.

4-62a   Gordon, D.N.   "Immigrants and Municipal Voting Turnout: Implications
for the Changing Ethnic Impact on Urban Politics." AMERICAN SOCIO-
LOGICAL REVIEW 35 (August 1970): 665-81.

Looks for trends in the relationship between the presence of
ethnic groups and voter turnout. Gordon uses data on the size
of ethnic populations and voter turnouts in 198 American cities
between 1934 and 1960. He concludes that the ethnic impact

on voter turnout has declined in partisan cities but not in nonpartisan cities.

4-63   Greenberg, Stanley B., ed. POLITICS AND POVERTY: MODERNIZA-TION AND RESPONSE IN FIVE POOR NEIGHBORHOODS. New York: John Wiley & Sons, 1974.

A study of the political aspects of poor neighborhoods in five cities. Emphasizing the immediate attitudinal determinants of political expression: culture, alienation, group consciousness, and class ideology. The book covers the problems of lower class culture and political response, the alienated politics of poor neighborhoods, and the politics of class.

4-64   Greenstone, J. David, and Peterson, Paul E. "Class and Racial Inte-rests in the Politics of Community Participation." In their RACE AND AUTHORITY IN URBAN POLITICS: COMMUNITY PARTICIPATION AND THE WAR ON POVERTY, pp. 71-98. New York: Russell Sage Founda-tion, 1973.

Assesses the relationship between class and racial interests and community participation. The essay begins with an analy-sis of class interests which, in an industrial society, generally underlie the conflict between business and worker interests. The author concludes that these class interests seldom become manifest in community participation controversies. However, the situation is quite the opposite for the racial interests of blacks. The authors show that the "black power" ideology, which articulates a full range of black factional interests, is directly relevant to the politics of community action.

4-65   _____. RACE AND AUTHORITY IN URBAN POLITICS: COMMUNITY PARTICIPATION AND THE WAR ON POVERTY. New York: Russell Sage Foundation, 1973.

Attempts to show that in the five largest American cities, New York, Los Angeles, Chicago, Philadelphia, and Detroit, the anti-poverty program of the mid-sixties set off local poli-tical struggles which crystallized and dramatized changing alignments in American politics. According to the authors, race rather than class had become the source of most intense domestic conflicts; the structure of political authority had itself become a political issue; and, in many cases, these issues produced decidedly ideological controversies. The book is divided into four major parts: (1) a comparative approach to the politics of community action; (2) interests, ideologies, and participation; (3) implementing participation in community ac-tion programs; and (4) political structures, public policy, and policy-making processes. The authors present a modification of the pluralist theory of community power structure. Each part of the book is discussed in terms of traditional views, as compared to the evidence obtained from the cities studied.

4-66   Greer, Edward. "The New Mayors: Black Power in the Big Cities."
        NATION 219 (November 1974): 525-29.

        Gives a brief history of the rise of black mayors and discusses
        the problems faced by black administrators. From studying the
        demographic characteristics of large urban areas, Greer be-
        lieves that cities themselves do not have the resources to cure
        urban ills and must actively seek federal assistance.

4-67   Hahn, Harlan. "Ethnic Minorities: Politics and the Family in Subur-
        bia." In THE URBANIZATION OF THE SUBURBS, edited by Louis H.
        Masotti and Jeffrey K. Hadden, pp. 185-205. Beverly Hills, Calif.:
        Sage Publications, 1973.

        Explores the interplay between public and private values that
        perpetuate the dominance of the nuclear family model in
        American suburbs. The author observes that public policies,
        such as housing loans, schools, and highways, benefit the
        desires of white families to raise their children in a favorable
        homogenous location. Zoning, government policy, and other
        measures, such as socioeconomic position, combine to exclude
        minority families, which are larger and less nuclear. Hahn
        concludes that unless programs are instituted to increase the
        socioeconomic conditions of the minority groups, the suburbs
        could eventually decay like the central city. He recommends
        that government adopt an overall benefit-cost analysis when
        developing programs.

4-68   _____, ed. PEOPLE AND POLITICS IN URBAN SOCIETY. Beverly
        Hills, Calif.: Sage Publications, 1972.

        Four essays dealing specifically with the importance in urban
        politics of race and ethnic relations and the environment in
        which minorities are located. Issues include racial dissatis-
        faction, separation, stereotyping, and ghettos.

4-69   Hamilton, Richard F. "Liberal Intelligentsia and White Backlash." DIS-
        SENT 19 (Winter 1972): 225.

        Presents data on regional attitudes covering various issues and
        compares the responses of blacks and whites. Hamilton con-
        cludes from his research that literary-political intellectuals
        read their special preconceptions into the day's news. It is
        in this respect that they exhibit all the perceptual biases
        and distortions that have been documented by experiments in
        social psychology.

4-70   Harrington, Michael. "Old Working Class, New Working Class." DIS-
        SENT 19 (Winter 1972): 146.

        Concludes that there are two working classes in America; a

still vital old working class and a new class created by political and economic evolution. The old working class is primarily blue collar workers who do physical labor in the industrial economy. In Harrington's account of the politics and
organization of the labor force in the United States, the new
labor force emerges as a well-organized force. Although
status factors have kept these two groups far apart, Harrington presents evidence that both groups could form a new political coalition, dedicated to social and democratic planning.

4-71   Hatcher, Richard G. "Mass Media and the Black Community." BLACK
        SCHOLAR 5 (September 1973): 2-10.

        Article from the perspective of a black consumer of news by
        the mayor of Gary, Indiana. First, Hatcher cites the import-
        ance of a newspaper as an information base upon which deci-
        sions can be made. He goes on to say that racism is a per-
        vasive ideology in white America and that the press is equally
        guilty of fostering this view. Hatcher proposes that we look
        at racism in greater detail to understand why it is, what it
        is, and how to fight it.

4-72   Hawkins, Brett [W.], and Lorinskas, Robert A., eds. THE ETHNIC FACTOR
        IN AMERICAN POLITICS. Columbus, Ohio: Merrill, 1970.

        A collection of articles by various scholars providing evidence
        that ethnic communities and identifications remain and con-
        tinue to affect political life. The book presents an ordered
        way to consider the political impact of ethnicity. Topics dis-
        cussed include: ethnicity as a durable social structure, system
        input and ethnic voting and policy attitudes, and the impact
        of ethnicity on political forms and policy outputs. Findings
        are integrated in a systems framework.

4-73   Henderson, Lenneal J., ed. BLACK POLITICAL LIFE IN THE U.S.: A
        TEST AS A PENDULUM. San Francisco: Chandler Publishing Co., 1972.

        An anthology of articles written by various black scholars.
        The book has three major purposes: (1) to present the perspec-
        tives of black scholars on black political life in the United
        States; (2) to present a collection of significant literature and
        analysis for the growing discussions and debates about black
        politics; (3) to focus on a few of the aspects and implications
        of black politics for American politics. Discusses the nature,
        history, problems, and future of black politics.

4-74   Herbert, Adam W. "The Evolving Challenges of Black Urban Adminis-
        tration." JOURNAL OF AFRO-AMERICAN ISSUES 3 (Spring 1975):
        173-79.

        Evaluates the impact of community control agencies upon the

implementation of responsive public sector programs. Herbert
observes that traditional public administration and community
control advocates take different approaches to the management
areas of integration, hierarchy, legality, and political supre-
macy. He concludes that an increase in the number of minority administrators at the local level can be important in the
effort to achieve more responsive public sector programs.

4-75   Hill, Herbert. LABOR UNION CONTROL OF JOB TRAINING: A
CRITICAL ANALYSIS OF APPRENTICESHIP OUTREACH PROGRAMS AND
THE HOMETOWN PLANS. Washington, D.C.: Howard University
Institute for Urban Affairs and Research, 1974.

Contends that a major difficulty in reversing the pattern of
joblessness and alienation among young blacks is the rigid control of training and access to employment by many labor unions
committed to perpetuating the racial status quo. Hill, the
National Labor Director of the NAACP, also maintains that
the federal government aids and abets the discriminatory racial
practices. He believes that alternative access routes to training and employment must be developed in the construction industry; minority contractor organizations and independent community hiring halls could provide, he feels, a viable basis for
the emergence of such community development programs.

4-76   Hill, Lewis E. "Some Notes on the Political Economy of Ghetto Dispersion." ATLANTA ECONOMIC REVIEW 25 (July/August 1975): 25-
27.

Contends that many of the problems of the ghettos can only
be solved by creating economic opportunities outside the
ghetto and by encouraging the voluntary dispersion of disadvantaged persons in order to take advantage of these opportunities. The programs must be aimed at segregation, discrimination, and other factors which cause poverty among disadvantaged ethnic groups.

4-77   Hill, Richard C. "Separate and Unequal: Governmental Inequality in
the Metropolis." AMERICAN POLITICAL SCIENCE REVIEW 68 (December
1974): 1557-68.

Notes that there has been relatively little comparative research
on governmental inequality among metropolitan areas in the
United States. Hill focuses upon the increasingly class and
status differentiated suburban government structure. His study
measures inequality in the distribution of fiscal resources among
governments by the standard deviation in family income among
municipalities in the metropolitan area. It appears that there
is a great deal of income inequality among families in metropolitan areas.

4-78   Hill, Robert B. "Inflation and the Black Consumer." CIVIL RIGHTS
DIGEST 6 (Summer 1974): 33-37.

> Traces the trends of the economy since the early 1960s. Hill
> observes that blacks and poor minority groups were hardest hit
> by the recession, particularly in terms of unemployment. He
> concludes that: (1) black and poor communities should be de-
> clared disaster areas and special federal funds should be al-
> located for their relief; (2) public service employment programs
> should be expanded; (3) costs should be reduced for child care
> so women can seek employment; and (4) taxes should be re-
> duced for low-income persons in order to halt the decline in
> purchasing power.

4-79   Holden, Matthew, Jr. "Black Politicians in the Time of the New Urban Politics." REVIEW OF BLACK POLITICAL ECONOMY 2 (Fall 1971):
56-71.

> Claims that the solution to many urban problems depends upon
> the establishment of sound national policy, but the cities are
> not sufficiently represented in Congress to influence this policy.
> Holden also discusses some elective offices which blacks have
> not pursued sufficiently to advance their interest.

4-80   _____. THE POLITICS OF THE BLACK NATION. San Francisco:
Chandler Publishing Co., 1972.

> A collection of seven essays on blacks and ethnicity dealing
> with specific aspects of black politics.

4-81   Hopps, June G. "A Planning Model for Black Community Development."
REVIEW OF BLACK POLITICAL ECONOMY 4 (Winter 1974): 57-73.

> Claims that programs such as Model Cities and Black Capitalism
> have done little to change the basic economic conditions for
> the majority of the black population. Hopps argues that blacks
> must devise additional strategies for black community develop-
> ment which can be debated among those concerned with the
> future of the black community. She emphasizes the importance
> of black participation and offers a model for community de-
> velopment, centered around black leadership.

4-82   Hunter, David R. THE SLUMS; CHALLENGE AND RESPONSE. New
York: Free Press, 1964.

> Examines the causes of slums, emphasizing that they are a
> human problem, not only a problem concerning real estate and
> finance. The author assesses components of slums in addition
> to physical characteristics, such as the "feel" of the slum and
> the sight of poverty amidst affluence. He concludes that slums
> represent conditions inimical to a democratic society.

4-83   Ien Houten, Warren D.; Stern, John; and Ien Houten, Dana. "Political
        Leadership in Poor Communities: Applications of Two Sampling Methodol-
        ogies." In RACE, CHANGE, AND URBAN SOCIETY, edited by P.
        Orlens and W.R. Ellis, Jr., pp. 215-54. Urban Affairs Annual Reviews,
        vol. 5. Beverly Hills, Calif.: Sage Publications, 1971.

        Presents two sampling methods, site and snowball, for the
        study of informal political leadership. They are used to ana-
        lyze relationships between informal leadership structures, and
        political values and attitudes in a community action program
        evaluation.

4-84   Jedel, Michael Jay, and Kujawa, Duane. "Barriers to Minority Employ-
        ment: Case Studies of Selected Employers in Metropolitan Atlanta."
        ATLANTA ECONOMIC REVIEW 23 (November/December 1973): 28-37.

        Results of a study of employment processes in which key em-
        ployers in metropolitan Atlanta participated. A questionnaire
        was given to employees, detailed interviews were administered
        to top executives, and all documents related to hiring or pro-
        motion decisions were made available to the research team.
        The study yielded these conclusions: (1) The majority of black
        and white employees generally responded to the questions the
        way management would have expected; (2) In the area of
        hiring, overt discrimination is virtually nonexistent in the firms
        examined; (3) Barriers are still perceived to exist in hiring
        practices and promotions; (4) Management needs to continually
        review all practices related to any aspect of the employment
        process; and (5) Line managements are not sufficiently knowl-
        edgeable about and involved in the formulation and operation
        of the affirmative action effect.

4-85   Johnson, Tobe. METROPOLITAN GOVERNMENT: A BLACK PERSPEC-
        TIVE. Washington, D.C.: Joint Center for Political Studies, 1972.

        Examines various aspects of metropolitanization and assesses
        some of their implications for black control. Johnson argues
        that consolidation reduces the political power of blacks. In
        many cities blacks represent the majority and could control
        the political process; however, with consolidation, the blacks
        no longer control the majority interests and thus lose political
        power. Blacks must demonstrate greater political sophistication
        and work for greater unity if they are to maximize the effects
        of metropolitanization. With respect to the city-county con-
        solidation particularly, blacks will have to be vigilant to en-
        sure that they do not trade-off long-run strategic advantages
        for economic gains and a few more council seats. Finally,
        federal courts, as presently constituted, are unlikely to approve
        structural or procedural changes in government which demon-
        strably dilute the black vote.

4-86   Karnig, Albert K. "Black Representation on City Councils: The Im-
        pact of District Elections and Socio-Economic Factors." URBAN AFFAIRS
        QUARTERLY 12 (December 1976): 223-56.

        Studies 139 municipalities where blacks constitute over 15 per-
        cent of the population, and demonstrates that black represen-
        tation on the city council is highest in cities using districts
        and lowest in cities using at-large elections. Nevertheless,
        in southern cities using districts, blacks are only about half
        as well represented as their populations should entitle them.
        Further, as of 1972, blacks were not represented at all in
        47 percent of the southern cities nor in 23 percent of those
        in the North. The author also concluded that for blacks,
        income is significantly associated with representation on the
        council. Leonard Cole criticizes some of these conclusions
        and Karnig responds in the same issue.

4-87   Kirlin, John J. "The Impact of Increasing Lower-Status Clientele Upon
        City Governmental Structures: A Model from Organization Theory."
        URBAN AFFAIRS QUARTERLY 8 (March 1973): 317-43.

        Develops a model of governmental reaction to the emergence
        of unwelcome demands for change. Three general themes are
        analyzed: (1) cities often experience a growth of low-income
        clientele, which causes new service demands and difficulties
        in meeting those demands; (2) factors relevant to the city's
        governmental organizations are initially the controlling factors
        in its response to the service demands of the new lower-income
        clientele; and (3) political action will normally be required to
        ensure an adequate response to lower-income clientele. The
        author concludes by discussing the public policy implications
        of his analysis.

4-88   Kornblum, William, and Lichter, Paul. "Urban Gypsies and the Culture
        of Poverty." URBAN LIFE AND CULTURE 1 (October 1972): 239-53.

        Gives a brief historical description of gypsies, isolating some
        of the common values and beliefs shared by them. The authors
        then analyze a study of two gypsy groups, one located in Paris
        and the other in Seattle, Washington, and find that assimila-
        tion for both groups into urban environments has been minimal.
        They discuss the strategies used by each group to adjust to the
        environment.

4-89   Kramer, J., and Walter, I. "Politics in an All-Negro City." URBAN
        AFFAIRS QUARTERLY 4 (September 1968): 65-88.

        A study of the political institution of Black City, an autono-
        mous black town of about 7,200 people located in a suburban
        community in the urban North. Kramer deals with the town's
        political structure, history, and its competitive ideologies.
        The study concludes that the city may be used as a model of

scarcity politics. There is a shortage of funds to provide services and the local government is undermanned and underpaid.
Furthermore, residents are not in a position to change the present situation.

4-89a Larson, C.J., and Hill, R.J. "Segregation, Community Consciousness,
and Black Power." JOURNAL OF BLACK STUDIES 2 (March 1972):
263-76.

A study of the social structure of two black communities in
an Indiana city. The authors look at the relationship between
physical and social segregation and neighborhood consciousness. The link between neighborhood consciousness, political
experience, and the tendency toward radical social actions
is also examined.

4-89b Levine, Charles H. RACIAL CONFLICT AND THE AMERICAN MAYOR.
Lexington, Mass.: Lexington Books, 1974.

Case studies of the administrations of three mayors--Stokes
in Cleveland, Hatcher in Gary, and Seibels in Birmingham.
Levine highlights the conflict approach to management in racially troubled cities. Conflict is not always a limitation,
it can be used creatively in racially polarized communities.
Executive-centered coalitions appear to work more effectively
in pluralistic situations where there is a low level of conflict
while other models work better in cities characterized by a
high degree of conflict. In a pluralistic context the mayors
in this study are not considered successful. However, when
the pluralist and the conflict model are compared different
results are found and the management performance of the three
mayors becomes more effective.

4-90 Levy, Mark R., and Kramer, Michael S. THE ETHNIC FACTOR. New
York: Simon & Schuster, 1972.

Describes the effects that six minority groups have had on
American politics: blacks, Chicanos and Puerto Ricans, Jews,
Irish, Slavs, and Italians. Ethnicity, the authors argue, is
becoming increasingly crucial in our political scheme, and it
behooves policy makers to learn as much about it as possible.

4-91 Lewinson, Edwin R. BLACK POLITICS IN NEW YORK CITY. New
York: Twayne Publishers, 1974.

An examination of the phenomenon of black politics in New
York City. After providing an overview of black political
development in New York, the author describes briefly the
political conflicts of two black politicians, Adam Clayton
Powell and J. Raymond Jones. In the final analysis, he says,
the importance of the history of black political activity in

New York City is that it demonstrates the relationship between increased political recognition and the improvement in the quality of life for black people.

4-92   Ley, David. THE BLACK INNER CITY AS FRONTIER OUTPOST. Washington, D.C.: Association of American Geographers, 1974.

Attempts to describe the problems and characteristics of the black inner city, but due to the complexity of the subject spends much of the book discussing the methodology of his study. The book examines both the facts of daily life in a black inner city neighborhood and the cognitive and behavioral processes at work in environments of stress and uncertainty.

4-93   Lowe, Robert A. METROPOLITAN CONNECTICUT: A 1970 DEMOGRAPHIC PROFILE. Storrs: University of Connecticut, Institute of Urban Research, August 1973.

A description and analysis of selected demographic and socioeconomic characteristics of the population of Connecticut's eleven metropolitan areas. A map of Connecticut, indicating the location of the Standard Metropolitan Statistical Areas (SMSAs) is included.

4-94   McLemore, Leslie B. "Toward a Theory of Black Politics--the Black and Ethnic Models Revisited." JOURNAL OF BLACK STUDIES 2 (March 1972): 323-31.

Discusses the special strategy problems of blacks and concludes that the skin color difference and the existence of racist attitudes make the white ethnic model inapplicable to black political approaches.

4-95   Marshall, D.R.; Frieden, B[ernard].; and Fessler, D.W. MINORITY PERSPECTIVES. Washington, D.C.: Resources for the Future, 1972.

Includes one paper by each of the authors. Marshall appraises the impact of metropolitan consolidation on the political standing and economic environment of minority groups. Frieden gives a cost-benefit analysis of the members of minority groups who have escaped to the suburbs. Fessler argues that the law, as it bears on the inequities generated by government and tradition, is changing at a rapid pace, but that organizational structures are not.

4-96   Meyer, David R. "Blacks in Slum Housing." JOURNAL OF BLACK STUDIES 4 (December 1973): 139-52.

Claims that black housing has been stereotyped in scholarly literature like most matters concerning black Americans. Terms like "slum" and "ghetto" have been carelessly applied to black housing in a way which only reinforces the stereotype.

4-96a Midura, Edmund M., ed. WHY AREN'T WE GETTING THROUGH?
THE URBAN COMMUNICATION CRISIS. Washington, D.C.: Acropolis
Books, 1971.

Ten essays looking at the causes and solutions for the communication barrier between the urban poor and the rest of the
nation. Topics include: a description of the communication
behaviors of the urban poor; the problems of the mass media
in trying to reach the urban poor; ways in which the federal
government can facilitate communication within the city; the
rise of the Watts writer workshop; the future of communication
in megalopolis; and the model urban communication plan of the
"new city" of Columbia.

4-97 Nelson, Jack. "The Changing Economic Position of Black Urban Workers." REVIEW OF BLACK POLITICAL ECONOMY 4 (Winter 1974): 35-
48.

Examines the economic position of blacks using data from census materials. Although the results are mixed, definite improvement can be observed in some areas of education and
income.

4-98 O'Brien, David J. NEIGHBORHOOD ORGANIZATION AND INTEREST-
GROUP PROCESSES. Princeton, N.J.: Princeton University Press,
1975.

See 3-73.

4-99 Ohls, James C. "Public Policy Toward Low Income Housing and Filtering in Housing Markets." JOURNAL OF URBAN ECONOMICS 2 (April
1975): 144-71.

See 5-124.

4-100 Palley, Marian Lief; Russe, Robert; and Scott, Edward. "Subcommunity
Leadership in a Black Ghetto: A Study of Newark, N.J." URBAN AF-
FAIRS QUARTERLY 5 (March 1970): 291-312.

Attempts to discover who the black community perceives as its
leaders, since the traditional leaders, the church and business
elites, have lost much of their influence in the ghetto. The
study was based upon a survey of twenty-five black leaders
active in community affairs. Regardless of their different
backgrounds, they seemed to share a growing sense of urgency
and militancy. Age rather than economic status or occupational and educational achievement seems the clearest indicator
of militancy.

4-101 Patterson, Ernest. BLACK CITY POLITICS. New York: Dodd, Mead
& Co., 1974.

Attempts to provide uninformed blacks with a knowledge of
the operations of city government and politics. Patterson
believes that this knowledge will enable them to devise better
strategies for gaining policies that affect black people. Ethnic
political factors are examined in Atlanta, Chicago, Cleveland,
St. Louis, Cincinnati, Detroit, Los Angeles, New York, and
Philadelphia. Based upon data accumulated during the 1960s,
this provides a good description of city politics and structures.

4-102 Pendleton, William W. "Blacks in Suburbs." In THE URBANIZATION
OF THE SUBURBS, edited by Louis H. Masotti and Jeffrey K. Hadden,
pp. 171-84. Beverly Hills, Calif.: Sage Publications, 1973.

See 6-78.

4-103 Perry, David C., and Feagin, Joe R. "Stereotyping in Black and White."
In PEOPLE AND POLITICS IN URBAN SOCIETY, edited by Harlan Hahn,
pp. 433-64. Beverly Hills, Calif.: Sage Publications, 1972.

See 4-68.

4-104 Reid, John D. "Black Urbanization of the South." PHYLON 35 (September 1974): 259-67.

Outlines and describes some of the major redistribution trends
of the black population in the South, with particular reference
to urban growth. Black migration continues out of the rural
South, not only towards other regions of the country, but to
southern urban areas as well. Reid documents the growth of
black population in the largest southern urban centers, and
describes the characteristics of southern blacks resulting from
out-migration.

4-105 "The Responsibility of Local Zoning Authorities to Nonresident Indigents."
STANFORD LAW REVIEW 23 (April 1971): 774-98.

See 5-134.

4-106 Rex, John. "Community and Association Against Urban Migrants." In
his RACE, COLONIALISM, AND THE CITY, pp. 15-31. Boston: Rout-
ledge & Kegan Paul, 1973.

Examines community life in the zone of transition, where "community" means contact on the street or in shops, and less ca-
sual contact in bars. The community framework includes organizations that provide an escape from loneliness, a means of
obtaining group goals, and a means for managing conflict.
The author compares these associations to the primary community, where men reveal more of themselves.

4-107 Rich, Wilbur C. "Future Manpower in Urban Management: A Black
Perspective." JOURNAL OF AFRO-AMERICAN ISSUES 3 (Spring 1975):
160-72.

Notes the rise of a black majority in America's largest cities,
and examines why they are run by white professionals. Blacks
do not hold high administrative positions because they lack the
necessary education and training. Administrative jobs should
not be filled by blacks until they are qualified to hold them,
but blacks should be placed in positions that would enable
them to gain expertise on the job. Jobs that require technical skills and training should be identified and the others
should be declassified. If blacks were to fill the jobs freed
by this process, Rich argues, they could exercise real political power.

4-108 Rist, Ray C. "Poor Kids and Public Schools." In his THE URBAN
SCHOOL: A FACTORY FOR FAILURE, pp. 241-56. Cambridge:
M.I.T. Press, 1973.

Focuses upon the St. Louis educational system, where Rist discovered that the following assumptions were prevalent: middle-
class students can learn, lower class students cannot; white
schools are good, black schools are bad; control is necessary,
freedom is anarchy; violence works, persuasion does not;
teachers can save a few, but lose many; the school tries, the
home will not; and finally, only the naive will dispute these
beliefs. The study does not question the competency of teachers, but demonstrates that the real issue is the unequal accessibility of that competence to students. Rist concludes
that the best solution will not come from changes in the class-
room, but from changes in overall social positions.

4-109 Rose, Harold [M.]. "The All Black Town: Suburban Prototype or Rural
Slum." In PEOPLE AND POLITICS IN URBAN SOCIETY, edited by
Harlan Hahn, pp. 397-431. Beverly Hills, Calif.: Sage Publications,
1972.

Attributes most black migration to the suburbs to a desire to
improve education and employment opportunities. Rose indicates, however, that much of the increase is actually spillover from adjoining black areas within the central city.

4-110 _____. "The Development of an Urban Subsystem: The Case of the
Negro Ghetto." ANNALS OF THE AMERICAN ASSOCIATION OF
GEOGRAPHERS 60 (March 1970): 1-17.

Develops a model for the rise of residential ghettos in northern
metropolitan systems to predict the future state of the ghetto.
Although it has some predictive value, its real value is the
insight it affords into the ghetto development process. The

model, based upon data from Milwaukee, Wisconsin, proves deficient in some of its assumptions about ghetto spatial patterns and housing market areas. Other models, such as the conceptual model and the segregation model, are also discussed.

4-111 Sackrey, Charles. "On Revolutionary Politics." In his THE POLITICAL ECONOMY OF URBAN POVERTY, pp. 121-44. New York: W.W. Norton, 1973.

An introduction to the study of the urban poor and possible solutions to their most serious problems. The book combines an analysis of the economic factors which cause poverty with a discussion of the implications for political activity. The authors conclude that: (1) there is a great deal more urban poverty than government statisticians tell; (2) the problem is disproportionately one of black people; (3) the principal proposals implemented in the past for abolishing urban poverty have failed miserably in terms of their own goals; and (4) the most difficult task is to choose between the two opposing political responses--liberal reform and revolutionary change--both of which have enormous inherent limitations.

4-111a Savitch, H.V. "Powerlessness in an Urban Ghetto: The Case of Political Beasts and Differential Access in New York City." POLITY 5 (Fall 1972): 19-56.

A response to the pluralistic analysis of urban politics. The author claims that urban pluralism is closed to certain socioeconomic groups and highly resistant to change. This "restrictive pluralism" includes (1) accepted modes of operation which legitimatize some groups and disfavor others, (2) a dominant ideology which frustrates change demanded by the disfavored groups and (3) a cluster of interest groups with authority. The author concludes that these factors promote class and ethnic discrimination which renders the disadvantaged members of urban society powerless.

4-112 Sawyer, F.M. "Black Colleges and Community Development." JOURNAL OF BLACK STUDIES 6 (September 1975): 70-99.

Argues that black colleges should be leaders in community development because of their institutional flexibility, homogeneity of clientele, and singleness of purpose. If black colleges are to contribute significantly to our national life, he concludes, they must examine themselves and their mission, the political dynamics of their function, their programmatic capabilities, their economic resources, their administrative arrangements, and their dialectical relationships.

4-112a Schnore, Leo F. CLASS AND RACE IN CITIES AND SUBURBS. Chicago: Markham Publishing Co., 1972.

See 6-83a.

4-113 Schuman, Howard, and Gruenberg, Barry. "Dissatisfaction with City Services: Is Race an Important Factor?" In PEOPLE AND POLITICS IN URBAN SOCIETY, edited by Harlan Hahn, pp. 369-92. Beverly Hills, Calif.: Sage Publications, 1972.

See 4-68.

4-114 Seale, Bobby. "The Black Scholar Interviews Bobby Seale." BLACK SCHOLAR 4 (September 1972): 7-16.

Seale's views on his and the Black Panthers' organizing efforts in Oakland and about his candidacy for mayor of Oakland. He describes the organization of nonprofit corporations in black communities which would be run by people in the community to provide community services. He entered the race for mayor of Oakland because he believes it is essential to gain control of the political institutions in order to effectuate necessary changes.

4-115 Sherman, Richard B. THE NEGRO AND THE CITY. Englewood Cliffs, N.J.: Prentice-Hall, 1970.

Examines the plight of blacks from the late nineteenth century to the late 1960s. The book is divided into seven parts: (1) "The City"; (2) "A Place to Live"; (3) "Finding a Job"; (4) "Schools"; (5) "Way of Life"; (6) "Urban Violence"; and (7) "Politics and Protest." Each section traces the issue under consideration from 1900 to the present and draws upon personal data from active participants. Throughout the study, Sherman consistently isolates the governmental and judicial actions that affected the Negro.

4-115a Shipler, David K. "The White Niggers of Newark: Mirror Images of America's First Black City." HARPER'S MAGAZINE, August 1972, pp. 78-83.

Examines the problems and attitudes of the white minority in a predominantly black city. The author discusses cultural conflicts and race relations between the Italian Americans and the blacks in Newark.

4-116 Siembieda, William J. "Suburbanization of Ethics of Color." ANNALS OF THE AMERICAN ACADEMY OF POLITICAL AND SOCIAL SCIENCE 422 (November 1975): 118-28.

See 6-85.

4-117 Sklar, Morton H. "The Impact of Revenue Sharing on Minorities and the Poor." HARVARD CIVIL RIGHTS--CIVIL LIBERTIES LAW REVIEW 10 (Winter 1975): 93-136.

See 7-104.

4-118 Smith, Earl. "Racism and the Boston School Crisis." BLACK SCHOLAR 6 (1975): 37-41.

A brief history of the black's struggle for quality education from 1787 to the present. Numerous cases are cited documenting the efforts to block black education.

4-119 Sternlieb, George, and Burchell, Robert W. "Those Who Remain: The New Minority Owners." In their RESIDENTIAL ABANDONMENT: THE TENEMENT LANDLORD REVISITED, pp. 97-133. New Brunswick, N.J.: Rutgers University, Center for Urban Policy Research, 1973.

Examines black owners of buildings in Newark, New Jersey, between 1964 and 1971. The study analyzes who the owners are, what kinds of buildings they buy, why they buy them, and variations in operating procedures and in attitudes towards tenants.

4-120 Surlin, Stuart H. "Broadcasters' Misperceptions of Black Community Needs." JOURNAL OF BLACK STUDIES 4 (December 1973): 185-93.

Contends that radio stations do not represent the needs of the black community. Surlin believes that white middle class . broadcast executives cannot accurately perceive the needs of their listeners without actively participating in an ongoing, structured, and nonbiased dialogue with a representative from every significant subgroup in the community. He sees the need for black ownership of broadcast stations or for a revision of broadcast lisensing procedures in order to meet the needs of the black community.

4-121 Tabb, William K. THE POLITICAL ECONOMY OF THE BLACK GHETTO. New York: W.W. Norton, 1970.

Studies the black ghetto as an economic unit of a larger society and describes the economic factors that explain the origins of the ghetto, the process through which exploitation and deprivation are perpetuated, and plans of action that might end such discriminatory practices. Tabb is concerned with institutional racism in conjunction with labor, housing markets, government, and unions, and shows their effects on black Americans. He concludes that there are three possible futures for the ghetto: (1) present policies can be continued, resulting in two societies separate and unequal; (2) the ghetto can be rehabilitated and strengthened; (3) the ghetto can be opened,

so that society will be one rather than two nations. Two
obstacles in accomplishing meaningful social change are a
false consciousness among both whites and blacks which keeps
them from thinking in terms of fundamental change and a system which does not allow for the expenditure of significant
sums of money by corporations on socially useful but privately
unprofitable purposes.

4-122 Teagin, Joe R., and Hahn, Harlan. "The Continuing Struggle for Black
Power." In GHETTO REVOLTS: THE POLITICS OF VIOLENCE IN
AMERICAN CITIES, pp. 297-332. New York: Macmillan, 1973.

Examines the apparent trend in black communities toward self-
determination and black power. Ghetto rioting in many cities,
the resurgence of black consciousness, a growing sense of personal efficacy, and the drive for community control all appear
to be part of a mutually reinforcing trend in the black struggle.
The authors conclude that urban leaders are committed to white
domination of the urban area and to exploiting the poor. They
believe that this will lead to violent uprisings unless the focus
of power is changed.

4-123 Thompson, Daniel C. THE NEGRO LEADERSHIP CLASS. Englewood
Cliffs, N.J.: Prentice-Hall, 1963.

Elaborates and extends Floyd Hunter's thesis (COMMUNITY
POWER STRUCTURE, Chapel Hill: University of North Carolina Press, 1953) regarding the place of Negro leadership in
the decision-making process of a major southern metropolis.
The study by Thompson explores the status of Negroes in New
Orleans and assesses the role of leadership as a factor in
status changes. Thompson reaches the same basic conclusions
as Hunter.

4-124 Walton, Hanes, Jr. BLACK POLITICAL PARTIES: AN HISTORICAL AND
POLITICAL ANALYSIS. New York: Free Press, 1972.

Looks at black political parties in the past and present. Walton also indicates the prospects for successful future black organizations. The research indicates that black political parties
have largely been a by-product of the one-party systems that
are prevalent in many southern states. Black parties have
achieved the most success on a local level. Walton finds
that they serve as instruments for protest and behave much
like third parties in general.

4-125 Ward, Francis B. "The Black Press in Crisis." BLACK SCHOLAR 5
(September 1973): 34-36.

Examines the decline of and the problems faced by black newspapers. Ward accounts for the decline by noting that black

editors did not publish materials blacks wanted to read and
the white papers took over the role of championing the oppressed blacks. He also cites the difficulty black papers
have in raising advertising revenue.

4-126 Warren, Donald I. BLACK NEIGHBORHOODS: AN ASSESSMENT OF
COMMUNITY POWER. Ann Arbor: University of Michigan Press, 1975.

Tests a set of hypotheses about the distinctive nature of black
population centers. The research design is comparative, using
data gathered from black and white respondents in the Detroit
area in 1969. The perpetuation of black ghetto patterns is
tested in this study. Warren concludes that social structural
dynamics do not explain all of social reality. Topics discussed are: models of the black community; the black ghetto
as a spatial system; the significance of social stratification
for black ghettos; local neighborhoods and the structure of
the black ghetto; role of voluntary associations in the black
ghetto; leadership structures; alienation and activism; and social change and structure of the black ghetto.

4-127 Warren, Roland L.; Rose, Stephen M.; and Bergunder, Ann F. "Community Decision Organizations and Urban Reform." URBAN AND SO-
CIAL CHANGE REVIEW 7 (Spring 1974): 42-47.

See 3-95.

4-128 Williams, Roger M. "Atlanta's Solution to the Race Problem." WORLD
2 (May 1973): 18-22.

Traces the development of white-black relationships in Atlanta
from the late 1930s to the early seventies. Today's image is
composed of three elements: (1) a relaxed, outdoor activity-
oriented "good life", (2) an enlightened attitude on racial
matters, and (3) a fast pace of building and development.
Whites and blacks have joined together, with the economic
establishment as their common denominator, and have built
the city into what it is today.

4-129 Wilson, James Q. NEGRO POLITICS. Glencoe, Ill.: Free Press,
1960.

Examines black civic and political leadership, assesses its
strength and effectiveness, and considers its weaknesses. Wilson finds that black leaders confront the same problems that
confront any civic leader seeking to mobilize or to represent
a community. This study deals primarily with Chicago.

4-129a Wilson, M. "Black Politics. A New Power." DISSENT 18 (August
1971): 333-45.

Notes that the black ghetto has only recently become a politically institutionalized ethnic community. The two leadership groups that have emerged, lower strata militants and middle class politicians, are examined. The importance of political organization and a future role for the two leadership groups is discussed.

4-129b Wyman, R.E. "Middle-Class Voters and Progressive Reform: The Conflict of Class and Culture." AMERICAN POLITICAL SCIENCE REVIEW 68 (June 1974): 488-504.

Studies election statistics in Wisconsin, demonstrating that middle class voters supported conservative opponents of reform rather than progressive candidates. Wyman also shows that ethnic background remains the most powerful determinant of voter preference in urban general elections, but that class considerations often proved more influential in the primaries.

Chapter 5

URBAN PUBLIC POLICY ISSUES

Included in this chapter are entries relating to policy formation; the politics of planning, zoning, and land use; and urban public policy issues (environmental, transportation, health, police, etc.).

5-1   Ackerman, B. "Integration for Subsidized Housing and the Question of Racial Occupancy Controls." STANFORD LAW REVIEW 26 (January 1974): 245-309.

Examines the legal and political aspects of housing integration quotas. Ackerman argues that the only feasible method of housing integration is through federal government support of racial occupancy controls. He supports suburban integration by minorities and low income people, using the 1964 Civil Rights Act and the 1968 Fair Housing Act to reinforce his argument.

5-2   Alesch, Daniel J., and Levine, Robert A. GROWTH IN SAN JOSE: A SUMMARY POLICY STATEMENT. Santa Monica, Calif.: RAND, 1973.

Summarizes the findings of the San Jose project of the RAND urban policy program. The issues examined are the rapid twenty-year growth of the San Jose metropolitan area, the causes and effects of that growth, and the policy potential of controlling the rate and pattern of growth in the future. The authors conclude that the ability to control sprawl is more a function of changing economic and political pressures that stem largely from federal and state policies, than a failure on the part of local government. They therefore recommend improvement of the policy handed down by local government rather than any fundamental changes.

5-3   Alford, Robert R. "The Comparative Study of Urban Politics." In URBAN RESEARCH AND POLICY PLANNING, edited by L.F. Schnore and H. Fagin, pp. 263-302. Beverly Hills, Calif.: Sage Publications, 1967.

Studies of power and influence in urban political processes
often ignore the distinction between long-term structural/cul-
tural and short-term situational factors. The authors have
not tried to evaluate existing studies of urban politics, but
have examined the entire field of comparative urban politics.

5-4   Allensworth, Donald T. THE POLITICAL REALITIES OF URBAN PLAN-
        NING. New York: Praeger Publishers, 1974.

        Examines the urban planning process, focusing on how policy
        is made. The study looks at city politics, suburban politics,
        and the local bureaucracy as a political system. These are
        the city and suburban environments within which the most
        important planning powers are found and exercised. In the
        author's view the scope, content, and emphasis of planning
        has little meaning except in the organizational setting of the
        political system. Allensworth believes that politics and the
        political system dictate the actual outcome of planning.

5-4a   Altshuler, Alan A. THE CITY PLANNING PROCESS: A POLITICAL
        ANALYSIS. Ithaca, N.Y.: Cornell University Press, 1965.

        Presents one of the first serious analyses of the flaws in the
        planning process as a technical endeavor within a political
        arena. The case studies in the book point to many problems
        that inhibit the implementation of planning recommendations.

5-5   Anderson, James E. PUBLIC POLICY-MAKING. New York: Praeger
        Publishers, 1975.

        Presents a general scheme for the analysis of public policy
        making. He makes the following conclusions: (1) the process
        of policy making on most problems is continuous; (2) modern
        pluralistic political systems usually have a very complex pub-
        lic policy-making process; (3) the analysis of public policy
        making can provide much information and insight into the
        nature and operation of the political system and processes;
        (4) much remains unknown or unexplained about the process
        of political decisions and public policies, although knowledge
        has expanded substantially in the last several decades.

5-6   Aron, Joan B. "Decision Making in Energy Supply at the Metropolitan
        Level: A Study of the New York Area." PUBLIC ADMINISTRATION
        REVIEW 35 (July/August 1975): 340-45.

        Contends that although the spillover costs and benefits of
        energy supply are particularly acute, metropolitan areas typi-
        cally lack the capacity to deal with energy as a regional
        policy issue in common with many other urban services. The
        author examines the primary local decision makers in energy,
        their orientations, the kinds of influence they use, the decision

rules, and the decisions which emerge. She observes that local governments and regional planning agencies have given scant consideration to electric energy as an "urban problem" and therefore confine themselves to a weak, reactive role in energy decisions.

5-7   Ashmore, Richard D., and McConahay, John B. PSYCHOLOGY AND AMERICA'S URBAN DILEMMAS. New York: McGraw-Hill Book Co., 1975.

Gathers psychological research and theory pertinent to the understanding and alleviation of the major urban problems. A broad overview of the "urban crisis" is presented, and a case is made that psychology can contribute to ameliorating urban dilemmas. For example, conflict is a fundamental part of the political process, and psychology may help political actors to better deal with it.

5-8   "The Attack on Snob Zoning." SAVINGS AND LOAN NEWS 91 (November 1970): 30-36.

Presents arguments for and against "snob" or exclusionary zoning. Critics decry the exclusivity resulting from this practice. Conversely, communities which use exclusionary zoning claim that traditional home rule is at stake. Suburban residents are concerned with the effect of suburban migration by low income and minority groups on property values, tax rates, school enrollment, and community services. Zoning is beneficial when used to exclude nuisances, like junkyards, from the community, but can be a problem when used to dictate who may or may not reside in a jurisdiction.

5-9   Babcock, Richard [F.]. THE ZONING GAME. Madison: University of Wisconsin Press, 1967.

Deals with the participants in the zoning game and the political rules by which zoning decisions are made with emphasis on zoning in suburbia. The author examines the motives and biases of the actors, and contends that much of what takes place in zoning has not been susceptible to academic scrutiny. Zoning, he says, represents the unique American contribution to the solution of disputes arising from competing demands for the use of private land.

5-10   Babcock, Richard F., and Bosselman, Fred P. EXCLUSIONARY ZONING: LAND USE REGULATION AND HOUSING IN THE 1970'S. New York: Praeger Publishers, 1973.

A broad study of land use and housing policies in the United States. The authors present five aspects of exclusionary zoning policies: (1) the impact of land use restrictions on housing,

including the history and legal status of land use controls;
(2) the role of local governments in promoting a balanced
housing supply; (3) regional housing policies with guides to
the preparation of regional housing policies; (4) the role of
metropolitan agencies in implementing housing plans and the
use of the A-95 clearinghouse process; and (5) state government implementation of regional housing policies and state
land use regulations.

5-11   Baldinger, S. PLANNING AND GOVERNING THE METROPOLIS: THE
        TWIN CITIES EXPERIENCE. New York: Praeger Publishers, 1971.

Examines the 1967 reorganization of governments to form the
Metropolitan Council of the Twin Cities area. The Minneap-
olis-St. Paul area constructed a hybrid government composed
of seven counties, dozens of suburbs, and several special districts. The purpose of the study was to determine what the
Metro Council is and how effective it has been, to discover
why it came about in the first place, to determine the repli-
cability of the Metro Council reorganization, and to determine what planners and policy makers can learn from it.

5-12   Banfield, Edward C. THE UNHEAVENLY CITY REVISITED. Boston:
        Little, Brown and Co., 1974.

A sequel to THE UNHEAVENLY CITY. Banfield argues that
society does not know and can never know the real nature
of urban problems, let alone what might alleviate or solve
them. He states that critics misconstrued THE UNHEAVENLY
CITY. His assumption was that because of the nature of man
and society, particularly American culture and institutions,
America cannot solve its serious problems by rational management. The basic premises outlined in the first book continue
to appear in this book.

5-13   Barr, Donald A. "The Professional Urban Planner." JOURNAL OF THE
        AMERICAN INSTITUTE OF PLANNERS 38 (May 1972): 155-59.

Views urban planners as governmental functionaries, giving
insights into their work. Barr sees urban planning as a bureaucratic function and observes that urban planning has the potential to interpret not only our present urban condition but
also a future one. He concludes that the professional planner
prepares plans of what will be; the rest of society should
counter with alternative plans of what should be.

5-14   Beard, Rick. "An Island in Its Own Community: The Urban University
        as Land-Use Planner." URBAN EDUCATION 8 (January 1974): 351-
        79.

Describes how George Washington University played a major

role in transforming a residential neighborhood as it expanded
from one building in 1912 to an area encompassing more than
80 percent of four city blocks. GWU is used to show the
impact of a large land user on its environment. The author
believes that GWU has for too long adopted an insular attitude toward its immediate neighborhood. There has been
either a disregard for, or lack of awareness of, the impact
the university has upon its surroundings. Beard also observes
that the stated goals of the university are couched in moralis-
tic terms which promise a rigorous standard of judgment that
is rarely met.

5-15   Bent, Alan E. ESCAPE FROM ANARCHY: A STRATEGY FOR URBAN
        SURVIVAL. Memphis, Tenn.: Memphis State University, 1972.

        Applies the theoretical framework of systems models and cyber-
        netics analysis, developing an intersystem linkage between the
        urban and political systems by focusing on the performance,
        promise, and potential of planning. Bent concludes that there
        is hope for solving the urban crisis. Local governments need
        to be forced to take strong action so that they can be effec-
        tive partners in the American federal system. He believes that
        if rational inputs are made into the political and decision-
        making apparatus, rational decisions will result.

5-16   Bergman, Edward. ELIMINATING EXCLUSIONARY ZONING: RECON-
        CILING WORK PLACE & RESIDENCE IN SUBURBAN AREAS. Cambridge,
        Mass.: Ballinger, 1974.

        See 6-8.

5-17   Berry, Mary F. "Homesteading: New Prescription for Urban Ills."
        HUD CHALLENGE 5 (January 1974): 2-5.

        Observes that urban homesteading relieves housing agencies of
        abandoned and dilapidated buildings and provides enlarged
        opportunity for homeownership by offering abandoned homes
        to qualified recipients for a term of years. Although care-
        fully designed homesteading can be effective, Berry notes that
        giving slum houses to poor people without making resources
        available for neighborhood revitalization creates problems.

5-17a   Beyle, T.L., and Lathrop, G.T., eds. PLANNING AND POLITICS:
        UNEASY PARTNERSHIP. New York: Odyssey, 1970.

        An interesting collection of readings exploring planning within
        a political framework. Such aspects as technique, style, and
        approach are covered. The authors also explore political
        ideology as a factor to be dealt with by planners. More of
        the latter should have been developed.

5-18   Bingham, W. Harold, and Bostick, C. Dent. "Exclusionary Zoning
       Practices: An Examination of the Current Controversy." VANDERBILT
       LAW REVIEW 25 (November 1972): 1111-50.

       Calls for recognition of the fact that the exclusion of racial
       and economic minorities from suburbs by restrictive land use
       practices will not be resolved unless it is perceived as an
       integral portion of the much larger overall urban dilemma.
       The authors believe its resolution will require innovative direc-
       tion and planning at the federal, state, and local level and
       a sensitive awareness by the courts that there are compelling
       social forces at work on both sides of the controversy. The
       formation of new, strong political coalitions in the suburbs is
       observed. The authors conclude that President Nixon's state-
       ment of June 11, 1971, and the Supreme Court's decision in
       James v. Valtierra demonstrate that executive and judicial
       coercion of the suburbs is not likely to occur in the near
       future.

5-19   Birch, David, et al. "Real Estate." In their PATTERNS OF URBAN
       CHANGE: THE NEW HAVEN EXPERIENCE, pp. 57-77. Lexington,
       Mass.: D.C. Heath and Co., 1974.

       Predicts the future of urban areas over several years. The
       authors analyze a study of New Haven and conclude that the
       city will act in certain ways, regardless of who the political
       leaders are on the local, state, and federal levels.

5-20   Blair, John P. "A Review of the Filtering Down Theory." URBAN AF-
       FAIRS QUARTERLY 8 (March 1973): 303-16.

       Discusses the filter down theory of economic activity, empha-
       sizing three questions: (1) What are the theoretical foundations
       and causal relationships involved? (2) What empirical evidence
       exists in support of the filter-down theory? and (3) What policy
       implications are implied by the theory? Blair concludes that
       it needs to be recognized that the source of the problem for
       rural areas and medium-sized cities is that they not only fail
       to attract industries in general, but also fail to attract indus-
       tries which provide a basis for future growth at least as fast
       as the national average.

5-21   Bolan, Richard S., and Nuttall, Ronald L. URBAN PLANNING AND
       POLITICS. Lexington, Mass.: D.C. Heath and Co., 1975.

       Presents a theoretical description of the decision-making pro-
       cess in urban areas in New York, Boston, and Pittsburgh based
       upon the findings, interpretations, and analyses of previous
       research. The model proposed four indices influencing com-
       munity decision-making outcomes: (1) characteristics of organi-
       zations and institutions engaged in the decision-making pro-

cess; (2) characteristics of actors' roles and the skill and effort devoted to their enactment; (3) the nature of planning
and action strategies; and (4) the characteristics of the issues
in the decision-making process. Only the first two indices
were tested in this study.

5-22   Bosselman, Fred P.   "The Local Planner's Role under the Proposed Model
Land Development Code." JOURNAL OF THE AMERICAN INSTITUTE
OF PLANNERS 41 (January 1975): 15-20.

A revision enabling legislation for local land development
planning in both the long- and short-range by The American
Law Institute's Proposed Model Land Development Code. The
Institute concluded that it was undesirable to mandate planning
by local governments and chose to offer incentives that would
encourage such planning. The author discusses incentives to
planning, alternative forms of planning, and short- and long-
term planning.

5-23   Bosselman, Fred [P.], and Callies, David. THE QUIET REVOLUTION
IN LAND USE CONTROLS. Washington, D.C.: Government Printing
Office for the Council on Environmental Quality, 1971.

Reviews state approaches to the difficult problem of reallocat-
ing land use responsibilities between state and local governments. The report examines the land use and environmental
control laws of Hawaii, Vermont, California, Minnesota, Mas-
sachusetts, and Maine, and summaries of the laws of many
other states. A summary of key issues in state land use regulation is presented.

5-24   Boyd, William L., and O'Shea, David. "Theoretical Perspectives on
School District Decentralization." EDUCATION AND URBAN SOCIETY
7 (August 1975): 357-76.

Discusses the development, consequences, and prospects of
school district decentralization. The authors contend that urban decision making tends to heavily favor the interests of
public bureaucracies and their usually well-organized employees.
They conclude that the decentralization movement appears to
have contributed to popularizing the notion of citizen participation in education policy making and responsive, community-
oriented schools.

5-25   Boyd, William L., and Seldin, Florence. "The Politics of School Reform
in Rochester, New York." EDUCATION AND URBAN SOCIETY 7
(August 1975): 439-63.

See 4-15.

5-26   Bramhall, Billie. "Planners Advocate for Communities Within Planning Department." PLANNERS NOTEBOOK 4 (June 1974): 1-8.

A case study explaining the structure and workings of the Pittsburgh community planners program. In 1970, Pittsburgh created a community planning division within its city planning department to bring more responsiveness through increased City Hall sensitivity to the needs of the local communities in the city. Bramhall observes that everything seems to take longer when the community is involved and that sometimes a small group can talk a neighborhood into rejecting something good for misleading reasons. Insufficient resources presents the biggest problem.

5-27   Branfman, Eric; Cohn, Benjamin; and Trubek, David. "Measuring the Invisible Wall: Land Use Controls and the Residential Patterns of the Poor." YALE LAW JOURNAL 82 (January 1973): 483-508.

Observes that in order to formulate policy, it is necessary to discover to what extent the observed degree of clustering in the United States results from public land use controls, private convenants, racial discrimination by individual lessors and sellers, and the unconstrained market in which the quality of real properties varies and buyers have varying incomes.

5-28   "Breaking the Noose: Suburban Zoning and the Urban Crisis." SOCIAL ACTION 36 (April 1970): entire issue.

Deals with suburban zoning and land use policies. Separate articles discuss snob zoning, possible citizen action to alter the imbalance in current urban policy regarding the use of suburban resources, and the possibility of state help for the suburbs.

5-29   Brilliant, Eleanor L. THE URBAN DEVELOPMENT CORPORATION. Lexington, Mass.: Lexington Books, 1975.

See 7-19.

5-30   Burchell, Robert W., and Listokin, David, eds. FUTURE LAND USE. New Brunswick, N.J.: Rutgers University, 1975.

Contains several essays which outline the task before decision makers in the field of land use. The articles discuss the future of land use controls, the equity concept on land use decisions, the conflict between growth and preservation of the environment, the multiple dimensions of the national energy policy, and the shape of metropolitan areas in the twenty-first century.

5-31   Caldwell, Lynton C., ed. ENVIRONMENTAL STUDIES; PAPERS ON

THE POLITICS AND PUBLIC ADMINISTRATION OF MAN-ENVIRON-
MENT RELATIONSHIPS. 4 vols. Bloomington: Indiana University,
1967.

Presents the results of seminars conducted by the Conservation
Foundation at Indiana University in 1965. The articles examine the political dynamics of environmental control; intergovernmental action on environmental policy; politics, professionalism, and the environment; and research on policy
and administration in environmental quality programs.

5-32   Cantor, Arnold. "State-Local Taxes: A Study of Inequity." THE
AMERICAN FEDERATIONIST 81 (February 1974): 14-21.

Contends that state and local taxes have doubled in the last
six years, aggravating long-standing inequities in the tax structure of America's state and local governments. According to
the author, the inequities have become major impediments to
the achievement of economic and social justice. Reactions to
these increases in revenue from inequitable tax systems have
ranged from meaningful reform measures to unrealistic statutory
or constitutional restrictions on government revenue raising.

5-33   Caputo, David C. "Evaluating Urban Public Policy: A Developmental
Model and Some Reservations." PUBLIC ADMINISTRATION REVIEW 33
(March/April 1973): 113-19.

Develops an evaluation model of urban public policy, stressing
component interaction and time variables. The author cautions
that subjective considerations, such as political decisions, may
thwart objectivity in the evaluation process; and that complexities of program evaluation may require research testing.
He describes his model for urban public policy evaluation and
explains why it would be workable.

5-33a   Catanese, Anthony J[ames]. PLANNERS AND LOCAL POLITICS: IM-
POSSIBLE DREAMS. Beverly Hills, Calif.: Sage Publications, 1974.

Presents a well-known analysis of the political basis for planning failures in the United States. The argument is made that
changes are necessary in planning process and ideology if we
are to expect implementation of planning. Also discusses planning process.

5-33b   Clark, Terry N. "Citizen Values, Power, and Policy Outputs. A Model
of Community Decision Making." JOURNAL OF COMPARATIVE AD-
MINISTRATION 4 (February 1973): 385-427.

A study of fifty-one American cities using a model of the political system that emphasizes the values of citizens in a community context, the structure of leadership, the centralization

of power and decision making, and policy outputs. The results
imply a series of specific policy recommendations.

5-33c ·Colman, William G. CITIES, SUBURBS, AND STATES. New York:
Free Press, 1975.

An overview of the issues of governing and financing cities,
and the fiscal and legal effects on service delivery. Colman
deals with problems of demographics, housing, education, and
employment. He examines the root causes, proposed solutions,
and the suitability of present government structures to revitalize
the cities.

5-34   Conant, Ralph W., and Molz, Kathleen, eds. THE METROPOLITAN
LIBRARY. Cambridge: M.I.T. Press, 1972.

Articles dealing specifically with how public libraries function
in urban areas. Of particular interest are chapters 9, 10, 12,
and 13. Chapter 9 studies trends in urban politics and government that affect library functions, acknowledging that the allocation of funds to urban libraries from scarce city financial
pools is most definitely a political function. Chapter 10
covers the financial capacity of local governments to provide
public library service needed by various types of communities.
Chapter 12 concerns the library as a provider of public services,
examining who receives the services and why. Chapter 13
examines the suburban library.

5-35   Costonis, John J. "The Cost of Preservation." ARCHITECTURAL FORUM
140 (January/February 1974): 61-67.

Examines the economic feasibility of the Chicago plan, which
proposed the transfer of development rights, rather than general
tax revenues, to fund municipal preservation programs. It
concludes that the cost of preservation restrictions on land
properties is a function of two factors: (1) the relative size
of the landmark and the replacement building, and (2) the
relative return on investment of the landmark and the replacement building.

5-36   _____. "Development Rights Transfer: An Exploratory Essay." YALE
LAW JOURNAL 83 (November 1973): 75-128.

Argues that the development potential of private property is a
community asset to be used to serve the community's needs.
This proposition, called development rights transfer, vastly
expands government's economic and planning power over private land-use decisions. Development rights transfer entails
zoning adjustments or development changes of the police power
and taxing approaches. Expanded governmental land-use tools
must be utilized to prevent further environmental deterioration.

5-37   Council on the Environment of New York City. A CITIZEN'S POLICY
        GUIDE TO ENVIRONMENTAL PRIORITIES FOR NEW YORK CITY, 1974-
        1984. New York: December, 1973.

        Considers the environmental impact of energy policies and the
        relationship between the current crisis and long-term energy
        planning. The three most important energy priorities in New
        York City in the next decade are: (1) to reduce energy con-
        sumption; (2) to. develop alternative sources of fuel, even
        locally; and (3) to apply all reasonable and attainable en-
        vironmental safeguards, including pollution control and clean
        fuel requirements.

5-38   Cow, Peter, ed. THE FUTURE OF PLANNING. Beverly Hills, Calif.:
        Sage Publications, 1973.

        Deals with planning as a dynamic process which affects pat-
        terns of urbanization and as a political process which concerns
        the allocation of resources. The book focuses on planning in
        Great Britain, but is applicable to the United States. It
        covers such issues as planning and the government, planning
        and the public, planning and the market, and how planning
        can respond to new issues.

5-39   Cox, Kevin R. CONFLICT, POWER, AND POLITICS IN THE CITY:
        A GEOGRAPHIC OVERVIEW. New York: McGraw-Hill Book Co.,
        1973.

        Contends that the major interest for urban geographers is the
        locational nature of many urban political issues, for example,
        the restrictive residential zoning practices of the suburbs. The
        author describes the nature of the political conflicts among
        localized urban populations and discusses the problem of fiscal
        disparities. He also evaluates the politics of redressing the
        locational inequity in government services and environmental
        quality within cities.

5-40   Crenson, Matthew A. THE UNPOLITICS OF AIR POLLUTION: A
        STUDY OF NON-DECISION MAKING IN THE CITIES. Baltimore:
        Johns Hopkins Press, 1971.

        Seeks answers to why many cities and towns in the United
        States failed for so long to make a political issue of air pol-
        lution problems. The author concludes that a lack of open-
        ness in American local politics, and politically enforced in-
        action are reasons for municipal neglect. This political im-
        mobility has become a major consideration for air pollution
        policy makers.

5-41   Danielson, Michael N., ed. METROPOLITAN POLITICS: A READER.
        Boston: Little, Brown & Co., 1966.

        A collection of thirty-seven essays covering the politics of
        transportation, water supply, planning, special districts, inter-
        local agreements, state and federal involvement in metropoli-
        tan problems, and metropolitan government. The focus is on
        political behavior rather than institutional reform.

5-42   Dantzig, George B., and Soaty, Thomas L. "Urban Models." In their
        COMPACT CITY: A PLAN FOR A LIVEABLE URBAN ENVIRONMENT,
        pp. 111-24. San Francisco: W.H. Freeman and Co., 1973.

        Explores the possible uses of computers, mathematical models,
        and operation research in solving urban problems. The authors
        examine the concept of total-system planning through which
        planning is a self-corrective, adaptive process and suggest use
        of computers to help plan highways and other urban problems.

5-43   _____. "Why the Compact City?" In their COMPACT CITY: A PLAN
        FOR A LIVEABLE URBAN ENVIRONMENT, pp. 3-15. San Francisco:
        W.H. Freeman and Co., 1973.

        An essay on the problems of excessive growth in the cities.
        Socioeconomic pressures that accelerate urban sprawl are
        studied including population increase, density of the inner
        city, industry relocation, and urban transportation problems.
        Some goals for urban society are outlined including the elimi-
        nation of slums and blight, and a viable center for business,
        culture, and government.

5-44   David, Stephen M., and Peterson, Paul E., eds. URBAN POLITICS
        AND PUBLIC POLICY: THE CITY IN CRISIS. New York: Praeger
        Publishers, 1973.

        Contends that urban political policy must be examined if the
        distribution of power in cities is to be determined. It can
        then be seen to whose demands government responds. The
        book covers the major political problems, urban governance and
        citizen participation, discussing them in the context of housing,
        transportation, and education policy and politics. It examines
        the possibilities for change in power relationships and public
        policy.

5-45   Davidoff, Linda; Davidoff, Paul; and Gold, Neil. "Suburban Action:
        Advocate Planning for an Open Society." JOURNAL OF THE AMERI-
        CAN INSTITUTE OF PLANNERS 36 (January 2, 1970): 12-21.

        See 6-26.

5-46   Davy, Thomas J. "Education of Urban Administrators: Considerations in Planning and Organizing Graduate Degree Programs." PUBLIC MANAGEMENT 54 (February 1972): 5-9.

See 2-10.

5-47   Denton, Eugene H. "How a City Determines Its Environmental Quality." PUBLIC MANAGEMENT 56 (March 1974): 10-11.

Contends that the quality of a city's environment is dependent on the city's design. The author, the assistant city manager of Dallas, discusses environmental changes in Dallas, emphasizing the decision-making process and the role of members of the community, and how the unique climate and character of Dallas itself forms a framework for its visual image.

5-48   DeQuine, Jeanne M. "The Interlocal Agreement: A Tool for Growth Management." FLORIDA ENVIRONMENTAL AND URBAN ISSUES 2 (October/November 1974): 8-9, 18-19.

Describes the interlocal agreement, which has been in existence for over one hundred years and is the most widely used method of interlocal cooperation in the United States. Counties, municipalities, and special districts are looking to the interlocal agreement to address problems of service delivery and growth rate. Outlined are decision-making steps for administrators and officials contemplating case studies of interlocal agreements.

5-49   Dixon, Robert G., Jr. "Rebuilding the Urban Political System." GEORGETOWN LAW REVIEW 58 (1970): 955-86.

An examination of the possibilities for structural reform of local government. The author analyzes existing institutions, the movement toward citizen participation inspired by the Office of Economic Opportunity and the Department of Housing and Urban Development, the use of new proportional devices to ensure minority representation, the growing councils of government movement, and the impact of the one man–one vote constitutional doctrine. He concludes that the keys to successful local reform movement and the essence of a functional government are concerns for the community in the political sense and the effective political representation of actual interests.

The concept of a general urban political community must be renewed and encompassed in a structure that is responsive to the continuing subcommunities of the older neighborhoods and the new service units, and that welds the whole into a sense of common enterprise. Failing this development, society may enter a post-political urban era, the result being a novel "formless form" of government, with high visibility for the immediate participant but no visibility for the general public.

5-50   Dolbeare, Kenneth. TRIAL COURTS IN URBAN POLITICS. New York: John Wiley & Sons, 1967.

An examination of the effect of court decisions on public policy, government processes restricted by legal constraints and vice versa, local political structure, court structure, judges, and the selection thereof. Questions include: Who uses the courts? Who is most successful in the courts? How is decision making affected by the judge and also by the counsel? Dolbeare examines the impact of the courts on zoning and land use, education, taxation, and local government policy.

5-51   Donnison, David. "What is the 'Good City'." NEW SOCIETY 26 (December 13, 1973): 647-49.

A look at urban planning in Britain. The author proposes four areas for empirical research which may help to correct the present day confusion: (1) accessibility of the city to newcomers; (2) availability of better or different opportunities in employment, education, and so forth; (3) relationship between one's opportunities and factors such as education and jobs; and (4) measurement of nobility in historical perspective.

5-51a   Donovan, John C. THE POLITICS OF POVERTY. 2d ed. Indianapolis: Bobbs-Merrill, 1973.

Deals with the genesis and implementation at the federal level of the Office of Economic Opportunity and the Johnson administration's poverty programs. While grand in concept, it is pointed out that the failures of these programs is largely due to a lack of commitment in implementation. Maximum feasible participation is also discussed, and it is pointed out that not only legislators did not recognize its implications, but that it was also misinterpreted by almost all program designers.

5-52   Downes, Bryan T., ed. CITIES AND SUBURBS. Belmont, Calif.: Wadsworth Publishing Co., 1971.

Presents a working hypothesis that there is a relationship between contextual/political differences of local municipalities and their policy outcomes. The editor suggests that students of local politics systematically examine the linkages among the concepts and variables in his model.

5-53   Downes, Bryan T., and Greene, Kenneth R. "The Politics of Open
Housing in Three Cities: Decision Maker Responses to Black Demands
for Policy Changes." AMERICAN POLITICS QUARTERLY 1 (April 2,
1973): 215-43.

See 3-29.

5-53a   Downs, Anthony. URBAN PROBLEMS AND PROSPECTS. Chicago:
Markham, 1970.

Presents a series of important articles that Downs had written
for a number of journals over an eight-year period. This is
an important book because of the unorthodoxy inherent in
many of his concepts. Downs can range from the conservative
on urban growth to the radical on transportation to the prag-
matist on ghetto development.

5-54   Downs, Edward R., Jr. "The Impact of the Robinson-Patman Act on
Minority Business Development." REVIEW OF BLACK POLITICAL ECON-
OMY 4 (Fall 1973): 1-19.

See 4-38.

5-55   Dreyfus, Daniel A. "Needed: A National Land Use Policy." CIVIL
ENGINEERING 42 (May 1972): 52-54.

See 7-42.

5-56   Ecker-Racz, Laslo L. THE POLITICS AND ECONOMICS OF STATE-
LOCAL FINANCE. Englewood Cliffs, N.J.: Prentice-Hall, 1970.

See 7-44.

5-56a   Eddy, William B., and Murphy, Thomas P. "Applied Behavioral Science
in Local Governments." In THE HUMAN RESOURCES OF CITY GOV-
ERNMENTS, edited by Charles H. Levine. Vol. 13, Urban Affairs Annual Review. Beverly Hills, Calif.: Sage Publications, 1977.

See 1-23.

5-56b   Eldredge, H. Wentworth, ed. WORLD CAPITALS: TOWARD GUIDED
URBANIZATION. Garden City, N.Y.: Anchor Press-Doubleday, 1975.

See 4-43a.

5-57   Ellickson, R.C. "Alternatives to Zoning: Convenants, Nuisance Rules,
and Fines as Land Use Controls." UNIVERSITY OF CHICAGO LAW RE-
VIEW 40 (Summer 1973): 681-781.

Contends that land use control in the United States is neither

as efficient nor as equitable as other alternatives. Detailed
mandatory zoning standards impair efficient urban growth and
discriminate against migrants, lower classes, and landowners
with little political influence. The alternative to zoning controls depends on a consensual system of internalization to handle external costs and would work particularly well in undevel-
oped areas. Injury caused by noxious land use should be de-
terred through fines and selected uniform mandatory standards.
The internalization devices could be administered by metropolitan nuisance boards that would perform rule-making, administrative, and adjudicatory functions within the guidelines of
state law.

5-58   Erie, Steven P., et al. REFORM OF METROPOLITAN GOVERNMENTS.
Washington, D.C.: Resources for the Future; distributed by Johns Hopkins University Press, 1972.

See 6-34.

5-59   Ernst, Robert T., et al. "Competition and Conflict Over Land Use
Change in the Inner City: Institution vs. Community." ANTIPODE 6
(July 1974): 70-97.

Examines the competition for land and the conflict over land-
use changes at the neighborhood community level. The author
identifies the major players in the inner city land-use issues
and demonstrates the effects on inner city communities.

5-60   Ershkowitz, Miriam. "Environmental Politics in the Metropolis." BU-
REAUCRAT 4 (July 1975): 147-62.

A case study of air resource management with New York City
and the Consolidated Edison Company, illuminating problems
local governments face in regulating large and politically influential public corporations like utilities. The author reports
that New York City's Department of Air Pollution Control had
several mechanisms to curtail emissions from Con Edison stacks
but failed to employ them. The city asked only for an explanation by the utility for the heavy emissions. Three factors
contributed to the lack of enforcement--a strong pollutor in
Con Edison, lack of widespread public support for enforcement,
and isolation of the actors from centers of governmental power
in New York City.

5-61   Fantini, Mario; Gittell, Marilyn; and Magat Richard. COMMUNITY
CONTROL AND THE URBAN SCHOOL. New York: Frederick A. Praeger, 1970.

See 3-33.

5-62   Finkelstein, Phillip. REAL PROPERTY TAXATION IN NEW YORK CITY.
        New York: Praeger Publishers, 1975.

        Argues that the property tax will not be replaced, and should
        thus be reformed as best as possible. Recommendations are:
        reassess upward land values to achieve a greater equalization
        of the tax burden and to provide an incentive for improvements,
        establish correct land values, and set differential tax rates for
        land and improvements as an alternative to the selection abate-
        ments now granted.

5-63   Fischel, William A. "Fiscal and Environmental Considerations in the
        Location of Firms in Suburban Communities." In FISCAL ZONING AND
        LAND USE CONTROLS, edited by Edwin S. Mills and Wallace E.
        Oates, pp. 119-73. Lexington, Mass.: D.C. Heath and Co., 1975.

        See 6-39.

5-64   Fisher, Anthony C., and Krutilla, John V. "Managing the Public
        Lands: Assignment of Property Rights and Valuation of Resources." In
        THE GOVERNANCE OF COMMON PROPERTY RESOURCES, edited by
        Edwin T. Haefele, pp. 35-59. Baltimore: Johns Hopkins University
        Press, 1974.

        Considers the issue of whether there should be public owner-
        ship or intervention in the allocation and management of the
        remaining large natural areas; discusses the concepts of common
        property, public goods, and externalities; and the effect of
        different assignments of property rights on the valuation of
        these areas. The authors conclude that the valuation problem
        could be resolved through a market but the resulting distribu-
        tion of land would not be socially optimal.

5-65   Fleming, Harold C. "The Social Constraints." CENTER MAGAZINE 9
        (January/February 1976): 16-22.

        See 4-50.

5-66   Fondinelli, Dennis A. URBAN AND REGIONAL DEVELOPMENT PLAN-
        NING: POLICY AND ADMINISTRATIONS. Ithaca, N.Y.: Cornell
        University Press, 1975.

        Examines urban and regional planning in terms of the develop-
        ment of urban policy. Part one introduces the discussion with
        an overview of planning, policy making, and the political pro-
        cess. The second part deals with the formulation of policy,
        including the political strategy and reformulations of develop-
        mental policy. Part three examines the administration of
        policy and the organizational structure of urban regions. Spe-
        cifically, the author examines the politics of economic develop-

ment and the organizational structure of northeastern Pennsylvania. The fourth section analyzes organizational interaction
and the dynamics of policy making. The author concludes by
examining politics, policy analysis, and policy development
in terms of the future of urban and regional planning.

5-67   Fowler, Edmund P., and Lineberry, Robert L. "The Comparative Analy-
        sis of Urban Policy: Canada and the United States." In PEOPLE AND
        POLITICS IN URBAN SOCIETY, edited by Harlan Hahn, pp. 345-68.
        Beverly Hills, Calif.: Sage Publications, 1972.

        See 5-76.

5-68   Francis, Mark. "Urban Impact Assessment and Community Involvement:
        The Case of the John Fitzgerald Kennedy Library." ENVIRONMENT
        AND BEHAVIOR 7 (September 1975): 373-404.

        See 3-37.

5-69   Fredericks, Steven J. "Curriculum and Decentralization: The New York
        City Public School System." URBAN EDUCATION 9 (October 1974):
        247-56.

        Develops several conclusions about curriculum development in
        the decentralized New York City school system: (1) the trans-
        ferral of power and the struggle to retain this power is a real
        threat to education in New York City, and (2) there is a
        demand for more involvement in curriculum development.
        Citizens felt they were not encouraged to participate.

5-70   Galany, Gideon, and Walden, Daniel, eds. THE CONTEMPORARY
        NEW COMMUNITIES MOVEMENT IN THE UNITED STATES. Urbana:
        University of Illinois Press, 1974.

        A compilation of essays by academics and planners in the field
        of new community development. Topics discussed include pub-
        lic enterprise and new towns, social planning and research in
        new communities, and the difficulties in planning and building
        new communities.

5-71   Gallagher, John F., and Bay, John P. A STATE ROLE IN LAND USE
        MANAGEMENT. Columbus, Ohio: Legislative Service Commission,
        1974.

        See 7-51.

5-72   Gapp, Paul. "Chicago 21." ARCHITECTURAL FORUM 140 (January/
        February 1974): 32-37.

        Details Chicago's plan for rejuvenating the declining inner

city. The plan offers alternatives to the economic, social, and cultural rigor mortis now overtaking the legendary Loop and the fringe areas. The new design involves a series of super blocks with renovations in transportation, urban renewal, and zoning.

5-73   Ginzberg, Eli, ed. THE FUTURE OF THE METROPOLIS: PEOPLE, JOBS, INCOME. Salt Lake City, Utah: Olympus Publishing Co., 1975.

An interdisciplinary approach to the "urban crisis" examining several metropolitan concerns, including demography, management, economics, public finance, minorities, and manpower. The editor concludes that three responses are essential for cities and metropolitan areas to overcome their crises: (1) the ability to articulate their plans for the future, (2) the ability to secure a broad consensus to support city goals, and (3) effective decision-making apparatus. He develops a strategy framework for solving metropolitan problems and suggests ways to implement it.

5-74   Gittell, Marilyn, et al. LOCAL CONTROL IN EDUCATION. New York: Praeger Publishers, 1969.

An evaluative documentary history of the creation of three demonstration school districts established in New York in 1967 for political and educational purposes. The authors record the impact of the program upon those it was designed to help, upon the institutions it was designed to change, and upon those who designed and administered it.

5-75   Hadden, Jeffrey K.; Masotti, Louis H.; and Larson, Calvin J., eds. METROPOLIS IN CRISIS--SOCIAL AND POLITICAL PERSPECTIVES. 2d ed. Itasca, Ill.: Peacock, 1971.

Short essays on urban problems. Part one presents an overview of the urban crisis, while part two discusses the political implications of the urban crisis. The third part of the book deals with the dimensions of the crisis, and includes excerpts from several national commissions. Part four examines the role of power as it relates to the urban crises, and explores community control in four essays. "Perspectives on Urban Change," a look at methods of change, concludes the volume.

5-76   Hahn, Harlan, ed. PEOPLE AND POLITICS IN URBAN SOCIETY. Beverly Hills, Calif.: Sage Publications, 1972.

Four essays dealing with the urban policy process and selected policy issues such as pollution, economic and human resource development, and policy expenditures.

5-77   Hanson, Royce. THE POLITICS OF METROPOLITAN COOPERATION.
       Washington, D.C.: Washington Center for Metropolitan Studies, 1964.

       A case study of the life and problems of the Metropolitan
       Washington Council of Governments (COG). The report looks
       closely at the evolution of the group, its leadership, and its
       politics. It describes the way COG works and examines the
       elements which compose the politics of metropolitan coopera-
       tion. Finally, it assesses the limits and potentialities of
       voluntary cooperation in resolving metropolitan conflicts. The
       study focuses a single institution, its members, and its activi-
       ties over a prolonged period of time, emphasizing critical
       decisions rather than structure and procedure.

5-78   Hartman, Chester W. HOUSING AND SOCIAL POLICY. Englewood
       Cliffs, N.J.: Prentice-Hall, 1975.

       See 7-59.

5-79   Hawkins, B[rett].W. POLITICS AND URBAN POLICIES. Indianapolis:
       Bobbs-Merrill, 1971.

       Attempts to provide a framework within which students of ur-
       ban affairs can understand urban public policy. Through com-
       parative studies Hawkins focuses on what is, not what ought
       to be, in an effort to provide research-based answers to sever-
       al important questions. He discusses the characteristics which
       distinguish cities that have adopted fluoridation, urban renewal,
       a city-manager form of government, and metropolitan govern-
       ment from other cities; the characteristics of the urban environ-
       ment that are associated with public spending for welfare and
       education; and the forces outside the city that shape its poli-
       cies.

5-80   Hill, Herbert. LABOR UNION CONTROL OF JOB TRAINING: A
       CRITICAL ANALYSIS OF APPRENTICESHIP OUTREACH PROGRAMS AND
       THE HOMETOWN PLANS. Washington, D.C.: Howard University In-
       stitute for Urban Affairs and Research, 1974.

       See 4-75.

5-81   Hirsch, Werner A., et al. FISCAL PRESSURES ON THE CENTRAL CITY:
       THE IMPACT OF COMMUTERS, NON-WHITES AND OVERLAPPING
       GOVERNMENTS. New York: Frederick A. Praeger, 1971.

       Examines the major fiscal problems of the central city. Three
       reasons are presented to account for city problems in financ-
       ing urban public services: (1) the large number of poor people
       living in cities results in slow growth of the revenue base but
       high expenditures; (2) certain physical and structural character-
       istics of the city, such as old buildings and diseconomies of

scale, deteriorate the revenue base, although costs do not decline; and (3) governmental fragmentation under federalism has been producing major spillovers of social costs and benefits, which have largely hurt the cities.

5-82   Hofferbert, Richard A., and Sharkansky, Ira, eds.   STATE AND URBAN POLITICS.   Boston: Little, Brown and Co., 1971.

Focuses upon the political, economic, and population characteristics that help shape the policies of state and local governments.   The editors believe that an understanding of the factors that shape policy can help social scientists reinforce good policies and change poor policies.   A conclusion that emerges is that the nature of the sociopolitical setting has measurable consequences for the patterns of policy followed by state and community decision makers.

5-83   Holden, Matthew, Jr.   "The Politics of Urbanization."   In PEOPLE AND POLITICS IN URBAN SOCIETY, edited by Harlan Hahn, pp. 557-600.   Beverly Hills, Calif.:   Sage Publications, 1972.

Examines the capacity of government to manage the political problems inherent in urbanization.

5-84   Holland, John J.   "County Government Can be an Effective Management Tool for Land-Use Planning."   NEW JERSEY COUNTY GOVERNMENT, April 1971, pp. 4-5, 8.

Proposes that counties in general, and specifically in New Jersey, are ready to participate effectively in the regional urbanization process, and should be assigned logical "middle management" responsibilities along with the authority to carry them out.   The author feels strongly that the pre-eminent barrier to sound land-use planning is the lone-standing predilection for the property tax as the basic source of local public funds.

5-85   Hughes, James W.   "Dilemmas of Suburbanization and Growth Controls."   ANNALS OF THE AMERICAN ACADEMY OF POLITICAL AND SOCIAL SCIENCE 422 (November 1975):   61-76.

See 6-59.

5-86   _____, ed.   NEW DIMENSIONS IN URBAN PLANNING: GROWTH CONTROLS.   New Brunswick, N.J.:   Rutgers University, Center for Urban Policy Research, 1974.

Examines many crucial questions concerning urban/suburban growth, focusing primarily upon growth controls.   Presenting both sides of the issue, Hughes argues that a community cannot be expected to continue to expand indefinitely; it has a

right to protect its neighborhoods. On the other hand, he
says, the effect of growth controls on those citizens outside
of the controlled community can be harmful. Clearly, this
is a complex and perplexing issue which citizens and professionals must address.

5-87   Imundo, Louis V., Jr. "Ineffectiveness and Inefficiency in Government
Management." PUBLIC PERSONNEL MANAGEMENT, March/April 1975,
pp. 90-95.

Contends that there are four basic causes of ineffectiveness
and inefficiency in all levels of government: (1) political ap-
pointees lack the expertise to manage and supervise well; (2)
standards of good work and measurement techniques, essential
for quality performance, have not been established; (3) budgets
based on past history lack the flexibility to adjust to new
demands; and (4) dependence on higher authority and/or rules
and regulations promotes inefficiency and smoother creativity.

5-88   "Innovations in Municipal Government." PUBLIC MANAGEMENT 55
(May 1973): 1-25.

Examines changes that have been occurring in municipal management. Of particular interest to students of urban politics
is "Intergovernmental Cooperation--A Community Approach,"
which discusses the provision of adequate services to the various users under a common arrangement and the accruement and
realization of savings of each entity in an intergovernmental
cooperation arrangement.

5-89   James, Judson L. "Federalism and the Model Cities Experiment."
PUBLIUS 2 (Spring 1972): 69-94.

See 7-64.

5-90   James, Ralph. "Is There a Case for Local Authority Policy Planning?
Corporate Management, the Use of Business Management Models, and
the Allocation of Resources in Local Government." PUBLIC ADMINIS-
TRATION 51 (Summer 1973): 147-63.

Argues that the potential for improvement by reworking the
information processes, as suggested by corporate management
advocates, is limited, due to the impossibility of defining
objective output standards for the great majority of local government services. There is often a trade-off between minimum
cost considerations and quality of service considerations. The
author believes that it would be helpful if the debate on
policy planning shifted to a consideration of decentralization
in relation to specific services. This would involve considera-

tion of optimum scale of operation for different services and
the critical relationships between services.

5-91   Jones, Charles O. CLEAN AIR: THE POLICIES AND POLITICS OF
POLLUTION CONTROL. Pittsburgh: University of Pittsburgh Press,
1975.

Describes the conflict between clean air and economic development, and assesses the problem at the local, state, and federal
level. Jones outlines the history of air pollution policy development. Increasing county and state participation in pollution control and the debates over policy is described. Jones
concludes by noting the implications for policy in other areas
of governmental control and regulation.

5-92   Jones, E. Terrence. "Mass Media and the Urban Policy Process."
POLICY STUDIES JOURNAL 3 (Summer 1975): 359-63.

Argues that in the later stages of the urban policy process,
and especially when studying the information about policy outcomes which is fed back into the initial stages of the next
round of urban policy-making, it is important to examine criti-
cally the role of the metropolitan mass media, such as the
major newspapers, television stations, and radio outlets ser-
vicing a metropolitan area. In particular, the author contends that we should: (1) study how the media describes urban
policy outcomes; (2) investigate the factors that influence the
quantity and quality of the media's coverage of outcomes; and
(3) analyze the ways in which the media's coverage of yester-
day's and today's outcomes affect tomorrow's policies.

5-93 Kaufman, Clifford. "Political Urbanism: Urban Spatial Organization,
Policy, and Politics." URBAN AFFAIRS QUARTERLY 9 (June 1974):
421-36.

Focuses upon the development of a field of political urbanism
concerned with political explanations for urban spatial organization. The author claims that such a focus draws our attention to the internal properties of urban areas. He attempts to
conceptualize and interrelate urbanism and urban policy. Dimensions of urbanism are used as a basis to classify forms of
urban resources related to the level and distribution of welfare
among urban actors.

5-94 Keller, Eugene. "Politicizing Statistics." DISSENT 20 (Spring 1973):
142-54.

Contends that the extent of "politicizing" government statistics
has been exaggerated. Keller explains that statistical programs
are central to the planning processes of all industrial coun-

tries, especially to those of the United States where decision making is relatively dispersed. He maintains that the statistics, as a rule, are not permitted to become suspect. However, some information may be withheld if it is deemed harmful to the bureaucracy affected by the statistics. The author disagrees with critics who charge that there is widespread "politicizing" of statistics.

5-95 Kendrick, Frank J. "Urban Transportation Policy: Politics, Planning, and People." POLICY STUDIES JOURNAL 3 (Summer 1975): 375-81.

Argues that the public is not cognizant of the tremendous effects that transportation policies can have on urban development and on the overall quality of life in metropolitan areas. Unless we begin to think of the whole urban environment and consider what we really want our cities to become in the future, we may someday have to look upon our urban freeway system as little more than a monument to our inability to deal successfully with a major facet of the urban crisis.

5-96 Kirkpatrick, Samuel, and Morgan, David. "Policy Support and Orientations Toward Metropolitan Politician Integration Among Urban Officials." SOCIAL SCIENCE QUARTERLY 52 (December 1971): 656-71.

Isolates the correlates of urban public officials' evaluations of urban policies and services, and describes the effects of their orientations upon various aspects of metropolitan political integration. The analysis suggests that: (1) community characteristics and life-styles have an impact on officials' evaluations of urban services; (2) individual characteristics of decision-making elites also shape policy evaluations; (3) evaluations of existing service outputs reflect relative degrees of budgetary commitment to these services; and (4) attitudes toward metropolitan integration may reflect community and individual ties to current levels of policy support in a variety of service areas.

5-97 Kirlin, John J. "The Impact of Increasing Lower-Status Clientele Upon City Governmental Structures: A Model from Organization Theory." URBAN AFFAIRS QUARTERLY 8 (March 1973): 317-43.

See 4-87.

5-98 Kirlin, John [J.], and Erie, Steven. "The Study of City Governance and Public Policy Making: A Critical Appraisal." PUBLIC ADMINISTRATION REVIEW 32 (March-April 1972): 173-84.

Reviews the existing studies of municipalities and suggests new research directions which they believe should be pursued if the study of urban governance is to contribute to public policy making. The authors examine models of municipal governance.

5-99   Knox, Michael D.; Kolton, Marilyn S.; and Dwarshwis, Louis. "Com-
        munity Development in Housing: Increased Tenant Participation." PUBLIC
        WELFARE 32 (Summer 1974): 48-53.

        See 3-55.

5-99a   Lakshmanan, T.R. "The New Technical Competence for Urban Manage-
        ment." In EMERGING PATTERNS IN URBAN ADMINISTRATION, edited
        by F. Gerald Brown and Thomas P. Murphy, pp. 172-92. Lexington,
        Mass.: Lexington Books, 1970.

        See 6-18a.

5-100   "Land Use Control in Metropolitan Areas: The Failure of Zoning and a
        Proposed Alternative." SOUTHERN CALIFORNIA LAW REVIEW 45 (1972):
        335.

        Evaluates the need for zoning laws by focusing upon the eco-
        nomic function of zoning and examining the assumptions which
        underlie the use of zoning as a land use control technique.
        The procedural and substantive abuses of zoning are considered,
        and a proposal is made for an alternative system of land use
        controls which can yield greater benefits.

5-101   Leach, Richard H., and O'Rourke, Timothy G., eds. DIMENSIONS
        OF STATE AND URBAN POLICY MAKING. New York: Macmillan,
        1974.

        Presents an overall analysis of state and urban policy making
        in four parts, each dealing with various aspects of the urban
        crisis. Part one deals with issues such as reformism and public
        policy in U.S. cities. The second part describes the political
        aspects of state legislative activities. The third part discusses
        political machines and the preconditions of mayoral leadership.
        The last part assesses various urban problems and controversies,
        such as crime, pollution, and finance.

5-102   Lehne, Richard, and Fisk, Donald M. "The Impact of Urban Policy
        Analysis." URBAN AFFAIRS QUARTERLY 10 (December 1974): 115-38.

        Examines the impact of detailed studies of local government
        operations in order to explore the domain of urban policy
        analysis. By reporting the circumstances under which analyses
        of urban policies were accepted into the deliberations of local
        decision makers, the authors hope to contribute to a more ef-
        fective use of local resources and to sketch quite tentatively
        those areas in which officials will accept analysis as compatible
        with local conditions. The case histories are examined to as-
        sess the impact that policy analysis can have on local govern-
        ment operations.

5-103 Lindsay, John V. THE CITY. New York: W.W. Norton, 1970.

A book by twice-elected mayor of New York City on his experience running the largest city in the United States. He argues that large cities need money, basic changes in their method of government, and the courage and foresight to give citizens a greater voice. Lindsay makes an urgent call to save the cities, claiming that the imbalance between what the cities receive and what other areas of the country get must be remedied or the cities will never solve the massive problems which confront them.

5-103a Lineberry, Robert L., and Masotti, Louis H., eds. URBAN PROBLEMS AND PUBLIC POLICY. Lexington, Mass.: Lexington Books, 1975.

Fifteen chapters by different specialists on urbanization, the politics of policy change, the policy-making system, and the federalization of urban policy.

5-104 Lineberry, Robert L., and Sharkansky, Ira. URBAN POLITICS AND PUBLIC POLICY. New York: Harper and Row, 1971.

A behavioral analysis of politics and public policies in American cities focusing on the realities of political behavior. The authors deal with urban politics and the policy choices of decision makers in urban governments. Urban problems that constitute the urban crisis are discussed to the extent that their existence is recognized in public policies designed to deal with them. The authors believe that urban issues can be influenced by public policy and that the cities have the human and financial resources needed to make improvements.

5-105 Linowes, R. Robert, and Allensworth, Don T. THE STATE AND LAND USE CONTROL. New York: Praeger Publishers, 1975.

See 7-75.

5-106 Long, Norton E. "Making Urban Policy Useful and Corrigible." URBAN AFFAIRS QUARTERLY 10 (June 1975): 379-97.

Argues that urban policy cannot be useful unless we clarify our priorities. Policy can be improved only if we are able to learn from our experiences in attempting to implement it. It is the function of urban policy analysts to observe what we are and are not doing and examine the consequences of our actions and inactions on the lives of specific people.

5-107 Lotz, Aileen. "An Island Acts to Save Itself: The Sanibel Story." FLORIDA ENVIRONMENTAL AND URBAN ISSUES 2 (April 1975): 7-8.

Assesses the future of Sanibel Island in view of the large number of building permits issued in the first half of the 1970s.
The island's population will probably grow from 1,000 in 1970
to 25,000 in 1980. City council steps to slow growth rate
include a court decision against developers of the Hilton Hotels;
a firm stand on the issuance of building permits by scrutinizing
each application for its impact on the island; the enactment of
a ninety-day zoning moratorium regulating digging and dredg-
ing that would damage the quality of fresh and salt water; and
a "no-burning" ordinance.

5-108 Loveridge, Ronald O. "The Environment: New Priorities and Old Politics." In PEOPLE AND POLITICS IN URBAN SOCIETY, edited by Harlan Hahn, pp. 499-530. Beverly Hills, Calif.: Sage Publications, 1972.

See 5-76.

5-109 Lowi, Theodore. "Decision Making vs. Policy Making: Toward an Antidote for Technology." PUBLIC ADMINISTRATION REVIEW 30 (May/June
1970): 314-25.

A review of four books on public policy and policy making.
According to Lowi, Mancur Olson's book deals with the problem of coercion, and Charles Lindbloom's is an "inadequate"
and brief treatment of American government. Yehezekel Dror's
work calls for the use of science and scientific decision making, but offers little in the way of a real model for operation.
Finally, he observes that Prof. Raymond Bauer's work is merely
a restatement of a "few principles of social psychology with a
bit of utility theory thrown in."

5-110 McDowell, Bruce D. "Land Use Controls and the Federal System." In
FUTURE LAND USE, edited by Robert W. Burchell and David Listokin,
pp. 43-57. New Brunswick, N.J.: Rutgers University, 1975.

Argues that since land use decisions are so complex, they must
be developed as part of a comprehensive planning process involving ordinary citizens at the local and regional levels.
The state and federal executive branches should resolve any
conflicts arising among local and regional land use decisions
and the courts should mediate any disputes. Citizens must
have input early in the process. The planning process can
absorb citizen input by means of a systematic, informed, and
publicly open policy development process.

5-111 McKeever, J. Ross. SHOPPING CENTER ZONING. Washington,
D.C.: Urban Land Institute, 1973.

Deals specifically with zoning as it applies to shopping centers,
developing useful points applicable to a method of land-use

control in general. The report bridges the communications gap between zoning officials who are struggling with the task of interpreting and enforcing existing regulations, and those developers who are trying to conform to them. The investigation reveals that zoning regulations in force for shopping center development are virtually chaotic. The author suggests certain guidelines to help municipal and regional legislatures adopt ordinances that will provide better planned shopping centers.

5-112 Mahood, H.R., ed. URBAN POLITICS AND PROBLEMS; A READER. New York: Charles Scribner's Sons, 1969.

Provides analyses of some of the critical urban issues confronting American political institutions and presents an overview of the nature and scope of urban policy. Mahood takes a pragmatic approach to the study of urban politics and administration, stressing the process rather than the technique of decision making at various levels of problem identification and policy making.

5-113 Mandel, David J. "Zoning Laws: The Case for Repeal." FREEMAN 22 (July 1972): 437-43.

Argues that zoning laws do not accomplish what they are supposed to, that their premises are faulty, that they create new problems, and since zoning is an irredeemable failure, zoning laws ought to be repealed.

5-114 Mandelker, Daniel R. "Critical Area Controls: A New Dimension in American Land Development Regulation." JOURNAL OF THE AMERICAN INSTITUTE OF PLANNERS 41 (January 1975): 21-31.

A discussion of the procedures that are an important part of the American Law Institute's Model Code provisions for state land development regulation. The statutory system for the administration of critical area controls is examined, problems of implementation are noted, and some possible revisions in the statutory proposals are suggested. Recent state legislation enacting the critical area concept is then compared to the American Law Institute proposals. The author does not argue the merits of state intervention in local government planning and land development control regulation. Instead, he assumes the need for an improved land development control process in areas where land development decisions have more than a local impact.

5-115 _____ . "Legal and Political Forums for Urban Change." ANNALS OF THE AMERICAN ACADEMY OF POLITICAL AND SOCIAL SCIENCE 405 (January 1973): 41-46.

See 3-61.

5-116 Mandelker, Daniel R., and Sherry, Thea A. "The National Coastal Zone Management Act of 1972." URBAN LAW ANNUAL 7 (1974): 19-37.

See 7-79.

5-117 Manheim, Marvin L. "Reaching Decisions about Technological Projects with Social Consequences: A Normative Model." TRANSPORTATION 2 (April 1973): 1-24.

See 3-62.

5-118 Marlan, Robert L., ed. CAPITAL, COURTHOUSE AND CITY HALL. 4th ed. Boston: Houghton Mifflin, 1972.

Comprises ninety-three short essays on a variety of political and governmental issues that affect local policy making. Of particular interest is chapter 15 which deals with the state-local political process. In one essay, James Q. Wilson says that an important and re-emerging theme in urban politics is the role of the community's class structure in determining the broad outlines of political conflict. Differences of income and ethnic background remain significant, although not as much as before. Lower class voters and upper class reformers still exhibit differences of rhetoric, life-style, and social purposes.

5-119 Mercer, John, and Barnett, Ross J. "Spatial Modifications to Models of the Urban Policy Process." POLICY STUDIES JOURNAL 3 (Summer 1975): 320-25.

Argues that local governments are important agents of income redistribution as far as upward and downward mobility, as a result of allocational and locational decisions. The authors attempt to incorporate the locational consequences of such decisions into a simple model of the urban policy process, an important effort since the decision-making process is likely to be sensitive to those who receive benefits and costs from such decisions and to the manner in which these costs and benefits are distributed.

5-120 Mitchell, Robert E. "Sociological Research on the Economic Myths of Housing." SOCIAL PROBLEMS 22 (December 1974): 259-80.

Reviews the basis of several arguments in support of high levels of government housing investments. The author contends that conventional wisdom, tradition, and political power have kept decision makers from developing alternative ways of funding housing programs for low- and moderate-income families. Two possible, but politically infeasible, methods of funding housing are examined in this study. One assumes that many families can probably pay more than they do now for housing, and the other entails genuine national commitment to housing for low- and moderate-income people.

5-120a Moore, Vincent J. "Politics, Planning, and Power in New York State: The Path from Theory to Reality." JOURNAL OF THE AMERICAN IN-STITUTE OF PLANNERS 37 (March 1971): 66-77.

An analysis of planning and implementation in New York State through the Rockefeller administration. These consisted of a detailed state land use and settlement policy, and four implementation strategies: regionalization, PPBS (planning-program-ming-budget system), governmental reorganization, and the use of public benefit corporations.

5-121 Morrison, Peter A. TOWARD A POLICY PLANNER'S VIEW OF THE URBAN SETTLEMENT SYSTEM. Santa Monica, Calif.: RAND, 1975.

Considers the interplay among three types of influences that affect the national system of urban development: (1) cultural predispositions--the basic values and axioms that define a society's aspirations and directions; (2) migratory predisposi-tions--the highly focused but still inactivated streams of poten-tial migration that are defined by the history of past popula-tion movements; and (3) government activities and programs, whose inadvertant secondary effects exert a powerful but un-directed influence on the redistribution of population. The author also examines the concept of "significant cultural geog-raphy," and the affect it may have on public policy.

5-122 Mott, George Fox. "Communicative Turbulence in Urban Dynamics--Media, Education, and Planning." ANNALS OF THE AMERICAN ACADEMY OF POLITICAL AND SOCIAL SCIENCE 405 (January 1973): 114-30.

See 3-65.

5-123 Murphy, Thomas P. "Urban Governmental Manpower." In his UNIVER-SITIES IN THE URBAN CRISIS, pp. 49-70. New York: Dunellen Pub-lishing Co., 1975.

Describes current manpower trends in state and local govern-ment and argues the need for technical personnel. Murphy believes that certain changes are necessary in undergraduate and graduate education for urban occupations and spells out desirable curriculum requirements. While acknowledging the funding problems in public administration and public affairs, he refers to the HUD Fellowship Program, and the increasing awareness of the need for intergovernmental coordination and for exchange programs between the federal government and univer-sities.

5-123a _____ . "The Urban Observatory Program." MIDWEST REVIEW OF
PUBLIC ADMINISTRATION 5 (August 1971): 110-32.

> A summary of activities of the first observatory cities (Atlanta,
> Albuquerque, Baltimore, Boston, Cleveland, Denver, Kansas
> City, Missouri, Milwaukee, Nashville, and San Diego). In-
> cludes comments by Brett W. Hawkins, William H. Cape,
> Dale A. Neuman, and John Taylor. (See also 5-123c.)

5-123b Murphy, Thomas P., and Rehfuss, John. URBAN POLITICS IN THE
SUBURBAN ERA. Homewood, Ill.: Dorsey Press, 1976.

> Chapters 6 and 10 deal with the delivery of governmental ser-
> vices in the suburbs as public policy issues.

5-123c Murphy, Thomas P., and Zarnowiecki, James. "The Urban Observatory:
The University-City Research Venture." In UNIVERSITIES IN THE URBAN
CRISIS, edited by Thomas P. Murphy, pp. 15-48. New York: Dunellen
Publishing Co., 1975.

> An analysis of the projects of the ten urban observatory cities
> and of the future for urban observatories. (See also 5-123a.)

5-124 Ohls, James C. "Public Policy Toward Low Income Housing and Filtering in Housing Markets." JOURNAL OF URBAN ECONOMICS 2 (April
1975): 144-71.

> Presents a model of a housing market in which dwelling units
> are constructed for relatively high income families and then
> gradually become available to lower income groups as they
> depreciate in quality and price. The author reaches five con-
> clusions: (1) it is neither surprising nor inefficient that the
> private market does not build new housing for poor people;
> (2) buildings are abandoned in the private market while they
> are still potentially livable; (3) substantial increases in govern-
> ment programs which draw poor people away from the regular
> market for filtered-down housing help to explain the abandon-
> ment of lower quality housing; (4) rent vouchers may substan-
> tially upgrade poor housing through accelerated filtering and
> through better maintenance; and (5) government programs, such
> as rent vouchers which work through existing markets, may be
> able to increase housing consumption by the poor more ef-
> ficiently than programs which involve new construction.

5-125 Peters, Terry S. THE POLITICS AND ADMINISTRATION OF LAND
USE CONTROL. Lexington, Mass.: D.C. Heath, 1974.

> Devises a conceptual framework and an administrative program
> for the effective implementation of the Fairfax County, Vir-
> ginia, Supervisor's Planning and Land Use System (PLUS). Part
> one of the book deals with local, regional, state, and national

factors that have promoted or stymied public activism in land use control. Part two addresses current public activities relating to land use control. The PLUS program is appraised in terms of legitimization, policy making, program development, and implementation.

5-126 Peterson, George E. "Voter Demand for Public School Expenditures." In PUBLIC NEEDS AND PRIVATE BEHAVIOR IN METROPOLITAN AREAS, edited by John E. Jackson, pp. 99-115. Cambridge, Mass.: Ballinger, 1975.

See 3-77.

5-127 Pollack, Patricia Varon. "The Planning Pretense." MAXWELL REVIEW 8 (Spring 1972): 65-71.

Written in response to an essay by E. Barbara Phillips in the winter issue of this magazine. Pollack agrees that liberals accept assumptions about social change and in the field of urban planning they have followed a strategy of adjusting "around the edges" without questioning the institutions that define the social and economic structure. Consequently, urban planners have served powerful socioeconomic interests in the name of "overriding public interest." Pollack believes that we need a different model of planning, one that would include political mobilization of the poor and other presently disenfranchised groups as a prelude to humanistic social change.

5-128 PROPOSED ALTERNATIVES TO TAX EXEMPT STATE AND LOCAL BONDS. Washington, D.C.: American Enterprise Institute for Public Policy Research, 1973.

An examination of alternatives to tax-exempt state and local bonds. One alternative would offer an interest subsidy to state and local governments in return for issuing taxable bonds instead of tax-exempt bonds. The subsidized bonds would be issued on a taxable basis at competitive market rates of interest. An important purpose of the proposal is to provide a wider market for state and local bonds and to close partially the tax loophole through which interest derived from such bonds is exempt from federal income tax. A bill (S.3215) introduced in the 92d Congress (1972) by Sen. William Proxmire, which would have broadened the market for state and local debt obligations through the use of an optional taxable bond alternative, is discussed at length, along with other proposals.

5-129 Rabinovitz, F.F. CITY POLITICS AND PLANNING. New York: Atherton, 1969.

Discusses the role of the urban planner in political and developmental decision making. Based on a comparative analy-

sis of six cities, Rabinovitz reaches three main conclusions:
(1) the urban planner is definitely an actor in the urban political arena, (2) the level of planning effectiveness is related
to the role of the planner, and (3) it appears that the planner can be an effective actor in various political systems.

5-130 Ranney, David C. PLANNING AND POLITICS IN THE METROPOLIS.
Columbus, Ohio: Charles E. Merrill Publishing Co., 1969.

Provides an understanding of the development of public planning policy in metropolitan governments. The following questions are examined: (1) What is the planner's role in local
government? (2) What factors influence the planner in making
decisions? (3) How are these decisions transformed into planning policy through the local government? The author also
decides the impact of metropolitanism on the development of
planning policy. Chapters 6 and 7 deal specifically with the
politics of planning.

5-131 Real Estate Research Corporation. "Detailed Cost Analysis." In THE
COSTS OF SPRAWL. Washington, D.C.: Government Printing Office,
1974.

Concludes that "sprawl" is one of the most expensive forms of
residential development in terms of economic costs, environmental costs, natural resource consumption, and many types
of personal costs. The study indicates that better planning
will reduce all types of costs, and increasing density will
increase some of them, though not nearly in proportion to the
increased number of households.

5-132 Reily, William K., ed. THE USE OF LAND: A CITIZENS' POLICY
GUIDE TO URBAN GROWTH. New York: Thomas Y. Crowell Co.,
1973.

Describes the work of the Task Force on Land Use and Urban
Growth, created in 1972 by the Citizen's Advisory Committee
on Environmental Quality, and sponsored by the Rockefeller
Brothers Fund. The report urges more responsible land use
with respect to natural systems and cultural values, the legiti-
mate rights of others to move where they want, and the need
to leave a rich and enduring environment to posterity. The
main problem the task force addressed was how to organize,
control, and coordinate urban development to protect what we
value most in the enviroment while meeting the essential
needs of the population for new housing, roads, power plants,
shopping centers, parks, businesses, and industrial facilities.

5-133 Reinstein, Robert J. "A Case of Exclusionary Zoning." TEMPLE LAW
QUARTERLY 1 (Fall 1972): 7-39.

Examines the land use policies of Bucks County, Pennsylvania, a large and rapidly developing suburb of Philadelphia. It is based on an amicus brief in a suit against Bucks County and its municipalities challenging the system of zoning ordinances; their consequences in terms of economic and racial segregation; the extent to which they preclude access of minority groups to adequate jobs, housing, and education; their sociological impact in polarizing communities; and the extent to which they achieve countervailing governmental purposes.

5-134 "The Responsibility of Local Zoning Authorities to Nonresident Indigents." STANFORD LAW REVIEW 23 (April 1971): 774-98.

Discusses the background of residential zoning, describing some of the zoning practices that are exclusionary in nature. Some of the judicial and legislative responses to the problem are considered, particularly the case of Southern Alameda Spanish Speaking Organization v. Union City. The Ninth Circuit's decision in that case required that the zoning actions of the local authorities reflect the needs of indigent community residents on a par with the desires of others in the community. The author examines the significance of that decision and explores the possibilities and problems that could arise if a responsibility to nonresident indigents was imposed upon local zoning authorities.

5-135 Ripley, Randall B. "Political Patterns in Federal Development Programs." In PEOPLE AND POLITICS IN URBAN SOCIETY, edited by Harlan Hahn, pp. 531-56. Beverly Hills, Calif.: Sage Publications, 1972.

See 5-76.

5-135a Robson, William A., and Regan, D.E., eds. GREAT CITIES OF THE WORLD. Vols. 1 and 2, 3d ed. London: George Allen and Unwin; Beverly Hills, Calif.: Sage Publications, 1972.

See 1-59.

5-136 Roe, Charles E. "Land Use: The Second Battle of Gettysburg." APPRAISAL JOURNAL 42 (January 1974): 90-102.

Describes the battle between a builder and environmentalists concerning the construction of a 307-foot observatory on the grounds of the Gettysburg National Military Park. Local political officials and the builder argued that the tower would bring more money into the community and would be a significant educational contribution to visitors of the park, since it would provide a panoramic view of the battlefield. After many court battles, the tower is now a part of the Gettysburg landscape.

5-137 Rose, Douglas D. "National and Local Forces in State Politics: The Implications of Multi-level Policy Analysis." AMERICAN POLITICAL SCIENCE REVIEW 67 (December 1973): 1162-73.

See 7-98.

5-137a Rosenthal, D[onald].B. "Power, Politics and Public Policy in American Urban Research." POLITY 5 (Summer 1973): 531-46.

Contends that many of the questions of urban politics, which once seemed settled by environmental determinism, have become repoliticized. These include the effects of political structure on decision making; the political behavior of bureaucracies; and how policy affects local groups. Urban research must study the role of intellectual activity in defining problems and promoting alternatives to existing societal arrangements.

5-138 Rubenstein, Laurence D. "Regulating Community Growth." HUD CHALLENGE 6 (January 1975): 2-4.

Quotes a recent Gallup Poll report that the majority of Americans believe local governments are not doing enough to anticipate and plan for future growth. Many want a halt to haphazard growth, others see controls on growth as crippling to continued economic development. Local officials who find themselves caught in the middle must be aware of the various growth-related issues and the problems they may encounter in attempting to enact a successful growth control program.

5-139 Salamon, Lester M., and Wamsley, Gary L. "The Politics of Urban Land Policy: Zoning and Urban Development in Nashville." In GROWING METROPOLIS: ASPECTS OF DEVELOPMENT IN NASHVILLE, edited by James F. Blumestein and Benjamin Walter, pp. 141-90. Nashville, Tenn.: Vanderbilt University Press, 1975.

An attempt to determine whether urban policy merely adapts passively to existing development trends or actively seeks to shape these trends according to some vision of the public good. The authors study Nashville, which has a political structure institutionally amenable to effective policy leadership by public officials. They conclude that there seems to be at least one thing in Nashville land-use policy about which every participant can complain, but also something about which everyone can rejoice. It is precisely this mixture of bitterness and joy that makes the policy politically variable. Therefore, the impact of public policy on urban development is inevitably mixed.

5-140 Schooler, Dean, Jr. "Political Arenas, Life Styles and the Impact of Technologies on Policy Making." POLICY SCIENCES 1 (Fall 1970): 275-87.

Distinguishes behavioral and physical technology and discusses their contributions to policy making. The author maintains that the attractiveness of a technology to policy makers depends upon how politically significant groups view the technology's impact on life-styles, as well as its value implications. Physical technologies are generally perceived as "distributive" by these groups and, therefore, will be more widely used in public policy than behavioral technologies, which are generally perceived as "redistributive" and "regulative."

5-141 Schultze, William A. URBAN AND COMMUNITY POLITICS. North Scituate, Mass.: Duxbury, 1974.

See 2-50.

5-142 Seevers, Gary L., and Pulsipher, Allan G. "Environmental Resources and Energy Supplies." In FUTURE LAND USE, edited by Robert W. Burchell and David Listokin, pp. 281-303. New Brunswick, N.J.: Rutgers University, Center for Urban Policy Research, 1975.

Identifies and analyzes some of the problems which complicate the efficient harmonization of energy policy and environmental policy. The authors explain why these problems have frustrated the policy-making process. Because of the complexity of energy-environment problems, the institutions designed to deal with them must be able to amalgamate, evaluate, and respond to a wide range of information and interests.

5-143 Sharma, Navin C.; Kivlin, Joseph E.; and Fliegel, Frederick C. "Environmental Pollution: Is There Enough Public Concern to Lead to Action?" ENVIRONMENT AND BEHAVIOR 7 (December 1975): 455-71.

A report based on a survey taken in a northern Illinois town of about three thousand. The town was selected because it had an acute pollution problem which had to be solved within a given period of time to comply with the law. The article examines the extent to which the public was informed, what the public thought about alternative solutions, and what was learned about the problem-solving process which could be useful to other communities. The results indicated that pollution is treated less as a political issue than a passing topic of conversation, and that the usual political process was not effective in generating antipollution sentiment.

5-144 Sheldon, Nancy W., and Brandwein, Robert. THE ECONOMIC AND SOCIAL IMPACT OF INVESTMENTS IN PUBLIC TRANSIT. Lexington, Mass.: D.C. Heath and Co., 1973.

See 7-102.

5-145 Shepard, W. Bruce. "Metropolitan Political Decentralization: A Test of the Life-style Values Model." URBAN AFFAIRS QUARTERLY 10 (March 1975): 297-313.

Argues that patterns of metropolitan political fragmentation are not satisfactorily explained by citizen preferences for different life-styles. Shepard's study suggests that political decentralization is a function of the availability of resources necessary to protect local autonomy through interaction and conflict with other metropolitan political subunits and state entities.

5-146 Skogan, Wesley G. "Groups in the Policy Process: The Police and Urban Crime." POLICY STUDIES JOURNAL 3 (Summer 1975): 354-58.

See 3-87.

5-147 Snyder, James C. "Financial Management and Planning in Local Government." ATLANTA ECONOMIC REVIEW 23 (November/December 1973): 43-47.

Reviews some of the implications of a new approach for intermediate and smaller local units of government. The public sector is currently developing a major new concept of public management which describes a number of improvements over the last twenty years. These include systemic planning, program budgeting, cost-effectiveness, and PPBS (planning-programming-budgeting system).

5-148 Spiegel, Arthur H. III. "How Outsiders Overhauled A Public Agency." HARVARD BUSINESS REVIEW 53 (January/February 1975): 116-24.

Describes how the New York City Department of Human Resources employed a management firm to streamline the record-keeping system of the welfare bureaucracy. The management team implemented a top-to-bottom overhaul that included an introduction of integrated, system-wide automation, a complete revamping of welfare center operations, and a general tightening of management controls. The author concludes that private-sector techniques are necessary for the management of government in many areas because the public sector seems incapable of self-reform.

5-149 Spiegel, Hans B.C., ed. DECENTRALIZATION: CITIZEN PARTICIPATION IN URBAN DEVELOPMENT. Vol. 3. Fairfax, Va.: Learning Resources Corp., National Training Laboratories, 1974.

See 3-88.

5-150 Stearns, Forrest W., and Montag, Tom, eds. THE URBAN ECOSYSTEM: A HOLISTIC APPROACH. Stroudsburg, Pa.: Hutchinson and Ross, 1975.

An interdisciplinary examination of the American city which clarifies the principles underlying the urban ecosystem. The book represents the insights of nearly one hundred scholars who held a conference to study the city in a comprehensive manner and is the first of a two-part study resulting from the conference. Twenty-six recommendations were made including: performance criteria should gradually be substituted for land-use standards and zoning, and teams of environmental extension personnel of varying disciplines should be established in urban and urbanizing areas.

5-151 Stenberg, Carl W. "The Regionalization of Environmental Management." PUBLIC MANAGEMENT 56 (March 1974): 15-18.

Decries the fact that local governments are not dealing with environmental issues on a regional basis. Overlapping jurisdictions duplicate activities, with confused responsibilities at the multi-county level resulting from a lack of intergovernmental cooperation. Stenberg believes that there are at least three possible directions for the regionalization of environmental management in the near future: (1) continuation of present ambivalent federal and state policies; (2) establishment of umbrella multijurisdictional organizations; and (3) state assumption of a major share of the responsibility.

5-152 Sternlieb, George, et al. "Planned Unit Development: A Summary of Necessary Considerations." URBAN LAW ANNUAL 7 (1974): 71-100.

Presents factors which must be considered before developing a local planned unit development (PUD) ordinance. Although PUD is frequently assumed to promote better use of open space and more stringent controls, it may become a tool for those who currently occupy the suburban enclaves and a disservice to the poor. The most salient issue is the inclusion or non-inclusion of the poor in this latest manifestation of the suburbanization process.

5-153 Strong, Ann L. PRIVATE PROPERTY AND THE PUBLIC INTEREST: THE BRANDYWINE EXPERIENCE. Baltimore: Johns Hopkins University Press, 1975.

Describes evolution of the Brandywine plan, an attempt to develop a politically acceptable way of protecting the water resources of an urbanizing area while still providing for normal growth. The author believes this case is applicable to all attempts to plan for urban growth. The central issue of the book is how to find the most democratic way of making decisions about the future use of urban fringe land. The author believes that the people of the entire urban area, through a representative council of elected officials, should make the major decisions about where, when, and how urbanization shall occur.

5-154 Taebel, Delbert A. "Citizen Groups, Public Policy, and Urban Transportation." TRAFFIC QUARTERLY 27 (October 1973): 503-15.

See 3-93.

5-155 URBAN AMERICA: GOALS AND PROBLEMS. Washington, D.C.: Government Printing Office, 1967.

A compliation of essays by more than twenty urbanologists who submitted the report to the Joint Economic Committee of the U.S. Congress. Part one discusses values, goals, and priorities for urban areas. Part two deals with functional problems, such as urban planning and policy questions. Part three, "Rules of the Game: Public Sector," examines many institutional and political questions of urban America. Part four suggests what the private sector can do to help solve urban problems.

5-156 Veatch, James F. "Federal and Local Urban Transportation Policy." URBAN AFFAIRS QUARTERLY 10 (June 1975): 398-422.

Argues that localities would establish better transportation programs without federal incentives. Veatch favors general revenue sharing, but believes that local governments need to use their money in ways that achieve clear objectives if they are to use it effectively.

5-157 Viteritti, Joseph P. POLICE, POLITICS, AND PLURALISM IN NEW YORK CITY: A COMPARATIVE CASE STUDY. Beverly Hills, Calif.: Sage Publications, 1973.

Evaluates the assumptions, methodology, and conclusions of those political scientists who are members of the pluralist school of thought by studying two controversial issues concerning the New York City Police Department. The first involves an attempt by Mayor Lindsay to create a civilian complaint review board in 1966, and the second, his attempt to eradicate a fifty-eight-year-old state law which limited the authority of local police administrators to deploy manpower at their own descretion. These studies are then used as an instrument for analyzing the manner in which the government of New York City responds to the demands and needs of its nonwhite population.

5-158 Washington, R.O. "The Politicization of School Decentralization in New York City." URBAN EDUCATION 8 (October 1973): 223-30.

Argues that while it is too early to determine the virtues and weaknesses of school decentralization, it is essential for members of the community to participate in planning the program. Members of local community school boards must be knowledge-

able of the educational process so that they are able to run
their own affairs. Otherwise, they will have to defer to the
bureaucrats. Moreover, the local school board members must
see as their first obligation the improvement of the quality of
education in their respective communities.

5-159 Welfeld, Irving H. AMERICA'S HOUSING PROBLEM: AN APPROACH
TO ITS SOLUTION. Washington, D.C.: American Enterprise Institute
for Public Research, October 1973.

An examination of the housing situation in the United States
by a former employee in the Office of the Deputy Under
Secretary for Policy Analysis and Program Evaluation at HUD.
He offers some alternatives to current inadequate housing
policies.

5-160 Wilcox, Allen R. "Population and Urban Systems: The Blurring of
Boundaries." POLICY STUDIES JOURNAL 3 (Summer 1975): 340-45.

Observes that studies of the relationship between population
and urban politics and policy varied according to whether the
orientation has been normative or empirical, and whether the
population has been treated as an independent or dependent
variable. The inadequacy of the resulting typology for future
policy research is the subject of this article.

5-161 Willeke, Gene E. "Citizen Participation: Here to Stay." CIVIL EN-
GINEERING 44 (January 1974): 78-82.

See 3-100.

5-162 Williams, O.P. METROPOLITAN POLITICAL ANALYSIS. New York:
Free Press, 1971.

Discusses urban politics as "a means by which space and place
are socially controlled and allocated in order to facilitate or
limit accessibility:" Every city or urban center is characterized
by some pattern of spatial articulation, and in American society, these spatially specialized areas become legal jurisdictions, equipped with powers of self-government. Communities
are formed and are politically sound until the inhabitants become dissatisfied and either choose to stay or vote with their
feet and join another community. Williams concludes with a
discussion of decentralization and centralization in terms of
four urban policy matters with which every large city has to
deal: circulation, removal of waste, obsolescence, and
growth.

5-162a Williams, Robert L. "Planning Role in Urban Decision-Making." In
EMERGING PATTERNS IN URBAN ADMINISTRATION, edited by F.

Gerald Brown and Thomas P. Murphy, pp. 127-39. Lexington, Mass.: Lexington Books, 1970.

See 6-18a.

5-163 Wilson, James Q., ed. CITY POLITICS AND PUBLIC POLICY. New York: John Wiley & Sons, 1968.

A collection of essays on local government selected because they try to explain directly the impact of city government on urban policies. Part one, "Politics and Community Development," examines city councils, policy outcomes, community types, and policy differences. Part two, "Politics and Public Finance," looks at local government's response to the urban economy. The politics of education, politics and law enforcement, and the politics of health and welfare are considered throughout the remainder of the book. According to the editor, the book discusses what is generally true, not what may have been the case in one place at one time.

5-164 Wofford, John G. "Participatory Planning for Boston Metro-Area Transportation." CIVIL ENGINEERING 43 (April 1973): 78-81.

See 3-103.

5-165 Zikmund, Joseph II. "Impact of the Use of Models on Urban Planning." POLICY STUDIES JOURNAL 3 (Summer 1975): 325-32.

Explores the practical and political uses of urban models. The author contends that the introduction of computer modeling into planning has hastened the change in the character of urban planning, escalated markedly the costs of major urban planning projects, and created circumstances likely to make local planners even more dependent on federal funding. The rise of the mathematician-technician in the planning field has tended to widen the gap between planning and politics in the United States.

Chapter 6
METROPOLITAN ORGANIZATION
AND SUBURBANIZATION

This chapter includes entries relating to the reorganization of metropolitan areas; city-county consolidation; governmental fragmentation and service delivery; urban counties; governing suburbs; suburban-central city relationships; councils of governments; and interstate metropolitan matters.

6-1   Advisory Commission on Intergovernmental Relations. ALTERNATIVE AP-
PROACHES TO GOVERNMENTAL REORGANIZATION IN METROPOLI-
TAN AREAS. Washington, D.C.: Government Printing Office, 1962.

Provides a concise review of the major approaches to reorganization of local government in metropolitan areas that have
been used or given serious consideration. The strengths and
weaknesses of the approaches and the factors that make them
more or less likely to prove effective if adopted are indicated.

6-2   _____. FOR A MORE PERFECT UNION--COUNTY REFORM. Report
M-61. Washington, D.C.: Government Printing Office, April 1971.

Argument for a strong county government by commission member
Robert E. Merriam. Model state legislation developed by ACIR
is presented. Some of the eight draft state laws included are
based on existing state laws and affect commission recommendations for making counties more able to meet future responsibilities. Some of the issues included in the draft legislation are
county performance of urban functions, county consolidation,
state assistance for county consolidation, and county powers
in relation to local planning and zoning actions.

6-3   Baker, Earl M., ed. "The Suburban Transformation of American Politics:
The Convergence of Reality and Research." PUBLIUS 5 (Winter 1975):
1-14.

An outgrowth of a conference at Temple University in April
1973 on the phenomenon of suburbanization. Scholars such as
Oliver Williams, Robert Wood, Daniel Elazar, and Frederick
Wirt are among the contributors.

6-4   Baker, Gordon E. "Redistricting in the Seventies: The Political Thicket Deepens." NATIONAL CIVIC REVIEW 61 (June 1972): 277-85.

Examines the political and judicial consequences of reapportionment on the tenth anniversary of Baker v. Carr. Baker anticipates four developments: (1) The U.S. Supreme Court will tamper with at-large multimember districts only when a racial minority's representation is negated; (2) gerrymandering will proliferate if the Court does not change the tone set in the Wells v. Rockefeller case; (3) there is a need to shift the responsibility of redistricting from the legislators themselves; and (4) Congress could and should enact standards of compactness, contiguity, and approximate population equality for House districts.

6-5   Baldassare, Mark, and Fischer, Claude S. "Suburban Life: Powerlessness and the Need for Affiliation." URBAN AFFAIRS QUARTERLY 10 (March 1975): 314-26.

Reports the findings of a study to determine whether migration to the suburbs is related to personality type. The authors conclude that there are only very small differences in suburban and urban resident personalities. Suburban life-style differences are not explained in terms of personality differences.

6-6   Banfield, Edward [C.]. "The Politics of Metropolitan Area Organization." MIDWEST JOURNAL OF POLITICAL SCIENCE 1 (May 1957): 77-91.

Contends that much of the talk about the metropolitan area "problem" is spurious. The author believes that the important issue is one of creating or maintaining organization for the effective management of conflict. He recommends that this should occur, not through the creation of new bodies by consolidation or federation, but through negotiations among the political leaders of existing jurisdictions. Banfield believes that the problem can be solved by strong mayors and strong governors engaged in political negotiation.

6-7   "Battle to Open the Suburbs: New Attack on Zoning Laws." U.S. NEWS & WORLD REPORT, June 22, 1970, p. 39.

Summarizes legal, governmental, and political decisions that have impacted suburbs. It is observed that a broad effort is being made to break down the distinctions between city and suburb that have in the past caused millions of people to flock to the suburbs. More aggressive action than ever before is being taken to combat restrictive zoning ordinances. A political battle concerning urban/suburban growth is being waged, as city dwellers and city minorities are fighting for their right to relocate, and suburbanites, wary of an "invasion" by minorities, are resisting change.

6-8   Bergman, Edward. ELIMINATING EXCLUSIONARY ZONING: RECON-
CILING WORK PLACE & RESIDENCE IN SUBURBAN AREAS. Cambridge,
Mass.: Ballinger, 1974.

Develops an explicit workplace and residence standard for
zoning ordinances and tests that standard on a sample of developing townships. Bergman concludes that until basic changes
are made in the fabric of local governance, the performance
standard for zoning deserves serious consideration as an attrac-
tive measure to curtail the worst abuses associated with exclusionary zoning of municipalities.

6-9   Bingham, David A. "Some Alternative Patterns for Local Government."
ARIZONA REVIEW 23 (May 1974): 1-4.

Discusses numerous concepts of organization for the Tucson
metropolitan area. For many years Tucson area voters have
considered various governmental reorganization patterns. Little
has changed, however, except the growth of the status quo.

6-10   Birch, David, et al. "Individuals and Households." In their PATTERNS
OF URBAN CHANGE: THE NEW HAVEN EXPERIENCE, pp. 25-35.
Lexington, Mass.: D.C. Heath & Co., 1974.

Outlines some of the changes that have taken place in the
New Haven metropolitan region. The authors consider the
factors determining the location of people and the migration
to the suburbs. They observe that transportation availability
and workplace proximity no longer dominate residential choice.
They conclude that sociological and aesthetic considerations
such as race, social status, and the age of neighborhoods are
the factors that influence choice.

6-10a   Bish, Robert L. THE PUBLIC ECONOMY OF METROPOLITAN AREAS.
Chicago: Markham Publishing Co., 1971.

Applies economic methods to the analysis of governmental
activities. Bish examines the metropolitan area systems in Los
Angeles and Dade counties.

6-11   Bish, Robert L., and Ostrom, Vincent. UNDERSTANDING URBAN
GOVERNMENT: METROPOLITAN REFORM RECONSIDERED. Washington, D.C.: American Enterprise Institute for Public Policy Research,
1973.

Presentation of the public choice model of understanding urban
public policy by two political economists. Their concept
challenges other methods of metropolitan reform such as community control, consolidation, and federation. The philosophy
of public choice begins with the individual, considers the
nature of public goods and services, and examines how differently organized systems of urban government meet the needs

of individuals for goods and services. The authors recommend decentralized government in which a multiplicity of services, having different economies of scale, could be offered.

6-11a Black, Guy. "The Decentralization of Urban Government: A Systems Approach." In EMERGING PATTERNS IN URBAN ADMINISTRATION, edited by F. Gerald Brown and Thomas P. Murphy, pp. 222-47. Lexington, Mass.: Lexington Books, 1970.

See 6-18a.

6-12 Bollens, John C. "Overlapping Governments." In GOVERNING URBAN AMERICA IN THE 1970'S, edited by Werner Z. Hirsch and Sidney Sonenblum, pp. 85-96. New York: Praeger Publishers, 1973.

Discusses the nature of overlapping governments. Bollens feels that it results chiefly from the profusion of local jurisdictions in terms of both number and type and the lack of local territorial exclusivity. He notes a significant result of overlapping is a problem of areawide service delivery and regulation.

6-13 Bollens, John [C.]; Bayes, John R.; and Utter, Kathryn L. AMERICAN COUNTY GOVERNMENT. Beverly Hills, Calif.: Sage Publications, 1969.

Reviews the literature of county government, makes a general appraisal of existing county research, and presents an agenda of needed investigations. The book also contains a design for testing the political vitality of counties and evidence in support of the design. It includes a bibliographical commentary which describes and analyzes books, monographs, articles, and public documents published primarily since 1945.

6-14 Bollens, John C., and Schmandt, Henry J. THE METROPOLIS: ITS PEOPLE, POLITICS AND ECONOMIC LIFE: 3d ed. New York: Harper and Row, 1975.

Illustrates that the metropolis is a complex and multi-dimensional phenomenon and a dynamic system of interacting relationships among organizations, people, and institutions. This text book provides a broad and objective discussion of the metropolis and looks at the process and behavior of actors as well as the form and structure of governments.

6-15 Booth, David A. METROPOLITICS: THE NASHVILLE CONSOLIDATION. East Lansing: Michigan State University, Institute for Community Development, 1963.

A study in metropolitics combining and synthesizing the results of three field investigations conducted in the Nashville area during the four years prior to the publishing of the book. Booth examines the two attempts to consolidate Nashville and

Davidson County and explains reasons for its defeat in 1958
and the successful consolidation in 1962.

6-16   "Breaking the Noose: Suburban Zoning and the Urban Crisis." SOCIAL
ACTION 36 (April 1970): entire issue.

See 5-28.

6-17   Bromage, Arthur W. POLITICAL REPRESENTATION IN METROPOLITAN
AREAS. Ann Arbor: University of Michigan, 1962.

Examines political representation in selected metropolitan federations, authorities and agencies. The topics discussed are
schemes of urban representation, design for metropolitan federations, local and state orientation for metropolitan authorities,
and a design for metropolitan authorities.

6-18   Browder, Glen, and Ippolito, Dennis S. "The Suburban Party Activist:
The Case of Southern Amateurs." SOCIAL SCIENCE QUARTERLY 53
(June 1972): 168-75.

Examines Democratic and Republican party activists such as
county officials and precinct chairmen in DeKalb County,
Georgia, a large and affluent suburban county near Atlanta.
The authors conclude that the organizations in DeKalb County
are "amateur-oriented," that is the leaders usually started out
with amateur incentives, such as citizen duty.

6-18a Brown, F. Gerald, and Murphy, Thomas P., eds. EMERGING PAT-
TERNS IN URBAN ADMINISTRATION. Lexington, Mass.: Lexington
Books, 1970.

Includes three chapters on each of four themes: urban polity,
urbanization and the federal system, implications for metropolitan planning, and centralization-decentralization.

6-19   Caile, Charlene. "Bringing the City and County Together." THE
AMERICAN COUNTY, February 1972, pp. 8-19.

Summarizes an October 1971 seminar of the National Association of Counties. A panel presented consolidation as an approach to more effective local government. The seminar discussed issues such as property taxes, general services areas,
urban service budgets, problems concerning consolidation,
black power voting, increase of federal money through consolidation, and economies of scale.

6-20   Campbell, Alan K., and Sacks, Seymour. METROPOLITAN AMERICA.
New York: Free Press, 1967.

A look at the differences in local fiscal outputs from city to

city and between cities and their suburbs. The determinants
and patterns of the differences are analyzed. Special attention is given to the fragmentation of metropolitan America's
governmental system.

6-21   Carver, Joan. "Responsiveness and Consolidation--A Case Study."
       URBAN AFFAIRS QUARTERLY 9 (December 1973): 211-50.

       Examines the consolidated government in Jacksonville, Florida.
       Carver believes that consolidation has brought more responsive-
       ness to community needs. Public-regarding and professional
       values have a much larger role in determining the priorities
       of Jacksonville than in prereform days. The author concludes
       tentatively that metropolitan governments which have increased
       problem-solving abilities may fail to utilize these abilities
       fully to solve some of the difficult social problems of the com-
       munity due to a limited awareness of the needs and demands
       of its marginal members and to the slight involvement of those
       people in local political life.

6-22   Cole, Richard L., and Caputo, David A. "Leadership Opposition to
       Consolidation." URBAN AFFAIRS QUARTERLY 8 (December 1972): 253-
       58.

       Suggests that elite opposition, even in a single geographic
       area, may involve diverse and complex views. It may be a
       mistake to assume, as most observers have, that a broad gen-
       eralization is descriptive of such opposition. Both Republican
       and Democratic leaders may oppose consolidation; those con-
       sidered very liberal and those considered very conservative may
       unite in their opposition; and philosophical as well as personal
       and partisan motives may influence leadership attitudes.

6-23   Connolly, Harold X. "Black Movement into the Suburbs: Suburbs Dou-
       bling Their Black Populations During the 1970s." URBAN AFFAIRS QUAR-
       TERLY 9 (September 1973): 91-111.

       A study of twenty-four suburban communities that more than
       doubled the number of black inhabitants during the 1960s and
       in which blacks were at least 10 percent of the total popula-
       tion in 1970. It appears that black suburban growth was
       selective, occurring only in some parts of the country and only
       in some metropolitan areas. The socioeconomic level of blacks
       in the suburbs was higher than that of city blacks, and their
       income nearly equaled that of suburban whites.

6-24   Costikyan, Edward N., and Lehman, Maxwell. "Concept of Multiple
       Functional Regions." In their NEW STRATEGIES FOR REGIONAL CO-
       OPERATION: A MODEL FOR THE TRI-STATE NEW YORK-NEW JERSEY-
       CONNECTICUT AREA, pp. 1-14. New York: Praeger Publishers, 1973.

Discusses the need for a regional approach to the problems of the New York-New Jersey-Connecticut metropolitan area. The Task Force on Jurisdiction and Structure in New York City made several recommendations concerning the reorganization of metropolitan governments in the New York area, including: multijurisdictional governmental functions should be identified, their geographic areas delineated, and a central regional overhead agency established to coordinate planning and regional data collection. (See also 6-25.)

6-25 _____. RESTRUCTURING THE GOVERNMENT OF NEW YORK CITY: REPORT OF THE SCOTT COMMISSION TASK FORCE ON JURISDICTION AND STRUCTURE. New York: Praeger Publishers, 1972.

Claims that governmental reorganization in New York City is crucial to a better government. In this report the task force advocated restructuring the government to a two-tier structure, comprised of a central government of mayor and city council, and several local governments of district councils and an executive. Local communities would flourish in this system. Although the proposal may be of questionable practicability, it is instructive for students of metropolitan government reorganization. (See also 6-24.)

6-26 Davidoff, Linda; Davidoff, Paul; and Gold, Neil. "Suburban Action: Advocate Planning for an Open Society." JOURNAL OF THE AMERICAN INSTITUTE OF PLANNERS 36 (January 2, 1970): 12-21.

Describes an advocacy agency created to promote the use of suburban resources for solving metropolitan problems of race and poverty. The advocates are speaking for "outsiders" of the close-knit suburban community. Advocate planners, planning on behalf of specified individuals and groups rather than a broadly defined "public interest," have discovered the need for regionwide and national planning to deal with the problems of the blacks and the poor.

6-27 Dixon, Robert G., Jr. DEMOCRATIC REPRESENTATION: REAPPORTIONMENT IN LAW AND POLITICS. New York: Oxford University Press, 1968.

See 7-38.

6-28 Downes, Bryan T. "Issue Conflict, Factionalism, and Consensus in Suburban City Councils." URBAN AFFAIRS QUARTERLY 4 (June 1969): 471-97.

A study of the effects of changes in municipal population growth rate upon issue conflict, factionalism, and consensus in small decision-making groups, in this case, city councils in thirty-seven suburban communities. The authors hypothe-

sized that rapid increases in population may give rise to exclusive values, divergent interests, and strains in a community,
which may be reflected in higher levels of issue conflict and
factionalism in city councils.

6-29 _____. "Problem-Solving in Suburbia: The Basis for Political Conflict."
In THE URBANIZATION OF THE SUBURBS, edited by Louis H. Masotti
and Jeffrey K. Hadden, pp. 281-312. Beverly Hills, Calif.: Sage
Publications, 1973.

An examination of questions which give rise to controversy and
conflict in suburban politics. The process of who gets what,
when, and how is probably a continuous conversion process
occurring over a period of time in interrelated stages. Issues
in political change that are likely to bring conflict are: (1)
who is responsible for solving suburban problems?; (2) how can
suburbs which do not meet their responsibilities be held ac-
countable?; (3) and how can suburbs be assisted in their difficulties?

6-30 _____, ed. CITIES AND SUBURBS. Belmont, Calif.: Wadsworth
Publishing Co., 1971.

See 5-52.

6-31 Downs, Anthony. OPENING UP THE SUBURBS: AN URBAN STRATEGY
FOR AMERICA. New Haven, Conn.: Yale University Press, 1973.

Argues that it is crucial to break down the economic barriers
to the suburbs of the United States in order to counteract the
undesirable effects of the legal and political separation between
the central cities and the suburbs. Two main themes are: urban poverty cannot be attacked effectively without reducing
the spatial concentration of the poor; and practical means do
exist to achieve this without seriously threatening the quality
of middle- and upper-income life.

6-32 Dye, Thomas R., and Hawkins, Brett W., eds. POLITICS IN THE
METROPOLIS. 2d ed. Columbus, Ohio: Charles E. Merrill, 1971.

A reader on the major conflicts in urban society related to the
structures and processes that manage conflict and maintain order in the metropolis. It includes a broad overview of the
diversity of metropolitan life which creates national conflict;
a discussion of the issues subsumed in conflict, such as race,
poverty, violence, partisanship, and city-suburban dichotomy;
the interdependence of the parts of the metropolis as a basis
for metropolitan-wide cooperation in transportation, education,
finance, planning and public service; a description of the
structures and processes available, including city politics and

community power, to resolve conflict and bring order; and proposals for reform and reorganization of metropolitan government.

6-33   Elazar, Daniel J. "Fragmentation, a Local Organizational Response to Federal-City Program." URBAN AFFAIRS QUARTERLY 2 (June 1967): 30-46.

See 7-46.

6-34   Erie, Steven P., et al. REFORM OF METROPOLITAN GOVERNMENTS. Washington, D.C.: Resources for the Future; distributed by Johns Hopkins University Press, Baltimore, 1972.

Discusses metropolitan area policy problems including the relationship of a region to the rest of the world, and the relationship of independent communities in urban areas with each other in pursuing common goals. The spillover phenomenon populates the world of metropolitan communities with exploiters and victims--the former prosper, and the latter become the "urban problem."

6-35.   Esslinger, Dean R. IMMIGRANTS AND THE CITY: ETHNICITY AND MOBILITY IN A NINETEENTH CENTURY MIDWESTERN COMMUNITY. Port Washington, N.Y.: Kennikat, 1975.

See 4-46.

6-36   Fainstein, Susan S., and Fainstein, Norman I. "Local Control as Social Reform: Planning for Big Cities in the Seventies." JOURNAL OF THE AMERICAN INSTITUTE OF PLANNERS 42 (July 1976): 275-85.

Discusses organizational problems of large bureaucratic city structures and propose improvements which would result from decentralization. Specific cases are examined.

6-37   Farley, Reynolds. "The Changing Distribution of Negroes Within Metropolitan Areas--The Emergence of Black Suburbs." AMERICAN JOURNAL OF SOCIOLOGY 75 (January 1970): 512-29.

An examination of the hypothesis that cities and suburbs are coming to have racially dissimilar populations. The author reviews the historical trends in racial composition, examines black population growth in suburbia in recent years, analyzes the socioeconomic characteristics of blacks in suburbia and moving into suburbia, and describes the types of suburbs experiencing black population growth. Data from New York and Chicago suburbs indicate that young black families who are typically better educated, hold more prestigious jobs, and have larger incomes than central city whites, are moving to suburbs.

6-38 Fava, Sylvia F. "Beyond Suburbia." ANNALS OF THE AMERICAN ACADEMY OF POLITICAL AND SOCIAL SCIENCE 422 (November 1975): 10-24.

> Addresses questions raised by suburban growth, such as: what role suburbs will play in an increasingly urban society; what role blacks and other minorities will take in the suburbs; and what type of governmental restructuring will occur. What political structures will be used to deal with urban/suburban metropolitan problems is raised but left unanswered. Social theory as it concerns suburbs is discussed briefly.

6-39 Fischel, William A. "Fiscal and Environmental Considerations in the Location of Firms in Suburban Communities." In FISCAL ZONING AND LAND USE CONTROLS, edited by Edwin S. Mills and Wallace E. Oates, pp. 119-73. Lexington, Mass.: D.C. Heath and Co., 1975.

> Contends that the property tax provides the means of exchange between firms and residents of suburban communities. Residents voluntarily surrender some of their community environment by granting permission to firms to locate there in return for fiscal benefits from the firms. If the property tax system is an efficient exchange mechanism, then metropolitan zoning policies should deal only with inter-municipal spillovers. The authors conclude that decentralized zoning and property taxation may not be as bad as is frequently asserted.

6-40 Fisher, Claude S., and Jackson, Robert Max. SUBURBS, NETWORKS, AND ATTITUDES. Working Paper no. 235. Berkeley: University of California, Institute of Urban and Regional Development, August 1974.

> Considers the relationship of suburban residence to greater involvement and interest in the locality. The data suggest suburbanites tend to be more involved in their localities and with their neighbors than are city residents; the difference between city and suburb is explained by self-selection; the nature of the suburb as an outlying subarea of the metropolis contributes to localized social ties and interests. The authors conclude that small towns and suburbs are somewhat alike, and thus the suburbanization of America may mean its de-urbanization.

6-41 Fox, Jeanne. REGIONALISM AND MINORITY PARTICIPATION. 2d ed. Washington, D.C.: Joint Center for Political Studies, 1974.

> An overview of the prominent forms of regionalism and the advantages and disadvantages to minorities of the regional approach. If minorities boycott involvement with regional government, someone else will make decisions for them. The author proposes guidelines for the development of a minority regionalism strategy.

6-42   Francois, Francis B.   "The Dilemma of Regionalism for Local Elected Officials."   PUBLIC MANAGEMENT 56 (January 1974):   8-10.

Urges that local problems be addressed in regional terms.   The dilemma between regional and local interests is more illusory than real.   Regional councils or councils of governments help municipalities so that power will not be diverted to the state and federal levels.   Regionalism is an extension, not a dilution, of local power.

6-43   Frieden, Bernard J.   METROPOLITAN AMERICA: CHALLENGE TO FEDERALISM, A STUDY.   Committee Print, 89th Cong., 2d sess.   Washington, D.C.:   Government Printing Office, 1966.

See 7-50.

6-44   Friedman, John, and Miller, John.   "The Urban Field."   In THE URBAN FUTURE, edited by Ely Chinoy, pp. 73-94.   New York: Leiber-Atherton, 1973.

Contend that a new urban unit will emerge--the urban field-- as the metro area expands and penetrates into the intermetropolitan periphery.   This area, comprised of the core metropolitan area and the surrounding intermetropolitan periphery, will be roughly one hundred miles in radius from the center.   This emerging pattern, if well planned, can allow for a "wider community of interests."

6-45   Friesema, H. Paul.   "Cities, Suburbs, and Shortlived Models of Metropolitan Politics."   In THE URBANIZATION OF THE SUBURBS, edited by Louis H. Masotti and Jeffrey K. Hadden, pp. 239-52.   Beverly Hills, Calif.:   Sage Publications, 1973.

Assesses the theoretical consequences of the changes in metropolitan politics in recent years, including a series of legal cases which challenge the jurisdictional sovereignty of white and wealthy suburbs.   Several theoretical models are examined, including the diplomacy model of Matthew Holden, the market model, and the life-style hypothesis of Oliver Williams.

6-46   Frisken, Frances.   "The Metropolis and the Central City: Can One Government Unite Them?"   URBAN AFFAIRS QUARTERLY 8 (June 1973): 395-422.

Examines the adequacy of current approaches to metropolitan political and administrative reform in reconciling central-city and regional needs and priorities.   It includes a case study of the Northeast Ohio Areawide Coordinating Agency, which serves the large metropolitan Cleveland area.   Because local governments are unlikely to act on their own to reduce metropolitan disparities, initiatives for change can only come from

state and federal governments. Alleviation of some metropolitan disparities may have to precede rather than follow effective political unification.

6-47   Gans, Herbert J. "How to Succeed in Integrating New Towns." DE-
       SIGN AND ENVIRONMENT 3 (Winter 1972): 28-29.

       An excerpt from a paper presented at a University of Califor-
       nia at Los Angeles conference on the implementation of the
       Department of Housing and Urban Development's social policies
       for new towns. Although planners generally have favored inte-
       gration to duplicate the prevailing demographic mix in the
       metropolitan area, Gans does not consider balance to be a
       viable goal for current new town planning. He suggests two
       approaches to integration policy: (1) microintegration of
       blacks on neighborhoods, and (2) macrointegration on the
       community as a whole, maintaining individual black or neigh-
       borhood segregation.

6-48   Gilbert, Charles E. GOVERNING THE SUBURBS. Bloomington: Indi-
       ana University Press, 1967.

       A study of suburban governmental developments, focusing upon
       three counties adjoining Philadelphia and selected municipali-
       ties within them. Two principal factors are studied as possible
       explanations of governmental action: (1) political structure
       as it relates to electoral organization and competition; and
       (2) political structure as patterns of socioeconomic pluralism,
       or "power structure." The book deals with three broad vari-
       ables: (1) the socioeconomic context of policy, (2) political
       (electoral) organization, and (3) governmental functions and
       structure.

6-49   Glendening, Parris N., and Reeves, Mavis Mann. CONTROVERSIES
       OF STATE AND LOCAL POLITICAL SYSTEMS. Boston: Allyn and
       Bacon, 1972.

       See 7-52.

6-50   Glenn, Norval D. "Suburbanization in the United States Since World
       War II." In THE URBANIZATION OF THE SUBURBS, edited by Louis
       H. Masotti and Jeffrey K. Hadden, pp. 51-78. Beverly Hills, Calif.:
       Sage Publications, 1973.

       Discusses the trend of suburbanization since the Second World
       War. Glenn cautions that some people have exaggerated the
       importance of suburban expansion. Suburbanization in the le-
       gal or political sense primarily has meant that "conurbations"
       have grown more quickly than the political boundaries of the
       central cities. He predicts that families will continue to move
       from the central cities, but that the stereotype of rows upon

rows of single family detached homes in the suburbs is not characteristic of the American way of life.

6-50a Grant, Daniel R. "Political Stability in Metro Government." In EMERGING PATTERNS IN URBAN ADMINISTRATION, edited by F. Gerald Brown and Thomas P. Murphy, pp. 34-63. Lexington, Mass.: Lexington Books, 1970.

See 6-18a.

6-50b Greene, Lee S.; Grant, Daniel R.; and Jewell, Malcolm E. THE STATES AND THE METROPOLIS. University: University of Alabama Press, 1968.

See 7-55a.

6-51 Griffin, C.W. "Local Autonomy--Metropolitan Anarchy." In his TAMING THE LAST FRONTIER, pp. 110-48. New York: Pitman, 1974.

Argues that some type of metropolitan government is necessary to cope with suburban sprawl and the fragmentation of local governments. Griffin concludes that financial pressure from the federal government may be the most politically practicable method of reforming suburban governmental attitudes. Suburban governments receive a great deal of federal aid in the form of highway construction, FHA mortgage insurance, and the construction of sewage-treatment plants. To those governments which practice exclusionary zoning or which fail to cooperate with metropolitan government, federal aid should be discontinued.

6-52 Haar, Charles M., ed. SUBURBAN PROBLEMS: THE PRESIDENT'S TASK FORCE ON SUBURBAN PROBLEMS. Cambridge, Mass.: Ballinger, 1974.

Reprinting of the final report of the task force established in 1967 by President Johnson. It includes nine chapters on the suburbs, the federal role in suburbia, and various land, housing, and planning approaches.

6-52a Hanson, Royce. "Toward a New Democracy: Metropolitan Consolidation and Decentralization." GEORGETOWN LAW JOURNAL 58 (March-May 1970): 863-99.

Discusses some of the factors that should be considered when conceptualizing the modernization of urban governance. The author is realistic about the prospects of change in metropolitan government. Only after a long succession of partial successes, frequent setbacks, and occasional isolated achievements will the eventual reorganization of metropolitan areas be realized. It will probably be necessary, he concludes, to

develop a consistent and coordinated federal policy directed
toward metropolitan governance as part of an overall national
urban policy.

6-53   Hanson, Royce, et al.   REFORM AS REORGANIZATION.   Baltimore:
Johns Hopkins University Press, 1972.

Addresses the organizational aspect of metropolitan government
reform. The essays included suggest that reform efforts are
most likely to succeed if they address the demands emerging
in the political constituency, and that reform of metropolitan
government is really a process of discovering a more fruitful
relationship between a political ideal and the realities of
integrating the public's desires with production possibilities.

6-54   Hawley, Amos H., and Zimmer, Basil G.   THE METROPOLITAN COM-
MUNITY: ITS PEOPLE AND GOVERNMENT.   Beverly Hills, Calif.:
Sage Publications, 1970.

Attempts to explain why metropolitan residents have been unwilling to accept governmental consolidation as a solution to
some metropolitan problems. The findings of the study con-
firm that residents believe there are significant service defi-
ciencies in suburban areas, but they are opposed to resolving
those problems by means of a consolidation of governmental
units.

6-55   Hester, L.A.   "The Jacksonville Story."   NATIONAL CIVIC REVIEW 59
(February 1970): 76-80.

A study of the consolidation of the city of Jacksonville and
Duval County, which, at the writing of this article, was the
largest metropolitan area merger in the United States. The
author examines the merger after it was in operation for one
year to determine what improvements might be made, and
what other areas of the nation could learn from the consolidation experience. The real advantage of consolidated government is that it provides a powerful tool for future planning
and for the implementation of the plans.

6-56   Hobbs, Edward H.   "A Problem: Fragmentation--One Answer: Annexation."   NATIONAL CIVIC REVIEW, September 1971, pp. 427-33.

Contends that two actions must be taken to prevent further
governmental fragmentation in newly emerging metropolitan
areas. First, the central city must take strong and effective
steps to prevent the formation of suburban governments. Second, cities must annex the fringe areas of the central city as
they build up and become more urban in character. Hobbs
argues that the expansion of city borders should eliminate the
inefficiency, waste, frustrations, and poor government that
usually accompany the formation of suburban government.

6-57   Hogan, James B. "Metro Government Favored by Local Officials."
        ARIZONA REVIEW 23 (May 1974): 5-11.

        A study of the Tucson metropolitan area revealing that when
        the attitudes of appointed officials are compared with those of
        elected officials, the former are slightly more favorable toward
        area-wide government. There appears to be substantial support
        for metropolitan change among public decision makers. In
        fact, public officials would transfer willingly several critical
        services, now produced and distributed by their separate juris-
        dictions, to some areawide agency.

6-58   Holland, John J. "County Government Can Be an Effective Manage-
        ment Tool for Land-Use Planning." NEW JERSEY COUNTY GOVERN-
        MENT, April 1971, pp. 4-5, 8.

        See 5-84.

6-59   Hughes, James W. "Dilemmas of Suburbanization and Growth Controls."
        ANNALS OF THE AMERICAN ACADEMY OF POLITICAL AND SOCIAL
        SCIENCE 422 (November 1975): 61-76.

        Discusses the political and land-use issues involved in growth
        controls as they related to the suburbs. The author cites
        various examples of growth control mechanisms and assesses
        the possible negative effects if jurisdictions do not enact such
        measures.

6-60   _____, ed. NEW DIMENSIONS IN URBAN PLANNING: GROWTH
        CONTROLS. New Brunswick, N.J.: Rutgers University, Center for
        Urban Policy Research, 1974.

        See 5-86.

6-60a   _____. SUBURBANIZATION DYNAMICS AND THE FUTURE OF THE
        CITY. New Brunswick, N.J.: Rutgers University, Center for Urban
        Policy Research, 1974.

        Seventeen chapters dealing with the dimensions of urban change,
        the process of neighborhood change, racial-ethnic dynamics, and
        dilemmas regarding the future.

6-61   "Improving County Government." PUBLIC MANAGEMENT 53 (April
        1971): entire issue.

        Examines county government management using Santa Clara
        County as an example. Also included is the discussion of six
        county managers on the role of the county manager. Problems
        of money and structure greatly affect county managers, as they
        do managers in cities. Just as there is no one model of how
        a city government should be structured, variations in the struc-

ture of county governments must be made according to the
needs of each individual county.

6-62   Kasarda, J[ohn].D. "Impact of Suburban Population Growth on Central
City Service Functions." AMERICAN JOURNAL OF SOCIOLOGY 77
(May 1972): 1111-24.

Investigates the relationship between suburban population growth
and service functions performed in central cities of 158 Standard Metropolitan Statistical Areas (SMSAs). Cross-sectional
and longitudinal analyses demonstrate that the suburban population has a large impact on central city trade and services
provided by central city governments. The impact of suburban
population is strong when controls are introduced for central
city size and age, annexation, per capita income of central
city residents, and percentage of the central city population
that is nonwhite.

6-63   Kasarda, John D., and Redfearn, George V. "Differential Patterns of
City and Suburban Growth in the United States." JOURNAL OF URBAN
HISTORY 2 (November 1975): 43-66.

Analyzes patterns of central city and suburban growth from
1900 to 1970, controlling for all metropolitan boundary changes
including suburban population annexed by central cities. The
first part of the analysis is devoted to elaborating the differential occurrence of annexation by regional location, by historical period, and by city growth stage. Then annexation estimates are used to arrive at corrected rates of population increase and changing density for all metropolitan central cities
and suburban rings.

6-64   League of Women Voters Education Fund. SUPER CITY/HOMETOWN,
U.S.A.: PROSPECTS FOR TWO-TIER GOVERNMENT. New York:
Praeger Publishers, 1974.

See 1-43.

6-65   Liebman, L. "Metropolitanism and Decentralization." In REFORM OF
METROPOLITAN GOVERNMENTS. The Governance of Metropolitan
Areas, no. 1. Edited by L. Wings, pp. 43-56. Baltimore: Resources
for the Future, 1972.

Compares the strengths and weaknesses of metropolitan government and decentralization. The author, assistant professor of
law at Harvard University Law School, argues that the two are
not antithetical but potential allies, since they are both based
on rationalized service delivery and on a more appropriate
alignment of the local political community.

6-66   Lineberry, Robert L. "Reforming Metropolitan Governance: Requiem on

Reality?" GEORGETOWN LAW REVIEW 58 (March/May 1970): 675-717.

> An attempt to understand the various approaches to metropolitan government reorganization by examining the underlying legal and political obstacles. In political terms, the two major political bodies that must be satisfied in order for a reform movement to be successful are the state legislature and the electorate in the area concerned. Usually, the state legislatures have developed a "hands off" attitude to reforms such as consolidation. Political divisiveness, then, is the underlying obstacle to the reform of governments in metropolitan areas.

6-67 Lyons, W.E., and Engstrom, Richard L. "Life-Style and Fringe Attitudes Toward the Political Integration of Urban Governments." MIDWEST JOURNAL OF POLITICAL SCIENCE 15 (August 1971): 475-94.

> A study of conflicting hypotheses found in aggregate based literature concerning the relationship between life-style and attitudes towards various aspects of political integration in urban areas. A survey study of fringe dwellers in the greater Lexington, Kentucky, area reveals that the respondents' attitudes towards a massive annexation proposal were not related to variations in life-style.

6-67a McKay, Robert B. REAPPORTIONMENT: THE LAW AND POLITICS OF EQUAL REPRESENTATION. 2d ed. New York: Simon & Schuster, 1970.

> Examines the history of unequal representation in state legislatures and emphasizes the importance of the landmark U.S. Supreme Court case, Baker v. Carr. Since this case and others have direct effect upon cities, they influence urban and rural politics. Much of the text is devoted to a justification for the Court's intervention in the reapportionment issue. The author tries to demonstrate that judicially manageable standards can be enforced and that judicial remedies in the cases can be ensured.

6-68 Marando, V[incent].L. "Life-Style Distances and Suburban Support for Urban Political Integration: A Replication." SOCIAL SCIENCE QUARTERLY 53 (June 1972): 155-60.

> Examines support for consolidation of cities and counties. The author correlated life-style variables with voter support for consolidation. The life-style theory that the greater the social distance, the less support for consolidation, was not confirmed by the study. It was found that suburban voters approved consolidation, although they had high social status.

6-69 _____. "Voting in City-County Consolidation Referenda." WESTERN POLITICAL QUARTERLY 26 (March 1973): 90-96.

Examines city-county consolidation in comparative terms by focusing on some selected political and economic factors cited as important to voter support in case studies. The author studies political and economic correlates of the "yes" vote in cities and counties. The findings of this study suggest that the number of separately elected administrators and the number of special districts are strongly related to both the city and fringe "yes" vote. It seems that the inclusion of more than a single elected administrator is a necessary factor for voter support. The findings further support the conclusions of other case studies--that consolidation support is bound by certain political parameters.

6-70 Marando, Vincent [L.], and Wanamaker, Daniel. "Political and Social Variables in City-County Consolidation Referenda." POLITY 4 (Summer 1972): 512-22.

Examines both the social and political correlates of voter support for city-county consolidations. Although the authors admit that this type of research does not in itself clarify the character of the political process involved in integration issues,· they find that comparative statistical studies do enable them to examine more closely the process of urban political integration.

6-71 Marshall, D.R.; Frieden, B[ernard].; and Fessler, D.W. MINORITY PERSPECTIVES. Washington, D.C.: Resources for the Future, 1972.

See 4-95.

6-71a Martin, Roscoe C. METROPOLIS IN TRANSITION: LOCAL GOVERNMENT ADAPTATION TO CHANGING URBAN NEEDS. Washington, D.C.: Government Printing Office, 1963.

Examines how some local governments have adapted to changing metropolitan needs. The study focuses on voluntary local actions designed to improve the structure of local governments and highlights the arrangements that are necessary to make service performance more efficient under metropolitan conditions. The author offers suggestions on how to reform metropolitan government in order to meet the needs of a twentieth-century urban society.

6-72 Mathewson, Kent. "Councils of Government: The Potential and the Problems." In EMERGING PATTERNS IN URBAN ADMINISTRATION, edited by F. Gerald Brown and Thomas P. Murphy, pp. 195-221. Lexington, Mass.: Lexington Books, 1970.

See 6-18a.

6-72a Mogulof, Melvin B. GOVERNING METROPOLITAN AREAS. Washington, D.C.: Urban Institute, 1971.

An intensive analysis of the effectiveness of metropolitan councils of governments as clearinghouses for federal programs. Includes commentary on the role of state government in metropolitan affairs.

6-73 _____. "A Modest Proposal for the Governance of America's Metropolitan Areas." JOURNAL OF THE AMERICAN INSTITUTE OF PLANNERS 41 (July 1975): 250-57.

Assesses restructured government in metropolitan areas as an interesting, if illusive, option for the American urban scene. Mogulof argues that four elements are necessary for a restructured metropolitan government: authority, multifunctional capacity, a geographic scope approximating the urban area, and taxing powers. He believes that restructured metropolitan areas would represent a model of metro governance composed of the following elements: local units of government capable of making decisions concerning the character and responsiveness of public services; areawide special purpose districts; metropolitan governing councils with authority to constrain local governments and special districts and with policy makers responsive to state government; and state government serving as an arbiter between local governments and areawide governments.

6-74 _____. "Who Does What? A Performance Comparison of Metropolitan Governments." URBAN AND SOCIAL CHANGE REVIEW 6 (Spring 1973): 59-64.

Based on a report comparing five metropolitan reorganizations in North America. Mogulof believes all five are stronger structures than the currently dominant metropolitan mechanism of the "clearinghouse." The five areas are: Urban County--Dade County, Florida; Consolidation City/County--Jacksonville, Florida; Transfer of Functions to State Government--Portland, Oregon; and Federation--Metropolitan Toronto. These governmental forms are evaluated in terms of police and fire protection, transportation, water, sewer and environmental control, welfare, recreation, education, housing, and policy making and planning.

6-74a Murphy, Thomas P. "Intergovernmental Management of Urban Problems in the Kansas City Metropolitan Area." In EMERGING PATTERNS IN URBAN ADMINISTRATION, edited by F. Gerald Brown and Thomas P. Murphy, pp. 248-76. Lexington, Mass.: Lexington Books, 1970.

See 6-18a.

6-74b _____. "Jurisdictional Boundaries and Areawide Decision Making: The Interstate Metropolitan Problem." In URBAN PROBLEMS AND PUBLIC POLICY, edited by Robert L. Lineberry and Louis H. Masotti, pp. 19-38. Lexington, Mass.: Lexington Books, 1975.

> Finds that coordination and management of urban services is more complex in interstate areas. Discusses mechanisms for overcoming interstate barriers.

6-74c _____. METROPOLITICS AND THE URBAN COUNTY. Washington, D.C.: Washington National Press, 1970.

> Discusses the evolving role of the urban county using Jackson County, Missouri, as a case study. Includes a heavy intergovernmental relations analysis involving Kansas City and Independence, as well as input on the complexities of interstate metropolitan areas.

6-74d _____. "Urbanization, Suburbanization, and the New Politics." In his THE NEW POLITICS CONGRESS, pp. 209-24. Lexington, Mass.: Lexington Books, 1974.

> An analysis of the relationship of the urban and suburban issues in Congress and the influence of the increased number of seats in suburban areas on urban policy.

6-74e Murphy, Thomas P., and Rehfuss, John. URBAN POLITICS IN THE SUBURBAN ERA. Homewood, Ill.: Dorsey Press, 1976.

> An examination of metropolitics from a suburban viewpoint. Political, social, and economic data are integrated in an interdisciplinary approach to urban, suburban, and metropolitan decision making. There is substantial treatment of federal and state policy impact.

6-74f Murphy, Thomas P., and Warren, Charles R., eds. ORGANIZING PUBLIC SERVICES IN METROPOLITAN AMERICA. Lexington, Mass.: Lexington Books, 1974.

> A series of twelve essays commissioned by the National Academy of Public Administration on the feasibility of metropolitan reorganization. Includes essays by Warren, Murphy, Vincent Marando, William Wilken, Patricia Florestano, Donna Shalala, and Astride Merget.

6-75 NACO Round Table. "City-County Consolidations, Separations, and Federations." THE AMERICAN COUNTY 35 (November 1970): 12-13, 16-17, 30-31.

> An excerpt from the City-County Consolidations, Separations, and Federations Workshop held at the National Association of

Counties annual convention in Atlanta, Georgia, July 1970. It includes discussions of consolidations in Nashville-Davidson County, Jacksonville, Indianapolis, and Baton Rouge; separation in Virginia; and federation in Dade County, Florida.

6-76   New York Committee for Economic Development. RESHAPING GOVERNMENT IN METROPOLITAN AREAS. New York: 1970.

Concludes that the existing organization of metropolitan government can seriously impede the solutions to problems of the central city and the suburbs. This report investigates the difficulty of combining into one system of government the ability to handle both metropolitan and community problems. The committee examined the importance of federal and state support in urban areas, and provided a framework for confronting the difficulties of welfare, jobs for the hard-core unemployed, education for the disadvantaged, and other urban problems.

6-77   Orfield, Gary. "Federal Policy, Local Power, and Metropolitan Segregation." POLITICAL SCIENCE QUARTERLY 89 (Winter 1974-75): 777-802.

Contends local governments can accomplish school segregation, but the problem inevitably must be handled on a metropolitan-wide level. Stable school desegregation in the older urban centers of America means cooperation across district lines.

6-78   Pendleton, William W. "Blacks in Suburbs." In THE URBANIZATION OF THE SUBURBS, edited by Louis H. Masotti and Jeffrey K. Hadden, pp. 171-84. Beverly Hills, Calif.: Sage Publications, 1973.

Maintains suburbs are still primarily white and middle class. Suburbanization as a process has been characterized by the redistribution of residential patterns. Unfortunately, because of discrimination, the suburbanization process for blacks has been primarily selective redistribution. It appears that blacks participate in the demographic dimensions, but not in the social dimensions of suburbanization.

6-79   Pratt, Henry J. "Counties' Role Grown in Urban Affairs." NATIONAL CIVIC REVIEW 61 (September 1972): 397-402.

Presents the findings of a study of the role of suburban county governments in suburban politics and intergovernmental relations. He concludes that county leaders have the power to exert political leverage and can play a prominent role in addressing suburban interests. Recent fiscal demographic and constitutional changes have made counties more important than ever before.

6-80   Remy, Ray. "The Professional Administrator in Regional Councils." PUBLIC MANAGEMENT 56 (January 1974): 11-13.

Argues that as the role of COG becomes increasingly important in metropolitan governance, so does the role of the director and his staff. The author believes that the director of a
COG is more involved in the broader political arena than his
city manager counterpart. The COG director must work well
with people of varying viewpoints, but must not ally himself
too closely with any one in particular.

6-80a Roos, Lawrence K., and Kelly, Thomas C. "Executive Leadership in
the Urban County." In EMERGING PATTERNS IN URBAN ADMINIS-
TRATION, edited by F. Gerald Brown and Thomas P. Murphy, pp. 112-
24. Lexington, Mass.: Lexington Books, 1970.

See 6-18a.

6-81 Rosenbaum, Walter A., and Henderson, Thomas A. "Explaining the Attitude of Community Influentials Toward Government Consolidation--a Re-
appraisal of Your Hypotheses." URBAN AFFAIRS QUARTERLY 8 (December 1973): 251-75.

A study of two communities, Tampa and Jacksonville, to determine why supporters of consolidation advocate that type of
governmental reorganization. Three typical reasons were dis-
cerned. First, some supporters were community influentials
who had nothing to lose; second, arguments of "economy and
efficiency" were persuasive; third, the flow of benefits ac-
cruing to special interest groups from consolidation encouraged
some support.

6-82 Safen, Edward. THE MIAMI METROPOLITAN EXPERIMENT, A METRO-
POLITAN ACTION STUDY. 2d ed. Garden City, N.Y.: Anchor,
1966.

Examines the background, initiation, and first achievements of
the metropolitan government of Miami. The authors explain
the state and regional politics of Greater Miami, and the
struggles and conflicts which ensued in the campaign to bring
consolidation to Miami.

6-83 Schiltz, Timothy, and Moffitt, William. "Inner-City/Outer-City Relationship in Metropolitan Areas: A Bibliographic Essay." URBAN AF-
FAIRS QUARTERLY 7 (September 1971): 75-108.

Reviews the literature on the subject of inner-city/outer-city
relations. The essay is divided into four major sections: Part
one discusses the various forms of inner-city/outer-city disparities and offers a general critique of the "myth" of suburbia. Part two concerns governmental fragmentation, its causes
and effects, and includes a short discussion of southern metrop-
olises. Part three deals with the various responses which have
been made to governmental fragmentation-interlocal cooperation-

governmental annexation, and governmental consolidation. It discusses the politics and the effects of adoption. The concluding section deals primarily with the concept of urban development and offers suggestions for further research.

6-83a Schnore, Leo F. CLASS AND RACE IN CITIES AND SUBURBS. Chicago: Markham Publishing Co., 1972.

A good evaluation of city-suburb socioeconomic differences and their impact on urban policy.

6-84 Scott, Thomas M. "Implications of Suburbanization for Metropolitan Political Organization." ANNALS OF THE AMERICAN ACADEMY OF POLITICAL AND SOCIAL SCIENCE 422 (November 1975): 36-44.

Provides a general explanation of the pattern of suburban growth and its effect on metropolitan political reorganization. The author says that contributions of suburbs to metropolitan governance are often overlooked. He cites examples of suburban policies which have been used elsewhere in the political system: (1) the use of more professionals in government; (2) a focus on high-quality, "people-oriented" services, such as education; and (3) the determination to maintain local control over life-style issues.

6-85 Siembieda, William J. "Suburbanization of Ethics of Color." ANNALS OF THE AMERICAN ACADEMY OF POLITICAL AND SOCIAL SCIENCE 422 (November 1975): 118-28.

Indicates that the suburbanization of minorities is not random; segregation exists in suburbia just as it does in the society at large; and although there are ethics among the whites, the suburbs remain basically white and highly segregated.

6-85a Stone, Clarence N., and Feldbaum, Eleanor G. "Blame, Complacency, and Pessimism: Attitudes and Problem Perceptions Among Selected Street Level Administrators in Two Urban Countries." ADMINISTRATION AND SOCIETY 8 (May 1976): 79-106.

Examines attitudes of social service employees. Survey data indicate that personal characteristics are important in explaining employee reaction to job stress. The authors conclude that employees who see their work objective as receiving extrensic rewards will be satisfied and those who see their work objective as attaining intrinsic rewards will become frustrated and leave their jobs.

6-86 "Symposium on Restructing Metropolitan Area Government." GEORGETOWN LAW JOURNAL 58 (March/May 1970): 663-1012.

Presents the views of several authorities in the field of urban studies, focusing on structural reform to show that a city can deal with changing patterns of mobility. The need for increased and better cooperation between levels of government is emphasized. Sen. Edmund Muskie calls for a national urban policy, and his introductory remarks set the tone for the symposium.

6-87 "Urban County: A Study of New Approaches to Local Government in Metropolitan Areas." HARVARD LAW REVIEW 73 (January 1960): 526-82.

Sees recent eruption of urban development in unincorporated areas as subjecting counties to a new demand for local services which they are not equipped to furnish. This article suggests creation of a central governmental authority which reflects the organic coherence of a metropolitan area. The author observes that the resources of the entire area could be more effectively utilized if placed at the disposal of a governmental unit possessing areawide responsibilities, thereby advancing efficiency and economy by eliminating duplicative operations. This article analyzes Dade County, Florida, which has acquired substantial power to compel the transfer of functions from its cities, and Los Angeles County, which is wholly dependent upon the consent of the cities.

6-87a Walsh, Annamarie Hauck. THE URBAN CHALLENGE TO GOVERNMENT. New York: Praeger Publishers, 1969.

See 1-73.

6-88 Walter, Benjamin, and Wirt, Frederick M. "The Political Consequences of Suburban Variety." SOCIAL SCIENCE QUARTERLY 52 (December 1971): 746-67.

Examines the effects of social variety upon suburban policy and political life. The authors discuss the different pressures and constraints on the policy maker and the administrator.

6-89 Weicler, John C. "The Effects of Metropolitan Political Fragmentation on Central City Budgets." In MODELS OF URBAN STRUCTURE, edited by David C. Sweet, pp. 177-203. Lexington, Mass.: Lexington Books, 1973.

Investigates the effect of suburbanization and metropolitan political fragmentation on the fiscal positions of local governments within the metropolitan area. It is particularly concerned with the effect of suburban population on central city expenditures and revenues, and with the effect of business

activity on the city's budget. The author concludes that cities
spend more on providing services to manufacturing plants than
they receive in tax revenue from them. On the other hand,
cities receive more in tax revenue from retail stores than they
spend in providing services to them. The results indicate that
central cities are able to exploit suburbs.

6-90   Wirt, Frederick M., et al. ON THE CITY'S RUN: POLITICS AND
POLICY IN SUBURBIA. Lexington, Mass.: D.C. Heath and Co.,
1972.

Examines the political consequences of massive suburbanization.
Topics discussed include the diversity of life styles, the sensitivity of suburbanites to national election moods, the attitudes
which link many suburbs to one another regardless of jurisdictional boundaries, suburban community response to massive immigration, and federal efforts to respond to the suburban experience.

6-91   Wood, Robert C. SUBURBIA: ITS PEOPLE AND THEIR POLITICS. Boston: Houghton Mifflin, 1958.

Examines suburban political ideology, its history, values, and
consequences. The author is impressed by the suburban re-
sistance to twentieth-century ideals and values, and by the
consistency with which suburbanites look to the past for guidance. Accordingly, suburbs closely resemble long-established
American traditions, although not necessarily the best ones.

6-92   Yin, Robert K., and Yates, Douglas. STREET-LEVEL GOVERNMENTS.
Lexington, Mass.: Lexington Books, 1975.

See 1-80.

6-93   Young, Ed. "Nashville, Jacksonville and Indianapolis Examined for
Possible Lessons for Future." NATION'S CITIES, November 1969, pp.
26-32.

A general discussion of city-county consolidation with an
examination of three case studies. In each of the cases, the
county government merged with most, but not all, of the
municipal governments in the county. The similarities and
differences in the experiences of the three regions are pointed
out. Similarities include the leadership of ambitious, innovative leaders, and conspicuous cooperation on the part of
state legislatures. Differences include the amount and types
of changes effected by consolidation; the powers of the new
government; and the extent of citizen support, particularly
of blacks.

6-94   Zikmund, Joseph II.   "Suburbs in State and National Politics."   In THE
       URBANIZATION OF THE SUBURBS, edited by Louis H. Masotti and
       Jeffrey K. Hadden, pp. 253-73.   Beverly Hills, Calif.:   Sage Publica-
       tions, 1973.

       Argues that there are many different kinds of suburbs and no
       single type of suburban voter.   Suburban diversity is so great
       that any statement of general suburban pattern is empirically
       and theoretically misleading.   The author concludes that, in
       order to understand the impact of suburbs on national or state
       politics, the impact of suburbs on the real constituencies of
       electoral competition must be analyzed.   In effect, there is
       no national electorate, only state and local electorates.

6-95   _____.   "A Theoretical Structure for the Study of Suburban Politics."
       ANNALS OF THE AMERICAN ACADEMY OF POLITICAL AND SOCIAL
       SCIENCE 422 (November 1975):   45-60.

       Provides a general theoretical structure for the study of subur-
       ban politics.   The author contends that suburbanites, regardless
       of race or socioeconomic status, simply want to be left alone,
       to have secure financial (i.e., home) investments, and to en-
       sure the safety of their family.   The politics of suburbia, seen
       in those terms, is a striving for the goals of privacy, well-
       being, and safety.

6-96   Zimmerman, Joseph F.   "Metropolitan Reform in the U.S.:   An Over-
       view."   PUBLIC ADMINISTRATION REVIEW 30 (September/October
       1970):   531-43.

       Contends that political inertia, strong opposition to reorganiza-
       tion, and the failure of the federal and state governments are
       reasons why there is little meaningful metropolitan reform.
       Any reform of the local government system promoted by the
       federal or state governments will probably include the use of
       revenue sharing and grants-in-aid to encourage the creation
       of a two-tier system, as it is less disruptive to the existing
       system, and less likely to promote alienation between citizens
       and their governments.

Chapter 7

FEDERALISM AND URBAN GOVERNMENTS

This chapter includes entries relating to intergovernmental relations, national urban policy, revenue sharing and urban politics, and the role of the states.

7-1   Aaron, Henry. "The Honest Citizens Guide to Revenue Sharing." TAX REVIEW 32 (October 1971): 37-41.

An analysis of the contradictory claims and assumptions about revenue sharing. The author believes that the revenue sharing debate has been inconclusive for specific reasons: the objectives of revenue sharing contain contradictory assumptions about its consequences; and neither economists nor political scientists have answered the crucial economic and political questions about its consequences. Aaron offers an alternative procedure for local equalization among the states by basing our attitudes about revenue sharing not on vaguely stated objectives, but on the one national objective that the federal government has exclusive power to achieve fiscal equalization.

7-2   Advisory Commission on Intergovernmental Relations. REVENUE SHARING--AN IDEA WHOSE TIME HAS COME. Washington, D.C.: Government Printing Office, 1970.

Provides an overview of revenue sharing which the commission believes to be an important part of a comprehensive program to restore fiscal balance to the American federal system. The report presents arguments for and against revenue sharing, and the basic concept is explained, including its impact on decentralization of federal power.

7-3   _____. STATE ACTION IN LOCAL PROBLEMS, 1972. Report M-77. Washington, D.C.: Government Printing Office, 1973.

A summary of selected state constitutional and legislative actions of 1972. State actions are focused in five major categories dealing with efforts of states to help local governments. The report provides a reference of major developments which are characteristic of trends in the relationship between states and local governments and indicates the programs being undertaken by the various states.

7-4 _____. STATE AID TO LOCAL GOVERNMENTS. Washington, D.C.: Government Printing Office, 1969.

Addressed to the problem of financing local governments and the effect of state aid to localities in the federal system. The commission presented twelve recommendations for improving inequities in the distribution of funds. Three major themes emerged from their research: there is a mismatch among governmental levels in financial responsibility for the provision of public services; state aid formulas, except for public education, usually fail to recognize variations in local fiscal capacity to support public services; state aid rarely, if ever, constitutes a "system."

7-5 _____. A STATE RESPONSE TO URBAN PROBLEMS: RECENT EXPERIENCE UNDER THE "BUYING IN" APPROACH. Washington, D.C.: Government Printing Office, 1970.

Examines the extent to which state governments are "buying into" federal-local grants-in-aid for urban development. This report, which was released only as a staff document, also analyzes the roles of states in urban affairs. There are a number of objectives of "buying in," including the following: to relieve local financial burdens, to coordinate state and local planning efforts, to improve intergovernmental cooperation, and to encourage local units to assume broader responsibilities. ACIR argues against the proliferation of federal categorical grants and recommends several reforms.

7-6 _____. URBAN AMERICA AND THE FEDERAL SYSTEM. Washington, D.C.: Government Printing Office, 1969.

Analyzes the urban crisis and the role of the local, state, and federal governments in resolving the problems which confront urban areas. This report examines the major intergovernmental dimensions of the urban crisis which include the growth of functional government, unbalanced federal-state-local revenue sources, restoration of fiscal balance in the federal system, and political balkanization of the metropolitan area. Some dynamics of urban development, including mobility, migration, and immobility, are reviewed. The report makes recommendations concerning a national urbanization policy including the effort to unshackle local governments, and to help states fulfill their crucial role in meeting urban problems.

7-7 Agnew, Spiro T. "The Case for Revenue Sharing." GEORGETOWN LAW JOURNAL 60 (October 1971): 7-28.

Argues that revenue sharing is important not only to help local governments finance services, but is vital to keep the federal system healthy. Categorical grants are no longer sufficient means of funding local governments due to the excessive control of the federal government. The debate among proponents and opponents of general and special revenue sharing is presented. Acting as the spokesman for President Nixon's "New Economic Policy," Agnew asserted that revenue sharing was a high legislative priority in the Nixon administration.

7-8   Anderson, Wayne F. "Revenue Sharing--Now It's Up to Us!" PUBLIC MANAGEMENT 55 (January 1973): 8-10.

Contends that city managers and urban executives are the key to effective implementation of revenue sharing. The foremost implementation problem is that the amount of money is small in comparison to the needs and expectations of urban areas. Several pointers on assembling or evaluating a first year's revenue sharing program are offered including overall financial principles, financial strengthening, tax cuts, capital expenditures, and operating expenditures.

7-9   Baker, G.E. RURAL VS. URBAN POLITICAL POWER. New York: Doubleday, 1955.

An argument for giving urban interest more power in state legislatures, written before reapportionment was ordered in Baker v. Carr. Rural areas had an inflated amount of political power as the country urbanized and cities were short-changed. Antiquated boundaries and outmoded political practices were the main inequities observed by Baker in his call for reform.

7-10   Banfield, Edward C. "Revenue Sharing in Theory and Practice." PUBLIC INTEREST 23 (Spring 1971): 33-45.

Attempts to define the central issue in the revenue sharing debate. Many mayors and city officials focus on the fiscal crisis facing the cities, but Banfield contends that the problem is not that serious. The issue is that states have the capacity to offer cities more help but are unwilling to do so. He observes that revenue sharing is much less redistributive than the existing federal grant-in-aid programs. Under revenue sharing wealthier states, in terms of per capita income, would benefit more than poorer states.

7-11   Beckman, Norman. "Federal Policy for Metropolitan Governance." NATIONAL CIVIC REVIEW, March 1974, pp. 128-32.

Summarizes several important pieces of federal legislation dealing with metropolitan governance. Beckman states that areawide governance can be achieved through methods other than consolidated metropolitan government. He discusses the ways the federal government has tried to provide for resource equalization including the use of allocation and matching formulas in awarding grants, a progressive system of tax collections, and the socially oriented purposes for which many tax funds are used.

7-12   Beckman, Norman, and Harding, Susan. "The State and Urban Development." STATE GOVERNMENT 44 (Spring 1971): 121-29.

A survey of state legislative developments in formulating urban growth policy indicating that the states have been taking more responsibility in guiding the growth and development of urban areas. Examples include state action on snob zoning, tenants' rights, urban renewal, land-use regulations, planning, and revenue reform.

7-13   Belmonte, Robert M. "State and County Relationships: An Imperfection in the Fabric of American Federalism." PUBLIC ADMINISTRATION REVIEW 33 (November/December 1973): 561-63.

Advocates the practice of American "federalism" within the states with more political power on the part of county government. Belmonte believes that the states should exercise a healthy respect for the role of counties within states. He notes counties usually are not political subdivisions of the state, but more commonly are administrative subdivisions.

7-14   Benson, George C. THE POLITICS OF URBANISM: THE NEW FEDERALISM. Woodbury, Iowa: Barron's Educational Series, 1972.

Presents the difference between politics in urban areas and other American politics. Benson observes that both the national and state governments have failed to realize that they are dealing with units of government; innumerable uncoordinated grants have a chaotic effect on local administration; and conflicting federal and state policies often tend to divide communities. He sees a need to rethink intergovernmental relations and stress intergovernmental cooperation. In addition, he sees a need for greater participation by the "ordinary citizen" in the workings of government. He concludes that it is less important for the federal government to change its policies than the manner of its administration.

7-15   Bingham, Richard D. PUBLIC HOUSING AND URBAN RENEWAL: AN ANALYSIS OF FEDERAL-LOCAL RELATIONS. New York: Praeger Publishers, 1975.

Two federal grant programs, public housing and urban renewal, are examined. To see why some cities make extensive use of

federal grants while other cities virtually ignore them and to
analyze the actual impact of federal grants on cities. The
author's findings suggest that if renewal and housing grants
promote economic vigor, the time lag necessary for the grants
to produce any measurable change is much longer than was
heretofore believed. Bingham concludes that public housing
and urban renewal meet only some of their espoused goals and
both programs have certain spillover effects.

7-16   Boyer, Brian D. CITIES DESTROYED FOR CASH: THE FHA SCANDAL
AT HUD. Chicago: Follett Publishing Co., 1973.

Describes the Federal Housing Administration's (FHA) "murder"
of cities, and the ways in which men despoil the urban landscape to enrich themselves. According to Boyer, FHA money
was taken by real estate speculators, mortgage companies,
banks, and other capital sources who finance and run the
nation's housing. The author cites instances of corruption,
conflict of interest, fraud, and double-dealing in the housing
industry. He offers some suggestions for reform of the FHA.

7-17   Break, George F. "Revenue Sharing: Its Implications for Present and
Future Intergovernmental Fiscal Systems: The Case For." NATIONAL
TAX JOURNAL 24 (September 1971): 307-12.

Argues that revenue sharing is necessary because local and
state governments have demonstrated that they are not capable
of meeting the service delivery needs of their citizens. Break
concludes that revenue sharing would not only provide more
money to states and local jurisdictions, it would also help to
decentralize some of the enormous power of the federal government and make the federal system healthier.

7-18   Bridgeland, William. "A War on Poverty Program: Its Conflicts and
Collapse." URBAN LIFE 4 (April 1975): 79-98.

Examines observers' and participants' perceptions of the Cap
County agency set up to deal with poverty. The study also
considered the agency's relationship with the Office of Economic Opportunity. The study concluded that poverty is a reality
in the county and that there has been little success in com-
batting it. Programs were often haphazard, goals unclear,
and leadership nonexistent. The county poverty agency eventually developed into a stagnant organization and was terminated.

7-19   Brilliant, Eleanor L. THE URBAN DEVELOPMENT CORPORATION.
Lexington, Mass.: Lexington Books, 1975.

Analyzes the Urban Development Corporation (UDC) of New
York State and examines the mutual interaction of its policy

content and the policy process. Brilliant discusses UDC's
design and looks at how it defines urban policy and planning,
and how it attempts to avoid the restrictions of our political
system which inhibit comprehensive planning. She also examines the compromises and costs of the implementation of its
policies and plans.

7-20 Brown, F. Gerald, and Murphy, Thomas P., eds. EMERGING PATTERNS
IN URBAN ADMINISTRATION. Lexington, Mass.: Lexington Books,
1970.

See 6-18a.

7-21 Browne, Edmond, Jr., and Rehfuss, John. "Policy Evaluation, Citizen
Participation and Revenue Sharing in Aurora, Illinois." PUBLIC AD-
MINISTRATION REVIEW 35 (March/April 1975): 150-57.

Sees two potential consequences of revenue sharing as the application of policy analysis at the local level and the development of different forms of participation by citizens in governmental affairs. The article examines these consequences in
Aurora and their implications for other jurisdictions. Citizen
participation and policy evaluation of federalism and in more
citizen involvement in the decision-making process of government.

7-22 Bryant, Coralie. "The Politics of Housing and Housing Policy Research."
POLICY STUDIES JOURNAL 3 (Summer 1975): 397-401.

Predicts that if the current housing shortage shows no indica-
tion of abating, the reformed and overwhelmingly Democratic
Congress with its newly powerful House Budget Committee may
reverse this situation. It is likely that Congress will focus
on housing policy to generate employment rather than houses.
When Congress does come to focus on housing programs, the
requisite social science research on policy alternatives and
program implications will probably still be incomplete.

7-23 Byrnes, John W. "Federal Action to Strengthen State and Local Revenue
Capabilities." NATIONAL TAX JOURNAL 24 (September 1971): 363-
68.

Argues that general revenue sharing would weaken the federal
system and would undermine the basic objectives of our constitutional system of government. As an alternative to revenue
sharing the author proposes a system of federal tax credits for
states taxes. Tax credits provide additional taxing latitude to
states and localities consistent with our federal system.

7-24 Campbell, Alan K., ed. AMERICAN ASSEMBLY, THE STATES AND

THE URBAN CRISIS. Englewood Cliffs, N.J.: Prentice-Hall, 1970.

Examines the role of the states in the federal system and their relationship to urban problems. The states are in a unique and crucial position to assist urban areas. According to the authors, if the states do not assume a greater share of the responsibility in meeting urban problems, the American federal system will become nonfunctional.

7-25 Cantor, Arnold. "State-Local Taxes: A Study of Inequity." THE AMERICAN FEDERATIONIST 81 (February 1974): 14-21.

See 5-32.

7-26 Caputo, David A. "General Revenue Sharing and American Federalism: Towards the Year 2000." ANNALS OF THE AMERICAN ACADEMY OF POLITICAL AND SOCIAL SCIENCE 419 (May 1975): 130-42.

Examines the political context and the limitations of attempts to measure the impact of general revenue sharing. Political developments, specific legislation requirements, and comparisons with prior categorical programs are explored. In addition, the impact of general revenue sharing on expenditure decisions and political developments is reviewed. Caputo contends that general revenue sharing will significantly affect federalism only if it is a precursor of other federal programs which make available substantial amounts of unrestricted federal funds to state and local governments.

7-26a Caputo, David A., and Cole, Richard L. "Policy Implications of General Revenue Sharing." In URBAN PROBLEMS AND PUBLIC POLICY, edited by Robert L. Lineberry and Louis H. Masotti, pp. 175-82. Lexington, Mass.: Lexington Books, 1975.

Discusses the policy impact of general revenue sharing on our federal system, including questions of decentralization of programs and service delivery.

7-27 Caraley, Demetrios. "Congressional Politics and Urban Aid." POLITICAL SCIENCE QUARTERLY 91 (Spring 1976): 19-45.

Deals with congressional attitudes and responses to the cities' financial crunch. Caraley explains that city requests for federal aid are viewed differently by northern Democrats, southern Democrats, and Republicans, and the composition of Congress determines whether pro-urban or anti-urban action is taken. Party differences, the role of the president, and committee composition and behavior are examined.

7-28 Carról, Michael A. "The Impact of General Revenue Sharing on the Urban Planning Process--An Initial Assessment." PUBLIC ADMINISTRA-

TION REVIEW 35 (March/April 1975): 143-50.

Assesses the impact of general revenue sharing on the urban
planning process. Carrol cites areas in which changes are
needed in the revenue sharing program in order to strengthen
the role of urban planning.

7-29   Clark, Timothy B.; Lilley, William III; and Iglehart, John K.   "New
        Federalism Report."   NATIONAL JOURNAL 4 (December 1972):   1907-
        40.

        An overview of the New Federalism program--the philosophy
        of it, the opposition to it in Congress, the legislation itself,
        and pilot projects.   The authors examine a plan to restructure
        the federal bureaucracy to make the federal government more
        responsive to need defined at the state and local levels.

7-30   Cohen, David K.   "Segregation, Desegregation, and Brown."   SOCIETY
        12 (November/December 1974):   34-40.

        See 4-31.

7-31   Cole, Richard L.   "Revenue Sharing: Citizen Participation and Social
        Service Aspects."   ANNALS OF THE AMERICAN ACADEMY OF POLIT-
        ICAL AND SOCIAL SCIENCE 419 (May 1975):   64-74.

        Claims that revenue sharing has not led to a complete demise
        of citizen participation opportunities as feared, nor has it ig-
        nored social service concerns.   Rather, those interested in
        receiving more revenue sharing funds can organize and compete
        with other local groups at the local level.   The most signifi-
        cant consequence of revenue sharing may be its encouragement
        of previously ignored groups to participate in its urban decision-
        making process.

7-32   Cole, Richard L., and Caputo, David A.   URBAN POLITICS AND DE-
        CENTRALIZATION: THE CASE OF FEDERAL REVENUE SHARING.
        Lexington, Mass.:   D.C. Heath and Co., 1974.

        Explains the political and policy aspects of general revenue
        sharing.   The authors examine the forces behind revenue shar-
        ing, which groups are affected, how they are affected by de-
        centralized decision making, and the revenue sharing decisions
        reached by city governments over 50,000 in population.   An
        important finding is that American cities are allocating general
        revenue sharing funds in relatively few program areas.

7-33   Conot, Robert.   AMERICAN ODYSSEY.   New York: William Morrow &
        Co., 1974.

        The culmination of the author's work as a special consultant
        to the National Advisory Commission on Civil Disorders, ap-

pointed after the 1967 riots in Detroit. The commission's report explained <u>what</u> happened, but did not tell <u>how</u> and <u>why</u>, and did not take into account the social pathology or the city's institutions. Conot sought to fill that void. The history of the city is traced to demonstrate its continuity, unity, and logic.

7-34 "The Controversey Over Revenue Sharing." CONGRESSIONAL DIGEST 50 (April 1971): 99-128.

Presents a general explanation of the features of general and special revenue sharing with a section devoted to pro and con arguments. Proponents include Senators Howard Baker and Marlow Cook, opponents include Sen. Vance Hartke and the executive council of the AFL-CIO.

7-35 Corman, James C. "Grave Doubts About Revenue Sharing." GEORGETOWN LAW JOURNAL 60 (October 1971): 29-44.

Concedes that states and cities are in desperate economic shape, but maintains revenue sharing is not the solution. It would be inefficient, harmful, and could become an entrapment for state and local governments, says this congressman from California. Several alternatives are presented, including tax credits, the federal takeover of health and welfare programs, drawing rights, and piggyback agreements.

7-36 Danielson, Michael N., ed. METROPOLITAN POLITICS: A READER. Boston: Little, Brown and Co., 1966.

See 5-41.

7-37 Dillon, Conley H., ed. "A Symposium: Needs and Prospectus for Research on Intergovernmental Relations." PUBLIC ADMINISTRATION REVIEW 30 (1970): 264-76.

A symposium by the National Capital Area chapter of the American Society for Public Administration (ASPA) in October 1969 featuring Dr. Robert C. Wood and Wendell E. Hulcher as speakers and Dr. Harold Seidman and Dr. David Walker as panelists. ASPA made six general recommendations including a stronger role for the Advisory Commission on Intergovernmental Relations, a meaningful and continuing intergovernmental research program developed by the Executive Office of the President, and an intergovernmental research program developed by the states.

7-38 Dixon, Robert G., Jr. DEMOCRATIC REPRESENTATION: REAPPORTIONMENT IN LAW AND POLITICS. New York: Oxford University Press, 1968.

Covers U.S. Supreme Court reapportionment decisions and
their effect on political and legal aspects of democracy including substantial analysis of the Baker v. Carr decision.
The author presents ten themes which deal essentially with
the shift from a concern for malapportionment of people to
the malapportionment of interests.

7-39   Dommel, Paul R.   "Distributive Politics and Urban Policy."   POLICY
STUDIES JOURNAL 3 (Summer 1975):   370-75.

Examines the possibility for reducing the controls and the complexities of federal aid through revenue sharing and block
grant proposals.   Two alternatives to the present scheme of
allocation are: (1) give priority to governments with the
most severe problems and no money to less needy governments,
or (2) establish distribution formulae scaled to needs, but with
eligibility standards to assure funds to a wide range of recip-
ients.   The latter alternative is more politically marketable.

7-40   _____.   THE POLITICS OF REVENUE SHARING.   Bloomington: Indiana University Press, 1974.

Covers the history of revenue sharing, an overview of the
public policy process in the United States, and possible ways
of evaluating policy.

7-41   Downs, Anthony.   "The Successes and Failures of Federal Housing Policy."   PUBLIC INTEREST, no. 34 (Winter 1974):   124-45.

An evaluation of federal housing programs of the 1960s and
early 1970s.   The author concludes that no accurate or
widely accepted model has been developed which explains
how housing markets and urban development actually work;
housing production is affected more by indirect financial influences than by specifically directed federal policies; and
the most serious urban housing problems involve many factors
besides physical dwelling units, such as income poverty which
makes paying for decent housing impossible.

7-42   Dreyfus, Daniel A.   "Needed: A National Land Use Policy."   CIVIL
ENGINEERING 42 (May 1972):   52-54.

A discussion of the impact of the National Environmental
Policy Act of 1970; the need for comparing public preferences
for competing values prior to decisions; and the need for national land-use policy to ensure that federal programs are compatible with state plans and the pending national legislation.
Land-use planning, as a tool for comprehensive environmental
management, can succeed only if an inventory of resources is
prepared which recognizes the unique characteristics of natural
and developed land resources.

7-43   Duchacek, Ivo D. COMPARATIVE FEDERALISM. New York: Holt,
Rinehart and Winston, 1970.

A comparative analysis of the reasons for the different patterns
of territorial distribution of political authority in the world.
The book focuses on the fluidity of the process of territorial
distribution of authority under new technology such as communications and planning. The author's central concept is that
of the territorial community or the territorial interest group
which is an aggregate of groups and individuals that share
common experiences, values, fears, and purposes, and an
awareness of the territorial dimensions of their collective interests and actions. The author views political man as a
territorial animal.

7-44   Ecker-Racz, Laslo L. THE POLITICS AND ECONOMICS OF STATE-
LOCAL FINANCE. Englewood Cliffs, N.J.: Prentice-Hall, 1970.

Expresses the author's concern for the fiscal difficulties of
state and local governments and reviews their taxing powers.
The author argues for a restructuring of the methods of taxation. He recognizes the political barriers which impede
sound fiscal policies and suggests that the needs of the people
would be met more effectively if political issues were resolved.

7-45   Elazar, Daniel J. CITIES OF THE PRAIRIE: THE METROPOLITAN
FRONTIER AND AMERICAN POLITICS. Studies in Federalism series,
no. 1. New York: Basic Books, 1970.

Examines ten medium-sized metropolitan communities. The
author finds that local political systems of the "cities of the
prairie" do not exist in a vacuum, but interact with the other
governmental levels and are continually shaped by the Upper
Mississippi Valley region. The focal point of a city is a
"civil community," i.e., the totality of governmental and
political institutions within a certain geographical area.

7-46   _____. "Fragmentation, a Local Organizational Response to Federal-
City Program." URBAN AFFAIRS QUARTERLY 2 (June 1967): 30-46.

Studies local-federal programs of airport planning, public housing programs, and urban renewal in the metropolitan areas of
Illinois to evaluate the federal role in local governmental fragmentation. Elazar concludes that there is no one best way
for a city to exercise its right of political access and control
as a means of influencing the federal programs. Cities should
use their congressional representatives in Washington to lobby
for urban concerns and there is no administrative or organizational substitute for quality leadership.

7-47   _____, ed. THE POLITICS OF AMERICAN FEDERALISM. Lexington,

Mass.: D.C. Heath and Co., 1969.

A collection of essays examining federalism at the federal, state, and local levels. The politics of federalism and the impact of federal principles in fields not generally associated with federalism are highlighted. Articles discuss legal and constitutional material, administrative operations, judicial proceedings, the making of policy, the representation of interests, and political appointments. The editor concludes that the American concept of federalism is intimately tied to a frontier society philosophy of change and progress.

7-48   Farkas, Suzanne. "The Federal Role in Urban Decentralization." AMERI-CAN BEHAVIORAL SCIENTIST 15 (September/October 1971): 15-35.

Contends that urban decentralization is more appropriately viewed as a concept for analyses of intergovernmental problems rather than as an approach to reforming or restricting local government. Federal urban policy has generated many of the problems which urban decentralization is intended to address. Farkas concludes that the most appropriate role for the federal government in urban decentralization might be as a countervailing force and as a redistributive agent in order to provide incentives for positive change, change the balance of political power between the advantaged and the disadvantaged, and equalize the financial capacities of the subunits to ensure equitable public services.

7-49   Fox, Douglas M., ed. THE NEW URBAN POLITICS. Pacific Palisades, Calif.: Goodyear, 1972.

A study of the relationships between the federal government and the cities. The author states unequivocally that policy will be the single most significant factor contributing to urban change in the United States. A commitment of national resources must be made if urban problems are to be met and solved, and the role of the federal government being crucial.

7-50   Frieden, Bernard J. METROPOLITAN AMERICA: CHALLENGE TO FEDERALISM, A STUDY. Committee Print, 89th Cong., 2d sess. Washington, D.C.: Government Printing Office, 1966.

Based on reports of the Advisory Commission on Intergovernmental Relations (ACIR). The author examines a wide range of metropolitan area problems, including metropolitan needs, government performance, the people and governments in metropolitan areas, the provision of urban services, metropolitan reorganization, and intergovernmental responsibilities. Several ACIR recommendations for structural change in metropolitan areas are summarized, including strengthening state-local relations in metropolitan areas, providing more federal aid to metropolitan areas, and improving the delivery of services in

metropolitan areas by using combined resources from all three
levels of government.

7-50a Frieden, Bernard J., and Kaplan, Marshall. THE POLITICS OF NE-
GLECT: URBAN AID FROM MODEL CITIES TO REVENUE SHARING.
Cambridge: M.I.T. Press, 1975.

A review of the Model Cities program from its origin to its
implementation and evaluation of two subsequent federal efforts, general and special revenue sharing. Frieden and Kaplan are both deeply involved in the implementation of federal
urban programs. They draw conclusions from Model Cities'
failures and the shortfall between aspirations and realization,
which can be applied to the future design of programs for urban aid.

7-51 Gallagher, John F., and Bay, John P. A STATE ROLE IN LAND USE
MANAGEMENT. Columbus, Ohio: Legislative Service Commission,
1974.

Focuses on government land-use management activities in Ohio
and other states. Topics include an overview of land use programs, local government land-use management in Ohio, zoning
procedures, and local land-use controls. The authors suggest
several methods of reform, including capital improvements,
planning and budgeting, public land trusts, land acquisition,
and tax and fiscal policy.

7-52 Glendening, Parris N., and Reeves, Mavis Mann. CONTROVERSIES
OF STATE AND LOCAL POLITICAL SYSTEMS. Boston: Allyn and
Bacon, 1972.

Presents opposing views of major issues facing state and local
governments. Topics discussed include conflict and cooperation in the American system of intergovernmental relations,
revenue sharing, the Supreme Court's reapportionment decision,
metropolitan government, and urban violence.

7-52a _____. PRAGMATIC FEDERALISM. Pacific Palisades, Calif.: Palisades Publishers, 1977.

An up-to-date analysis of the interrelationships of federal,
state, and local governments. Numerous insights into the
politics of intergovernmental relations and the impact on governmental decisions at the local level.

7-53 Goetz, Charles J. WHAT IS REVENUE SHARING? Washington, D.C.:
Urban Institute, 1972.

Examines the nature of revenue sharing and discusses important
implications of its legislation. The legislative history of reve-

nue sharing, which provides the framework for Goetz's discussion, illuminates many ambiguities that have not been resolved. He concludes that one of the most nagging questions about revenue sharing is the political effects it will have in urban governmental circles.

7-54 Goldman, Lawrence. "Federal Policy and the UDC." PLANNER 61 (May 1975): 176-79.

An article by the special assistant to the president of the Urban Development Corporation (UDC) highlighting the accomplishments of the New York Urban Development Corporation and contrasting them with the federal policy towards housing. The author provides a chronology of events concerning the birth and development of UDC and argues that because programs designed to provide housing for low-income families are dependent upon federal subsidies, the federal government, both Congress and the president, must work to provide more funds for low-income housing.

7-55 Grant, Daniel B. "Urban Needs and State Responses." In THE STATES AND THE URBAN CRISES, edited by Alan K. Campbell, pp. 59-84. Englewood Cliffs, N.J.: Prentice-Hall, 1970.

Examines state responses to city problems and proposes various alternatives for restructuring urban governments. The author claims that, although the political prospects for rational restructuring in metropolitan areas is not good, no area is so hopelessly fragmented that it cannot be reorganized to create greater interdependence. He argues that state governmental leaders must assume the task of reorganization.

7-55a Greene, Lee S.; Grant, Daniel R.; and Jewell, Malcolm E. THE STATES AND THE METROPOLIS. University: University of Alabama Press, 1968.

Contains five chapters on the condition of the states, the changing political environment of state government, the changing face of state legislatures, the decline of states' rights and the rise of state administration, and state governments and metropolitan areas.

7-55b Haar, Charles M. BETWEEN THE IDEA AND THE REALITY. A STUDY OF THE ORIGIN, FATE, AND LEGACY OF THE MODEL CITIES PROGRAM. Boston: Little, Brown and Co., 1975.

Explanation of what was right and wrong with the Model Cities program during the mid- and late-1960s by an insider in the Johnson administration. This rare evaluation of recent history by a participant-observer concludes with a proposal for a future national goals survey.

7-56   Hagman, Donald G.   "National Environmental Policy Act's Progeny Inhabit the States--Were the Genes Defective?"   URBAN LAW ANNUAL 7 (1974): 3-56.

Espouses the state provisions influenced by the National Environmental Policy Act of 1969 (NEPA), particularly California's Environmental Quality Act of 1970 (CEQA). CEQA was the first NEPA-like act to be adopted by a state, and has had more impact and been involved in more controversy than any other state act. The article describes the history of CEQA and then looks at the principal statutes and other documents that have brought provisions similar to NEPA to other states.

7-57   Haider, Donald.   "The Political Economy of Decentralization."   AMERICAN BEHAVIORAL SCIENTIST 15 (September/October 1971): 108-29.

See 1-34.

7-58   Hartke, Vance.   "Toward a National Growth Policy."   CATHOLIC UNIVERSITY OF AMERICA LAW REVIEW 22 (Winter 1973): 231-78.

Discusses why the necessity for a comprehensive national growth policy has arisen and the shape that policy should take in guiding this nation's future. Congressional legislative endeavors have failed as a result of their narrow scope, according to Hartke. He concludes that any truly constructive legislative effort must call for the development of a national growth policy at the highest level of government. Such a policy must be implemented by the Executive Office of the President.

7-59   Hartman, Chester W.   HOUSING AND SOCIAL POLICY.   Englewood Cliffs, N.J.: Prentice-Hall, 1975.

Proposes that economic and political interests that shape the housing system are fundamental social policy issues. The author delineates the nature and dimensions of the housing problem, the barriers to increased and lower-priced housing production, the difficulties in maintaining decent occupancy conditions in the existing housing stock, and the successes and failures of government intervention in the housing market over the past few years. The overriding issue raised in the book is whether the right to decent housing is compatible with the profit system.

7-60   Heller, Walter [W.], ed.   PERSPECTIVES ON ECONOMIC GROWTH.   New York: Random House, 1968

A collection of essays dealing with policies encouraging economic growth in the United States. Several prominent economists present their views on the effect that economic growth has had and will have on U.S. foreign policy, the use of direct federal programs, new initiatives for expanding the traditional role of state and local governments, and tax changes designed to stimulate the private sector.

7-61   Heller, Walter W., et al. REVENUE SHARING AND THE CITY. Baltimore: Johns Hopkins Press, 1968.

Discusses revenue sharing as it effects: (1) the future demand for urban public services; (2) the costs of supplying such services; (3) the ability of cities to raise needed revenues; (4) the appropriate division of functions among the various levels of government; (5) the capacity of the states to help their urban communities and the future of state governments in general; and (6) the relative advantages and disadvantages of federal block grants as compared to categorical grants. This book was the outgrowth of a conference sponsored by Resources for the Future.

7-62   Hentoff, Nat. A POLITICAL LIFE: THE EDUCATION OF JOHN V. LINDSAY. New York: Alfred A. Knopf, 1969.

See 1-36.

7-63   Hill, Richard C. "Separate and Unequal: Governmental Inequality in the Metropolis." AMERICAN POLITICAL SCIENCE REVIEW 68 (December 1974): 1557-68.

See 4-77.

7-64   James, Judson L. "Federalism and the Model Cities Experiment." PUBLIUS 2 (Spring 1972): 69-94.

Reviews and evaluates the Model Cities program which, according to the author, was one of the most substantial deliberate attempts ever undertaken by the federal government to strengthen the pattern of intergovernmental relations. The concept of Model Cities is discussed; an analysis of its major controversies reviewed; and the New Federalism concept proposed by President Nixon examined. Despite its problems, the Model Cities experiment was valuable and useful as a way to reduce governmental fragmentation and ease communication problems between administrators and citizens.

7-65   Jennings, M. Kent, and Zeigler, Harmon. "The Salience of American State Politics." AMERICAN POLITICAL SCIENCE REVIEW 64 (1970): 523-35.

Uses the concept of salience maps to explore the relationship of the citizenry to their state governments. The authors conclude that the states loom large in the perspectives of the American public and that attachments to the states as political entities are real.

7-66   Jones, Charles O. CLEAN AIR: THE POLICIES AND POLITICS OF POLLUTION CONTROL. Pittsburgh: University of Pittsburgh Press, 1975.

   See 5-91.

7-67   Jones, Leroy. "New Dimensions in State/Local Relations." PUBLIC MANAGEMENT 52 (August 1970): 16-19.

   Discusses the need for interlocal cooperation among governments. Describing the state as a "federation of municipalities similar to the federal arrangement for the states," the author, the commissioner of the Connecticut Department of Community Affairs, presents the role of states as coordinators and advocates of programs designed to solve urban problems. Jones contends that states are becoming more responsible and responsive to the needs of local governments.

7-68   Keyserling, Leon H. "Revenue Sharing: Its Implications for Present and Future Intergovernmental Fiscal Systems: The Case Against." NATIONAL TAX JOURNAL 24 (September 1971): 313-21.

   Contends it is a mistake to give money to state and local governments without attaching strings, as proposed under general revenue sharing. Keyserling argues that it is reckless to continue developing new programs to solve old problems when, if coordinated and used effectively, existing programs would meet the need. He presents ten national priorities and attempts to show that general revenue sharing would not help solve the problems, and would cause an additional expense to an already overburdened national treasury.

7-69   Leach, Richard H. AMERICAN FEDERALISM. New York: W.W. Norton, 1970.

   Explains the major characteristics of the American federal system essential for a basic knowledge of our political and governmental process. The author describes federalism as a partnership between the federal, state, and local governments, stressing that intergovernmental cooperation is crucial if the federal system is to remain viable and strong. The role of the states is examined at length as part of the dynamic federal system.

7-70   Levitan, Sar A. "The Art of Giving Away Federal Dollars." In his THE FEDERAL SOCIAL DOLLAR IN ITS OWN BACK YARD, pp. 1-20. Washington, D.C.: Bureau of National Affairs, 1973.

   Examines grants-in-aid to the local Washington, D.C., government and to independent institutions and groups serving the city. The article assesses the effectiveness of grant-in-aid programs and examines the urban problems to which these programs are addressed. It raises the following questions: (1) How do federal funds help solve the particular local problems to which they are addressed? (2) Are the results measurable? (3) How do the grant-in-aid funds change the actions and allocations of the city? and (4) Do they merely replace local efforts or do they have substantial leverage to alter the direction of such efforts?

7-71 Liebert, Roland J. "The Partial Eclipse of Community Government: The Trend Toward Functional Specialization." SOCIAL SCIENCE QUARTERLY 56 (September 1975): 210-24.

Explores causes for variation in the extent of city government effacement and specialization. Three factors that shape community development are assessed: local tradition, the power of the state, and the pressure of urbanization.

7-72 Lilley, William III. "Block-Grant Reforms Promise Revolution in Federal-City Relations." NATIONAL JOURNAL 4 (May 27, 1972): 891-901.

A critique of the 1972 Housing and Urban Development Act. The author examines many of the issues which necessitated the act and assesses its potential for alleviating some urban problems. The role of cities and counties in obtaining grants is outlined. A table reveals that small- and medium-sized cities actually received more of the urban renewal money than big cities. The political influence of the cities as compared to the counties is also examined; appears that the influence of the cities was much greater than that of the counties in getting legislation passed.

7-73 Lindsay, John V. THE CITY. New York: W.W. Norton, 1970.

See 5-103.

7-74 Lineberry, Robert L. "Reforming Metropolitan Governance: Requiem on Reality?" GEORGETOWN LAW REVIEW 58 (March/May 1970): 675-717.

See 6-66.

7-74a Lineberry, Robert L., and Masotti, Louis H., eds. URBAN PROBLEMS AND PUBLIC POLICY. Lexington, Mass.: Lexington Books, 1975.

See 5-103a.

7-75 Linowes, R. Robert, and Allensworth, Don T. THE STATE AND LAND USE CONTROL. New York: Praeger Publishers, 1975.

An examination of the planning role of state governments, a

relatively new field in American government. The authors trace the history of state planning and land-use control; and state involvement in regional, metropolitan, rural, and local planning; zoning; and subdivision regulation. They also demonstrate the interrelationship and interdependency between land-use controls and various public facilities and services. Political aspects of the land-use issue are examined, particularly the impact of state institutions, such as the legislature and courts, on state and local planning and land-use policy. The authors also assess the influence of private and public interests concerned with state land-use policy. The study concludes that the states can be most helpful in developing regional and metropolitan planning and in widening the perspectives of local planning agencies.

7-76 Long, Norton E. "The Three Citizenships." PUBLIUS 6, no. 2 (1976): 13-32.

Discusses the purpose and political power of state, local, and federal governments. The power of cities and states is small compared to federal power, because we view ourselves as members of a specific nation state as opposed to members of state A or city B. Major problems confronting us are tackled by the federal government due to its economic power and political superiority.

7-77 McDowell, Bruce D. "Land Use Controls and the Federal System." In FUTURE LAND USE, edited by Robert W. Burchell and David Listokin, pp. 43-57. New Brunswick, N.J.: Rutgers University, 1975.

See 5-110.

7-78 McLure, Charles E., Jr. "Revenue Sharing: Alternative to Rational Fiscal Federation?" PUBLIC POLICY 19 (Summer 1971): 457-78.

Argues that revenue sharing is not the answer to rational fiscal federalism. McClure contends that if revenue sharing is needed at all, it is needed only as a supplement or alternative to a more rational approach to financing federalism. Revenue sharing is useful not due to its inherent strengths, but because it is less irrational than other institutions that deal with fiscal federalism. McLure concludes that we really need to follow more closely the "layer-cake" model of federalism, which would diminish or even eliminate the need for revenue sharing.

7-79 Mandelker, Daniel R., and Sherry, Thea A. "The National Coastal Zone Management Act of 1972." URBAN LAW ANNUAL 7 (1974): 19-37.

Deals with those innovative sections of the CZMA which provide expanded exercise of state-based review and regulation.

The authors trace the history of the CZMA and outline the
major elements of the state planning and land use regulation
process mandated by the act. They pay special attention to
those sections of the act which present problems of implementation to state coastal zone administrators.

7-79a Marando, Vincent L. "An Overview of the Political Feasibility of Local
Governmental Reorganization." In ORGANIZING PUBLIC SERVICES IN
METROPOLITAN AMERICA, edited by Thomas P. Murphy and Charles R.
Warren, pp. 17-52. Lexington, Mass.: Lexington Books, 1974.

An analysis of the thirty-six major reorganization efforts between 1945 and 1972. Deals with voter reaction to the referenda on the city and county mergers with a summary of the
factors that are related to reorganization support and opposition.

7-80 Marshall, D.R.; Frieden, B[ernard].; and Fessler, D.W. MINORITY PER-
SPECTIVES. Washington, D.C.: Resources for the Future, 1972.

See 4-95.

7-81 Martin, Roscoe C. THE CITIES AND THE FEDERAL SYSTEM. New
York: Atherton Press, 1965.

Describes the American federal system as flexible enough to
accommodate changes without serious difficulties. Martin's
study assesses the roles of the three levels of government and
how they seek solutions to urban problems. Since the changes
in the cities have wrought great changes in the federal system,
Martin analyzes operational aspects of the federal system. In
discussing the centralization of power at the federal level, he
notes how it could help foster a sense of national urgency
with respect to crucial problems which deserve nationwide recognition and resources.

7-81a Mogulof, Melvin B. GOVERNING METROPOLITAN AREAS. Washington, D.C.: Urban Institute, 1971.

See 6-72a.

7-82 Moynihan, Daniel Patrick. MAXIMUM FEASIBLE MISUNDERSTANDING.
New York: Free Press, 1969.

Examines the origin, nature, and internal contradictions of the
social change programs put forth under the "Great Society,"
focusing primarily upon community action in the "war on poverty." As the title suggests, there were misunderstandings
with respect to the "maximum feasible participation" of residents in the community action programs, primarily because the
phrase referred to at least three distinct activities: organizing
the power structure, expanding the power structure, and as-

sisting the power structure. The author concludes that the
program failed primarily because the government did not know
what it was doing.

7-83 _____, ed. TOWARD A NATIONAL URBAN POLICY. New York:
Basic Books, 1970.

Presents the views of various social scientists who are concerned with formulating a deliberate and planned national
urban policy. Twenty-five essays are included, covering a
range of topics, such as intergovernmental relations in an urbanizing America and urban design. The book provides a
broad background to the issues discussed in the field of urban
studies and argues for a systematic policy to deal with urban
problems.

7-83a Murphy, Thomas P. "Intergovernmental Management of Urban Problems
in the Kansas City Metropolitan Area." In EMERGING PATTERNS IN
URBAN ADMINISTRATION, edited by F. Gerald Brown and Thomas P.
Murphy, pp. 248-76. Lexington, Mass.: Lexington Books, 1970.

See 6-18a.

7-83b _____. "Intergovernmental Relations Revolution." In his METROPOLI-
TICS AND THE URBAN COUNTY, pp. 206-53. Washington, D.C.:
Washington National Press, 1970.

An analysis of the impact of federal planning programs on
metropolitan Kansas City during the 1960s.

7-84 _____. "Urban Governmental Manpower." In his UNIVERSITIES IN
THE URBAN CRISIS, pp. 49-70. New York: Dunellen Publishing Co.,
1975.

See 5-123.

7-84a _____. "Urbanization, Suburbanization, and the New Politics." In
his THE NEW POLITICS CONGRESS, pp. 209-24. Lexington, Mass.:
Lexington Books, 1974.

See 6-74d.

7-84b Murphy, Thomas P., and Rehfuss, John. URBAN POLITICS IN THE
SUBURBAN ERA. Homewood, Ill.: Dorsey Press, 1976.

An intensive analysis of suburban government and politics including heavy attention to intergovernmental relations (chapters
8-11) and national urban policy (chapter 12).

7-84c Muskie, Edmund S. "Urban Administration and Creative Federalism."

In EMERGING PATTERNS IN URBAN ADMINISTRATION, edited by
F. Gerald Brown and Thomas P. Murphy, pp. 83-99. Lexington, Mass.:
Lexington Books, 1970.

See 6-18a.

7-85   Nathan, Richard P.   "Federalism and the Shifting Nature of Fiscal Relations." ANNALS OF THE AMERICAN ACADEMY OF POLITICAL AND
SOCIAL SCIENCE 419 (May 1975): 120-29.

Maintains that general revenue sharing is the most important
legislative enactment of New Federalism and that there is a
need to study closely its fiscal and structural effects. Nathan
describes a study by the Brookings Institution, under his direction, to examine three kinds of effects of revenue sharing on
recipient state and local governments: (1) distributional--how
was the money allocated? (2) fiscal--what have been its real
or net effects? and (3) political--what have been the effects
of revenue sharing on the processes and structure of state and
local governments? The author believes that such data will
enable us to accurately assess revenue sharing.

7-86   Orfield, Gary.   "Federal Policy, Local Power, and Metropolitan Segregation." POLITICAL SCIENCE QUARTERLY 89 (Winter 1974-75): 777-
802.

See 6-77.

7-87   Ostrom, Vincent, ed.   "The Study of Federalism at Work."   PUBLIUS 4
(Fall 1974): entire issue.

A journal containing six essays that examine aspects of the
American federal system. The first essay analyzes different
approaches to improving its operation. The second discusses
citizen evaluations of performances of leaders in Nashville--
Davidson County, Tennessee. Interjurisdictional cooperation
among police departments in the St. Louis metropolitan area is
the subject of the third essay and the question of policy analysis in federal systems is examined in the fourth article. The
fifth essay analyzes structural variations in interorganizational
arrangements, and the last chapter contains an analysis of
federalism in Canada.

7-88   Pierce, Neal R.   "State-Local Report/Fiscal Crises Illustrate Growing
Interdependence." NATIONAL JOURNAL 7 (February 22, 1975): 280-
92.

Argues that all levels of government must work in a coordinated
partnership to solve the fiscal problems of the nation. Pierce
examines the history of governmental expenditures from 1946-
74 to demonstrate how governments got where they are. Sev-

eral authorities are cited concerning their solutions to fiscal difficulties, and congressional legislation is reviewed.

7-89   Pressman, Jeffrey L. "Federal Programs and Political Development in Cities." In IMPROVING THE QUALITY OF URBAN MANAGEMENT, edited by Willis D. Hawley and David Rogers, pp. 583-605. Beverly Hills, Calif.: Sage Publications, 1974.

Examines the problems federal programs confront due to weak local leadership and the lack of arenas in which federal and local actors can bargain effectively. More money, increased administrative efficiency, and higher levels of participation may not make local governments or intergovernmental systems stronger or more open. Federal policy ought to be formulated with the specific intention of increasing the capacity and responsiveness of political institutions themselves. By building a framework for commitment to continuing joint action, the federal and local levels will benefit.

7-90   PROPOSED ALTERNATIVES TO TAX EXEMPT STATE AND LOCAL BONDS. Washington, D.C.: American Enterprise Institute for Public Policy Research, 1973.

See 5-128.

7-91   Qundry, Kenneth E., and Soule, Don M. "Revenue Sharing Between State and Local Governments." GROWTH AND CHANGE 1 (July 1970): 8-13.

Develops a state-to-local revenue sharing formula in which state aid is more closely related to local fiscal disparities with respect to the provision of general government services. The authors determined that a system of state-to-local revenue sharing based on the geographic origin of state tax revenue tends to accentuate the disparaties among local governments' ability to finance needed services. Federal-to-state revenue sharing would be a good supplement to state tax revenue as a source of transfer funds.

7-92   Reuss, Henry S. REVENUE-SHARING: CRUTCH OR CATALYST FOR STATE AND LOCAL GOVERNMENTS. New York: Praeger Publishers, 1970.

A call for a merger of revenue sharing and state-local government modernization by Congressman Reuss, a proponent of general revenue sharing. He examines proposals for general revenue sharing, which he thinks should be used as a catalyst for state and local governmental reform. (See also 7-93.)

7-93   _____. "Should We Abandon Revenue Sharing?" ANNALS OF THE

AMERICAN ACADEMY OF POLITICAL AND SOCIAL SCIENCE 419 (May 1975): 88-99.

Examines several questions concerning general revenue sharing: (1) Can revenue sharing really help to equalize fiscal capacities among rich and poor governments? (2) Can it give local governments greater flexibility in spending, yet guarantee that the needs of poor and minority groups will be met? (3) Can it be used to spur the reform of state and local government? (4) Can and should it induce states to rely on more progressive local tax systems? (5) Is revenue sharing the best way to achieve any or all of these goals? The author also examines the origin of revenue sharing, revenue sharing in use, and the future of the program. (See also 7-92.)

7-94 REVENUE SHARING AND ITS ALTERNATIVES: WHAT FUTURE FOR FISCAL FEDERALISM? 3 vols. Washington, D.C.: Government Printing Office, 1967.

A collection of articles and papers concerning the potential effect of revenue sharing on the three levels of the American federal system. It provides a comprehensive examination of revenue sharing, its alternatives, and fiscal federalism. The first volume, "Lessons of Experience," examines philosophical arguments in the FEDERALIST PAPERS as a background to the present day discussion of revenue sharing. The "Range of Alternatives for Fiscal Federalism" is discussed in volume 2. It focuses on various methods for sharing federally collected revenues with individuals, states and local governments. Volume 3 is a collection of revenue and expenditure projections at the federal, state, and local levels.

7-95 Ripley, Randall B. "Political Patterns in Federal Development Programs." In PEOPLE AND POLITICS IN URBAN SOCIETY, edited by Harlan Hahn, pp. 531-55. Beverly Hills, Calif.: Sage Publications, 1972.

Examines the federal government's efforts to promote economic and human resource development in the last few years, primarily in four specific programs: Model Cities, the Job Corps, the Appalachia program, and the programs of the Economic Development Administration. The author concludes by presenting a framework for future policy research.

7-95a Rissman, Frank, and Gartner, Allan. "Community Control and Radical Social Change." SOCIAL POLICY 1 (May-June 1970): 52-55.

See 3-80.

7-96 Robson, William A., and Regan, D.E., eds. GREAT CITIES OF THE WORLD. Vols. 1 and 2, 3d ed. London: George Allen and Unwin, Beverly Hills, Calif.: Sage Publications, 1972.

See 1-59.

7-97 Rondinelli, Dennis A. "Revenue Sharing and American Cities: Analysis of the Federal Experiment in Local Assistance." JOURNAL OF THE AMERICAN INSTITUTE OF PLANNERS 41 (September 1975): 319-33.

Argues that revenue sharing operates most effectively as a federal income supplement to local taxing powers and as a redistributive device for assisting central cities and smaller towns to expand limited revenue bases. The author believes that political limitations on increasing local taxes makes federal tax collection and revenue redistribution a more tolerable means of expanding local government income, avoiding complex administrative constraints and requirements. He concludes that general revenue sharing should be redesigned as an unrestricted grant of federal funds to state and local governments.

7-98 Rose, Douglas D. "National and Local Forces in State Politics: The Implications of Multi-level Policy Analysis." AMERICAN POLITICAL SCIENCE REVIEW 67 (December 1973): 1162-73.

Argues that studies of state politics which ignore other levels are severely limited in their usefulness for both methodological and substantive reasons. It is necessary to examine the external relations of states, particularly those with the federal government, if one is to understand state politics.

7-99 Rose, Harold [M.]. "The All Black Town: Suburban Prototype or Rural Slum." In PEOPLE AND POLITICS IN URBAN SOCIETY, edited by Harlan Hahn, pp. 397-431. Beverly Hills, Calif.: Sage Publications, 1972.

See 4-109.

7-100 Sanford, Terry. STORM OVER THE STATES. New York: McGraw-Hill Book Co., 1967.

Personal views of state government by the former governor of North Carolina. Based on having research for a study of American states, Sanford contends that the citizens of the United States must mobilize their resources to upgrade the quality of state governments. He makes ten recommendations for the reform of state government, which he believes would make the states stronger, thereby strengthening the federal system.

7-101 Sharkansky, Ira. REGIONALISM IN AMERICAN POLITICS. New York: Bobbs-Merrill, 1970.

Examines regional peculiarities in politics and public policies. Questions addressed are: (1) How do the state politics and public policies of each region differ? (2) How consistent are the patterns within each region? (3) To what extent do re-

gional traits in politics and policies merely reflect the regional
distribution of economic resources among the states? (4) For
those regional differences in politics and policies that cannot
be traced in current economic characteristics, what other experiences shared by neighboring states provide an explanation?

7-102 Sheldon, Nancy W., and Brandwein, Robert. THE ECONOMIC AND
SOCIAL IMPACT OF INVESTMENTS IN PUBLIC TRANSIT. Lexington,
Mass.: D.C. Heath and Co., 1973.

Provides data and guidelines on public transit, in order to assist governmental decision makers who must design policies for
allocating capital investments for urban transportation. The
study assesses the use of portions of federal highway excise
taxes to support capital investments in bus, rapid rail, and
commuter transit systems.

7-103 Shinn, C. "The Federal Grant Programs to Aid Construction of Municipal Sewage Treatment Plants: A Survey of the 1972 Amendments." TU-
LANE LAW REVIEW 48 (December 1973): 85-104.

Contends that the grant program has not been a successful
method of attacking the national water pollution problem. It
has suffered from inefficient allocation systems, insufficient ap-
propriations, and political opposition because of the indirect
subsidy to industries. Support is growing for adoption of a
federal system of river basin authorities empowered to construct,
operate, and maintain exclusive treatment facilities and to establish and enforce pollution abatement standards and programs.
But this program would conflict with the contemporary political
attitude of decentralizing governmental authority and returning
as much responsibility and control to the local governmental
units as possible.

7-104 Sklar, Morton H. "The Impact of Revenue Sharing on Minorities and the
Poor." HARVARD CIVIL RIGHTS--CIVIL LIBERTIES LAW REVIEW 10
(Winter 1975): 93-136.

Contends that since the first revenue sharing program became
law, there have been indications that this new approach to allocating federal aid has had an adverse impact on minorities
and the poor. An introduction briefly describes the general
structure of revenue sharing. Section 2 indicates that the distribution funds discriminate against the poor because the basic
formula and limiting provisions do not treat poorer communities
in a manner commensurate with their needs. Section 3 analyzes mounting evidence that local governments are not providing an equitable share of a failing aggravated by the proportional reductions and impoundments of other federal grant programs serving the poor. Finally, Section 4 discusses the vic-
timization of the poor and minorities by the absence of mean-

ingful federal performance requirements and the ineffectiveness of the Office of Revenue Sharing in policing the few standards that have been imposed.

7-105 Stenberg, Carl W. "The Regionalization of Environmental Management." PUBLIC MANAGEMENT 56 (March 1974): 15-18.

See 5-151.

7-106 _____. "Revenue Sharing and Governmental Reform." ANNALS OF THE AMERICAN ACADEMY OF POLITICAL AND SOCIAL SCIENCE 419 (May 1975): 50-62.

Examines the value of general revenue sharing to governmental reform. Stenberg contends that the program has had positive impacts in citizen participation in the budgetary process, the equalization of interstate and central city-suburban fiscal disparities, and interlocal cooperation in certain projects and programs. However, general revenue sharing has failed to encourage more vigorous state revenue-raising efforts, and to target funds to local jurisdictions with the greatest needs. It has worked at cross-purposes with regional planning programs and review processes, and with organizations responsibile for their conduct.

7-107 Tax Foundation. FISCAL OUTLOOK FOR STATE AND LOCAL GOVERNMENT TO 1975. New York: 1965.

A study of the financial picture of state and local governments projected to 1975. It provides a historical background to the economic situation of states and localities, and projects levels of activity for 1970 and 1975, under a specified set of assumptions. The study is useful in determining how projections of state and local finances can be made. The emphasis in the study is on overall national levels of activity, not individual government units. The fundamental assumption behind these projections was that there would be no revolutionary changes in any of the forces which influence the general economy.

7-108 Thurow, Lester. "Aid to State and Local Governments." NATIONAL TAX JOURNAL 23 (March 1970): 23-35.

Contends that many programs which give aid to states and localities have not adequately considered the effects of aid on fiscal federalism. He argues that aid systems such as federalization or a comprehensive system of grants-in-aid must be used as guides to change the present aid programs. Further, block grants should be substituted for the present system of specific grants-in-aid. Thurow belives that tax-free state and local bonds and state and local tax deductions should be abolished, and that the revenue generated in this way should be be placed into the distribution formula for unrestricted grants. This would increase the money available to state and local governments and would increase equity.

7-109 TRANSIT STATION JOINT DEVELOPMENT. Washington, D.C.: Department of Transportation and Department of Housing and Urban Development, May 1973.

A project designed to establish a stronger basis for joint development in the design and construction of U.S. transit systems. An interdisciplinary team examined institutional, legal, financial, design, and engineering factors associated with joint development. Current planning for transit stations in the United States tends to be narrowly focused on construction of the transit system. The project team found evidence, however, and financial assistance, cities would be interested in undertaking a more comprehensive approach to transit system planning. The team found six general categories of constraints to joint development: (1) fragmentation of governmental institutions; (2) inadequate planning; (3) inadequate transportation coordination; (4) the physical environment of transit stations; (5) the loss of potential economic benefits; and (6) inadequate implementation support for station area development.

7-109a Unruh, Jesse M. "State Government and the Urban Crisis." In EMERGING PATTERNS IN URBAN ADMINISTRATION, edited by F. Gerald Brown and Thomas P. Murphy, pp. 100-11. Lexington, Mass.: Lexington Books, 1970.

See 6-18a.

7-110 Veatch, James F. "Federal and Local Urban Transportation Policy." URBAN AFFAIRS QUARTERLY 10 (June 1975): 398-422.

See 5-156.

7-111 Veneman, John G. "Revenue Sharing Seen as Essential for Cities." NATIONAL CIVIC REVIEW, January 1972, pp. 11-14.

The undersecretary of HEW points out the need for revenue sharing. He cites four characteristics of revenue sharing: (1) the elimination of matching; (2) automatic funding formulae based on need; (3) hold-harmless provisions so no community gets hurt financially; and (4) the elimination of federal approval. As a spokesman for HEW, the author believes that revenue sharing will provide great benefits to states and localities.

7-112 Walker, David Bradstreet. "Interstate Regional Instrumentalities: A New Piece in an Old Puzzle." JOURNAL OF THE AMERICAN INSTITUTE OF PLANNERS 38 (November 1972): 359-68.

Assesses the major similarities and differences among the four categories of federal multistate regional commissions established between 1961 and 1971. Underlying reasons for the growing popularity of this new intergovernmental mechanism are probed, and some across-the-board tentative findings are offered regarding the record of the economic development commissions and the river basis commissions that were established in the sixties. Differing interpretations of their collective experiences are also cited.

7-112a Walsh, Annamarie Hauck. THE URBAN CHALLENGE TO GOVERN-MENT. New York: Praeger Publishers, 1969.

See 1-73.

7-113 Watterson, Wayt T., and Watterson, Roberta S. THE POLITCS OF NEW COMMUNITIES: A CASE STUDY OF SAN ANTONIO RANCH. New York: Praeger Publishers, 1975.

See 3-97.

7-114 Welfeld, Irving H. AMERICA'S HOUSING PROBLEM: AN APPROACH TO ITS SOLUTION. Washington, D.C.: American Enterprise Institute for Public Research, October 1973.

See 5-159.

7-115 Wright, Deil S. "Intergovernmental Relation in Large Council Managers Cities." AMERICAN POLITICS QUARTERLY 1 (April 1973): 151-87.

Explains a concept of intergovernmental relations using a research setting of large council-manager cities in the United States. Wright examines configurations of intergovernmental contact by different city officials; the problematic content and evaluations of these intergovernmental relationships; and the relationship between environmental, political, structural, and behavioral characteristics and variations in intergovernmental contacts, cooperation and consequences. He concludes that: (1) the significance of state action is paramount in defining the scope and setting patterns of intergovernmental relations for large cities; (2) there is a substantial gap between the performance of both state and national governments and municipal leadership expectations; and (3) there is a prominent but conditional role for the city manager in intergovernmental relations.

7-116 _____. "Revenue Sharing and Structural Features of American Federalism." ANNALS OF THE AMERICAN ACADEMY OF POLITICAL AND SOCIAL SCIENCE 419 (May 1975): 100-119.

Examines the impact of general revenue sharing on three struc-

tural features of American federalism: (1) governmental entities; (2) institutions and actors' roles; and (3) behavioral
perspectives. Wright observes that general revenue sharing
is both a cause and an effect of the pluralistic and fragmented
patterns present in the structures of separtion of powers and
federalism. He concludes that the most abstract and unap-
preciated effect of general revenue sharing has been some
reduction in the tension, competition, and rivalry pervading
the relationships among intergovernmental actors.

7-117 _____. "The States and Intergovernmental Relations." PUBLIUS 6
Winter 1972, pp. 7-68.

Develops five main arguments: (1) the states and the federal
and local governments are interdependent; (2) finance is crucial to intergovernmental relations and categorical grants-in-
aid are the basis of federal-state relations; (3) categorical
grants have had a significant effect on the states, primarily
in political terms; (4) because the states occupy the "middle-
man" position in the federal system, they are subjected to
much crossfire, and, on the whole, the states have made numerous progressive moves; and (5) due to intergovernmental relations, the states regularly are on the receiving end of conditions produced by their own responses to intergovernmental
impacts.

7-118 Zikmund, Joseph II. "Suburbs in State and National Politics." In
THE URBANIZATION OF THE SUBURBS, edited by Louis H. Masotti
and Jeffrey K. Hadden, pp. 253-73. Beverly Hills, Calif.: Sage
Publications, 1973.

See 6-94.

Appendix A
BIBLIOGRAPHIES

Many useful bibliographies on urban politics are included in bibliographies with a wider scope. The largest number of individual detailed bibliographies on narrow subjects is available from the Council of Planning Librarians. This list is a selected list including the best of the bibliographies from the Council of Planning Librarians and many other broader scope bibliographies that are relatively rich in selections on urban politics.

Adrian, Charles R., and Press, Charles, "Suggested Readings for Specific Localities." In their GOVERNING URBAN AMERICA. 4th ed., pp. 556-71. New York: McGraw-Hill Book Co., 1972.

Ashford, Douglas E. COMPARATIVE URBAN POLITICS AND URBANIZATION. No. 428. Monticello, Ill.: CPL*, 1973. 34 p.

Bicker, William. COMPARATIVE URBAN DEVELOPMENT: AN ANNOTATED BIBLIOGRAPHY. 1965. Washington, D.C.: American Society for Public Administration.

Branch, Melville C. COMPREHENSIVE URBAN PLANNING: A SELECTED BIBLIOGRAPHY WITH RELATED MATERIALS. 1970. Beverly Hills, Calif.: Sage Publications.

Brown, Ruth E. COMMUNITY ACTION PROGRAMS, AN ANNOTATED BIBLIOGRAPHY. No. 277. Monticello, Ill.: CPL, 1972. 37 p.

Bryfogle, Charles. CITY IN PRINT. Urban Studies Bibliography. Tucson: Dawson and Co., 1974.

---

*CPL refers to Council of Planning Librarians. See separate entry.

Bibliographies

Burg, Nan C. LOCAL GOVERNMENT: FORM AND REFORM, A SELECTED BIBLIOGRAPHY. No. 640. Monticello, Ill.: CPL, 1974. 71 p.

City University of New York, Graduate School and University Center, Urban Analysis Center. SELECTED REFERENCES: DECENTRALIZATION AND NEIGHBORHOOD GOVERNMENT. New York: 1972.

Council of Planning Librarians. Exchange Bibliographies.
> Publishes a large number of diverse urban-related bibliographies--about 1,000 since 1968. This listing contains those most relevant to urban politics. P.O. Box 229, Monticello, Illinois 61856.

Davis, Lenwood G., comp. BLACKS IN THE CITIES: 1900-1974: A BIBLIOGRAPHY. 2d ed. Nos. 787-88. Monticello, Ill.: CPL, 1975. 82 p.

_____. ECOLOGY OF BLACKS IN THE INNER CITY: AN EXPLORATORY BIBLIOGRAPHY. Nos. 785-86. Monticello, Ill.: CPL, 1975. 80 p.

Dinnerstein, Leonard, and Reimers, David M. "Bibliographic Essay on Ethnics." In their ETHNIC AMERICANS, pp. 157-60. New York: Dodd, Mead & Co., 1975.

Duncombe, Herbert Sydney. "Studies of County Government in Selected States and Counties." In COUNTY GOVERNMENT IN AMERICA, pp. 270-79. Washington, D.C.: National Association of Counties Research Foundation, 1966.

Ebner, Michael H. THE NEW URBAN HISTORY: BIBLIOGRAPHY ON METHODOLOGY AND HISTORIOGRAPHY. 1973. Monticello, Ill.: CPL.

Gamberg, Herbert. THE ESCAPE FROM POWER: POLITICS IN THE AMERICAN COMMUNITY. No. 106. Monticello, Ill.: CPL, 1969. 62 p.

Heikoff, Joseph M. URBAN POLITICS: SELECTED READINGS RELATED TO PLANNING. No. 177. Monticello, Ill.: CPL, 1971. 16 p.

Hoover, Dwight W. CITIES, AN ANNOTATED GUIDE TO THE AMERICAN URBAN EXPERIENCE. New York: R.R. Bowker, 1976.

McCurdy, Howard E. "Intergovernmental and Urban Policy." In PUBLIC ADMINISTRATION: A BIBLIOGRAPHY, pp. 147-52. Washington, D.C.: College of Public Affairs, American University, 1972.

McKelvey, Blake. "American Urban History Today." AMERICAN HISTORICAL REVIEW. Vol. 57, pp. 919-29, 1952.

Masotti, Louis H., and Dennis, Deborah Ellis, comps. and eds. SUBURBS, SUBURBIA AND SUBURBANIZATION: A BIBLIOGRAPHY, SECOND EDITION. Nos. 524-25. Monticello, Ill.: CPL, 1974. 108 p.

May, Judith V. CITIZEN PARTICIPATION: A REVIEW OF THE LITERATURE. Nos. 210-11. Monticello, Ill.: CPL, 1971. 82 p.

Murphy, Thomas P. "Urban Counties and Metropolitan Areas Bibliography." In his METROPOLITICS AND THE URBAN COUNTY, pp. 268-88. Washington, D.C.: Washington National Press, 1970.

Nilsen, Kirsti, comp. BIBLIOGRAPHY OF BIBLIOGRAPHIES PREPARED BY U.S. GOVERNMENT AGENCIES OF INTEREST TO COMMUNITY PLANNERS. No. 527. Monticello, Ill.: CPL, 1974. 23 p.

Novak, Michael. "Bibliography on Ethnics." In his THE RISE OF THE UN-MELTABLE ETHNICS, pp. 307-13. New York: Macmillan Co., 1972.

Powers, Susan, and Carpenter, Kelly. LEGAL, SOCIAL AND ECONOMIC AS-PECTS OF GROWTH MANAGEMENT--ANNOTATED READINGS AND CASE LAW. No. 843. Monticello, Ill.: CPL, 1975. 32 p.

Ross, Bernard H., and Fritschler, A. Lee. URBAN AFFAIRS BIBLIOGRAPHY. 3d ed. Washington, D.C.: The American University, 1974.

Ruchelman, Leonard I. "Selected References on Mayors and Urban Politics." In his BIG CITY MAYORS, pp. 369-71. Bloomington: Indiana University Press, 1969.

Schnore, Leo F. "Bibliography." In his SOCIAL SCIENCE AND THE CITY, pp. 303-30. New York: Praeger Publishers, 1968.

Stenberg, Carl W. AMERICAN INTERGOVERNMENTAL RELATIONS: A SELECTED BIBLIOGRAPHY. No. 227. Monticello, Ill.: CPL, 1971. 37 p.

Thompson, Bryan. ETHNIC GROUPS IN URBAN AREAS: COMMUNITY FOR-MATION AND GROWTH: A SELECTED BIBLIOGRAPHY. No. 202. Monticello, Ill.: CPL, 1971. 18 p.

Universal Reference System. BIBLIOGRAPHY OF BIBLIOGRAPHIES ON POLITI-CAL SCIENCE, GOVERNMENT, AND PUBLIC POLICY. POLITICAL SCIENCE, GOVERNMENT, AND PUBLIC POLICY SERIES. Vol. 3. Princeton: Princeton Research Publishing Co., 1967. These are annual supplements published by the Plenum Publishing Corp., New York.

Wallace, Rosemary H., ed. INTERNATIONAL BIBLIOGRAPHY AND REFER-
ENCE GUIDE ON URBAN AFFAIRS. Ramsey, N.J.: Ramsey-Wallace, 1966.

Walton, Hanes. "A Bibliography on Black Politics." In his BLACK POLITICS,
pp. 225-39. Philadelphia: J.B. Lippincott Co., 1972.

White, Anthony G. BIG-CITY MAYORS SPEAK OUT: A SELECTED BIBLIOG-
RAPHY. No. 635. Monticello, Ill.: CPL, 1974. 7 p.

_____. CITY-COUNTY CONSOLIDATION: A SUPPLEMENTAL SOURCE TO
BIBLIOGRAPHY NO. 294. No. 417. Monticello, Ill.: CPL, 1973.

_____. NONPARTISAN MUNICIPAL ELECTIONS: A SELECTED BIBLIOG-
RAPHY. No. 834. Monticello, Ill.: CPL, 1975. 6 p.

_____. A SELECTED BIBLIOGRAPHY: CITY-COUNTY CONSOLIDATION IN
THE UNITED STATES. No. 294. Monticello, Ill.: CPL, 1972. 53 p.

Xerox University Microfilms. "Urban Politics and Political Processes." In UR-
BAN PROBLEMS, A CATALOG OF DISSERTATIONS, pp. 31-35. Ann Arbor,
Mich.: Xerox University Microfilms, 1974.

Appendix B
ABSTRACTS AND INDEXES

In recent years there has been a significant increase in the number of abstracts and indexes including items on urban politics. There is no one abstract or index which deals exclusively with urban politics.

AMERICAN DOCTORAL DISSERTATIONS. Ann Arbor, Mich.: Association of Research Libraries, 1955/56-- . Annual.

COMPREHENSIVE DISSERTATION INDEX (1861-1972). Ann Arbor, Mich.: Xerox University. Annual updates.

CURRENT CONTENTS. Philadelphia: Institute for Scientific Information, 1961-- . Weekly.

DISSERTATION ABSTRACTS INTERNATIONAL. Ann Arbor, Mich.: Xerox University 1938-- . Monthly.

INDEX TO CURRENT URBAN DOCUMENTS. Westport, Conn.: Greenwood Press, 1971-- . Quarterly.

> Lists the official publications of the largest cities and counties in the United States and Canada.

INTERNATIONAL POLITICAL SCIENCE ABSTRACTS. Oxford: Blackwell, 1951-- . Quarterly.

NEWSBANK. Greenwich, Conn.: 1970-- . Quarterly.

> An indexed collection of articles from U.S. urban newspapers.

PUBLIC AFFAIRS INFORMATION SERVICE. New York: Public Affairs Information Service, 1915-- . Weekly.

Abstracts and Indexes

SAGE PUBLIC ADMINISTRATION ABSTRACTS. Beverly Hills, Calif.: Sage
Publications, 1974-- . Quarterly.

SAGE URBAN STUDIES ABSTRACTS. Beverly Hills, Calif.: Sage Publications,
1973-- . Quarterly.

>   Includes references to books, articles, and government publications.

SOCIAL SCIENCES CITATION INDEX. Philadelphia: Institute for Scientific
Information, 1973-- . 3/year.

>   Provides access to material reviewed or mentioned by other sources.

SOCIAL SCIENCES INDEX. New York: Wilson, 1974-- . Quarterly.

SOCIOLOGICAL ABSTRACTS. New York: Sociological Abstracts, 1952-- .
Frequency varies (now 6/year).

URBAN AFFAIRS ABSTRACTS. Washington, D.C.: National League of Cities/
U.S. Conferences of Mayors, 1971-- . Weekly.

>   Monitors 800 periodicals, journals, and newsletters.

URBAN AFFAIRS REPORTER. Chicago: Commerce Clearing House, 1967-- .
Biweekly.

>   Loose-leaf information on federal programs affecting state and
>   local governments.

Appendix C

REFERENCE WORKS

There are numerous reference works that relate to subjects of which urban politics is a part. The selected list which appears here will provide most of the information one might seek on statistics, organizations, and major government documents.

Brian, J.L. Berry, ed. CITY CLASSIFICATION HANDBOOK: METHODS AND APPLICATIONS. New York: Wiley-Interscience, 1972.

BRADDOCK'S FEDERAL-STATE-LOCAL GOVERNMENT DIRECTORY. Washington, D.C.: Braddock Publications, 1975-- . Annual.

Dushkin Publishing Group. AMERICAN GOVERNMENT ENCYCLOPEDIA. Guilford, Conn.: 1973-- . Annual.

International City Management Association. THE MUNICIPAL YEARBOOK. Washington, D.C.: 1933-- . Annual.

National Association of Counties and the International City Management Association. THE COUNTY YEAR BOOK. Washington, D.C.: 1975-- . Annual.

National Association of Regional Councils. ANNUAL DIRECTORY. Washington, D.C.: 1971-- .

NATION'S CITIES. Washington, D.C.: National League of Cities, 1963-- . Quarterly.

> December 1976 issue has an annual directory of agencies at all levels of government that specialize in urban affairs.

Scammon, Richard M., ed. AMERICA VOTES. 4 vols. New York: Macmillan, 1956-62.

Reference Works

U.S. Advisory Commission on Intergovernmental Relations. Numerous publications. See library index for specific issues. Outstanding volumes include: IMPROVING URBAN AMERICA, 1976; SUBSTATE REGIONALISM AND THE FEDERAL SYSTEM, 5 vols., 1973-74; and STATE LEGISLATURE PROGRAMS, annual.

U.S. Department of Commerce, Bureau of Census. CONGRESSIONAL DISTRICT DATA BOOK. 1960-- . Frequency varies.

Supplements are issued after censuses and when states are redistricted between censuses.

_____. Issues periodic population, urban finance, and voting reports.

U.S. National Commission on Urban Problems. BUILDING THE AMERICAN CITY. Report to Congress and the President of the United States. Washington, D.C.: Government Printing Office, 1969.

_____. HEARINGS. 5 vols. Washington, D.C.: Government Printing Office, 1968.

U.S. National Advisory Commission on Civil Disorders. REPORT OF THE NATIONAL ADVISORY COMMISSION ON CIVIL DISORDERS. Washington, D.C.: Government Printing Office, 1968.

U.S. Senate. Committee on Government Operations. CATALOGUE OF FEDERAL AIDS IN STATE AND LOCAL GOVERNMENTS. Washington, D.C.: Government Printing Office, 1966.

URBAN DATA SERVICE REPORTS. Washington, D.C.: International City Management Association, with a different topic each month. 1969-- .

Urban Institute. UNIVERSITY URBAN RESEARCH CENTERS. Washington, D.C.: 1972-- .

URBAN RESEARCH NEWS. Beverly Hills, Calif.: Sage Publications. Biweekly.

Whittick, Arnold, editor-in-chief. ENCYCLOPEDIA OF URBAN PLANNING. New York: McGraw-Hill Book Co., 1974.

Appendix D

SELECTED URBAN POLITICS TEXTBOOKS

There are a large number of textbooks on urban politics. They tend to become outdated rather fast. The books selected here give a good range of the field and in most cases are also related to urban policy questions.

Adrian, Charles R., and Press, Charles. GOVERNING URBAN AMERICA. 4th ed. New York: McGraw-Hill Book Co., 1972.

Baker, John H. URBAN POLITICS IN AMERICA. New York: Charles Scribner's Sons, 1971.

Banfield, Edward C. THE UNHEAVENLY CITY REVISITED. Boston: Little, Brown and Co., 1974.

Banfield, Edward C., and Wilson, James Q. CITY POLITICS. Cambridge: Harvard-M.I.T. Press, 1963.

Benson, George C.S. THE POLITICS OF URBANISM. New York: Barron's, 1972.

Bollens, John C., and Schmandt, Henry J. THE METROPOLIS: ITS PEOPLE, POLITICS AND ECONOMIC LIFE. 3d ed. New York: Harper and Row, 1975.

Downs, Anthony. URBAN PROBLEMS AND PROPSECTS. Chicago: Markham Publishing Co., 1970.

Dye, Thomas R. POLITICS IN STATES AND COMMUNITIES. 3d ed. Englewood Cliffs, N.J.: Prentice-Hall, 1977.

Feagin, Joe R., ed. THE URBAN SCENE. New York: Random House, 1973.

Fox, Douglas M. THE NEW URBAN POLITICS. Pacific Palisades, Calif.: Goodyear Publishing Co., 1972.

Glendening, Parris N., and Reeves, Mavis Mann. PRAGMATIC FEDERALISM. Pacific Palisades, Calif.: Palisades Publishers, 1977.

Hadden, Jeffrey K.; Masotti, Louis H.; and Larson, Calvin J. METROPOLIS IN CRISIS. Itasca, Ill.: Peacock Publishers, 1967.

Hahn, Harlan. PEOPLE AND POLITICS IN URBAN SOCIETY. Beverly Hills, Calif.: Sage Publications, 1972.

Hawkins, Brett [W.]. POLITICS AND URBAN POLICIES. Indianopolis: Bobbs-Merrill Co., 1971.

Lineberry, Robert [L.], and Sharkansky, Ira. URBAN POLITICS AND PUBLIC POLICY. 2d ed. New York: Harper and Row, 1974.

McCandless, Carl A. URBAN GOVERNMENT AND POLITICS. New York: McGraw-Hill Book Co., 1970.

Murphy, Thomas P., and Rehfuss, John. URBAN POLITICS IN THE SUBURBAN ERA. Homewood, Ill.: Dorsey Press, 1976.

Shank, Alan. POLITICAL POWER AND THE URBAN CRISIS. 3d ed. Boston: Holbrook Press, 1976.

Walton, Hanes. BLACK POLITICS. Philadelphia: J.B. Lippincott Co., 1972.

Wirt, Frederic M.; Walter, Benjamin; Rabinovitz, Francine F.; and Hansler, Deborah R. ON THE CITY'S RIM. Lexington, Mass.: D.C. Heath and Co., 1972.

Appendix E

PERIODICALS WITH CONTENT RELEVANT
TO URBAN POLITICS

In addition to the popular news weeklies, such as NEWSWEEK, TIME, and U.S. NEWS AND WORLD REPORT, there are a number of academic or professional journals with content relevant to urban politics. The most significant are listed below and their contents are generally indexed by Public Affairs Information Service and the Social Service Index.

ADMINISTRATION AND SOCIETY. Beverly Hills, Calif.: Sage Publications, 1974-- . Quarterly. (Formerly JOURNAL OF COMPARATIVE ADMINISTRATION.)

AMERICAN COUNTY GOVERNMENT. Washington, D.C.: National Association of County Officials, 1935-- . Monthly.

AMERICAN JOURNAL OF POLITICAL SCIENCE. Detroit: Wayne State University Press, 1973-- . Quarterly.

AMERICAN POLITICAL SCIENCE REVIEW. Menasha, Wis.: George Banta Co., 1906-- . Quarterly.

AMERICAN POLITICS QUARTERLY. Beverly Hills, Calif.: Sage Publications, 1973-- . Quarterly.

AMERICAN SOCIOLOGICAL REVIEW. Menasha, Wis.: American Sociological Society, 1936-- . Bimonthly.

ANNALS. Philadelphia: American Academy of Political and Social Science, 1890-- . Annual.

THE BLACK SCHOLAR. San Francisco, Calif.: Black World Foundation, 1969-- . Monthly, except July and August.

Periodicals Relevant to Urban Politics

BUREAUCRAT. Beverly Hills, Calif.: Sage Publications, 1972-- . Quarterly.

CITY. Washington, D.C.: Urban America, 1967-- . Annual.

COMPARATIVE URBAN RESEARCH. New York: City University of New York, Comparative Urban Studies Center, 1972-- . 2/year.

CONGRESSIONAL QUARTERLY WEEKLY REPORT. Washington, D.C.: Congressional Quarterly.

EDUCATION AND URBAN SOCIETY. Beverly Hills, Calif.: Sage Publications, 1968-- . Quarterly.

ENVIRONMENT AND PLANNING. London: Pion, 1969-- . Quarterly.

JOURNAL OF BLACK STUDIES. Beverly Hills, Calif.: Sage Publications, 1970-- . Quarterly.

JOURNAL OF POLITICS. Gainesville, Fla.: Southern Political Association, 1939-- . Quarterly.

JOURNAL OF REGIONAL SCIENCE. Philadelphia: Regional Science Research Institute, 1958-- . Biannual.

JOURNAL OF THE AMERICAN INSTITUTE OF PLANNERS. Cambridge, Mass.: American Institute of Planners, 1935-- . Quarterly.

JOURNAL OF URBAN ECONOMICS. New York: Academic Press, 1974-- . Quarterly.

LAW AND SOCIETY REVIEW. Denver, Colo.: Law and Society Association, 1966-- . Quarterly.

NATIONAL CIVIC REVIEW. Worcester, Mass.: National Municipal League, 1912-- . Frequency varies.

NATIONAL JOURNAL. Washington, D.C.: Center for Political Research, 1969-- . Weekly.

NATION'S CITIES. Washington, D.C.: National League of Cities, 1963-- . Quarterly.

THE PLANNER. London: Royal Town Planning Institute, 1973-- . 10/year.

POLICY AND POLITICS. London: Sage Publications, 1972-- . Quarterly.

POLICY SCIENCES. New York: American Elsevier, 1970-- . Quarterly.

POLICY STUDIES JOURNAL. Urbana: University of Illinois, 1972-- . Quarterly.

POLITICAL SCIENCE QUARTERLY. New York: Academy of Political Science, Columbia University, 1886-- .

POLITY. Amherst: University of Massachusetts, 1968-- . Quarterly.

PUBLIC ADMINISTRATION REVIEW. Washington, D.C.: American Society for Public Administration, 1940-- . Bimonthly.

PUBLIC AFFAIRS REPORT. Berkeley: Institute of Governmental Studies, University of California, 1960-- . Monthly.

PUBLIC FINANCE QUARTERLY. Beverly Hills, Calif.: Sage Publications, 1973-- .

THE PUBLIC INTEREST. New York: National Affairs, 1965-- . Quarterly.

PUBLIC MANAGEMENT. Chicago: International City Management Association, 1919-- . Monthly.

PUBLIUS. Philadelphia: Center for the Study of Federalism, Temple University, 1971-- . Frequency varies.

REVIEW OF BLACK POLITICAL ECONOMY. New York: Black Economic Research Center, 1970-- . Quarterly.

SOCIAL SCIENCE QUARTERLY. Austin: Southwestern Social Science Quarterly, University of Texas. 1919-- .

SOCIETY. Philadelphia: Transaction, 1972-- . Monthly.

URBAN AFFAIRS QUARTERLY. Beverly Hills, Calif.: Sage Publications, 1965-- .

URBAN LAWYER. Chicago: American Bar Association, 1969-- . Quarterly.

WESTERN POLITICAL QUARTERLY. Salt Lake City: Institute of Government, University of Utah, 1948-- .

Appendix F
URBAN PUBLIC INTEREST AND PROFESSIONAL ASSOCIATIONS

American Institute of Planners
1776 Massachusetts Avenue, N.W.
Washington, D.C. 20036

American Public Health Association
1015 18th Street, N.W.
7th Floor
Washington, D.C. 20036

American Public Welfare Association
1155 16th Street, N.W.
Suite 201
Washington, D.C. 20036

American Public Works Association
1313 East 60th Street
Chicago, Ill. 60637

    Washington Office
    1176 Massachusetts Avenue, N.W.
    Washington, D.C. 20036

American Society for Public
  Administration
1225 Connecticut Avenue, N.W.
Room 300
Washington, D.C. 20036

American Society of Planning
  Officials
1313 East 60th Street
Chicago, Ill. 60637

Council for International Urban Liaison
1612 K Street, N.W.
Room 904
Washington, D.C. 20036

Council of State Community Affairs
  Agencies
1612 K Street, N.W., Room 906
Washington, D.C. 20006

Council of State Governments
Iron Works Pike, P.O. Box 11910
Lexington, Ky. 40511

    Washington Office
    444 North Capitol Street
    2nd Floor
    Washington, D.C. 20001

International Association of Chiefs
  of Police
11 Firstfield Road
Gaithersburg, Md. 20760

International Association of Fire
  Chiefs
1329 18th Street, N.W.
Washington, D.C. 20036

International City Management
  Association
1140 Connecticut Avenue
Washington, D.C. 20036

International Personnel Management
  Association
1313 East 60th Street
Chicago, Ill. 60637

    Washington Office
    1776 Massachusetts Avenue,
    N.W.
    Washington, D.C. 20036

Associations

Labor-Management Relations Service
of Conference of Mayors
1620 Eye Street, N.W.
Room 616
Washington, D.C. 20036

Municipal Finance Officers Association
1313 East 60th Street
Chicago, Ill. 60637

> Washington Office
> 1730 Rhode Island Avenue,
> N.W.
> Suite 512
> Washington, D.C. 20036

National Academy of Public Administration
1225 Connecticut Avenue, Room 300
Washington, D.C. 20036

National Association of Counties
1735 New York Avenue, N.W.
Washington, D.C. 20036

National Association of Housing and
Redevelopment Officials
2600 Virginia Avenue, N.W.
Room 404
Washington, D.C. 20037

National Association of Regional
Councils
1700 K Street, N.W., Room 1306
Washington, D.C. 20036

National Conference of State Legislatures
1405 Curtis Street
Denver, Colo. 80202

> Washington Office
> 444 North Capitol Street,
> N.W.
> Washington, D.C. 20001

National Governors' Conference
1150 17th Street, N.W.
Washington, D.C. 20036

National Institute of Municipal
Law Officers
839 17th Street, N.W.
Washington, D.C. 20006

National League of Cities
1620 Eye Street, N.W., 4th Floor
Washington, D.C. 20006

National Municipal League
47 East 68th Street
New York, N.Y. 10021

National Recreation and Park Association
1601 North Kent Street
Arlington, Va. 22209

National School Boards Association
1055 Thomas Jefferson Street
Washington, D.C. 20007

National Training and Development
Service for State and Local
Government
5028 Wisconsin Avenue, N.W.
Washington, D.C. 20016

Public Administration Service
1313 East 60th Street
Chicago, ill. 60637

> Washington Office
> 1776 Massachusetts Avenue,
> N.W.
> Washington, D.C. 20036

Public Technology, Inc.
1140 Connecticut Avenue
Washington, D.C. 20036

United States Conference of Mayors
1620 Eye Street, N.W.
Washington, D.C. 20006

AUTHOR INDEX

This index is alphabetized letter by letter and references are to entry numbers. It includes authors, editors, translators, compilers, and contributors.

Author Index

Beyle, T.L. 5-17a
Biddle, William W. 2-4
Bingham, David A. 6-9
Bingham, Richard D. 7-15
Bingham, W. Harold 5-18
Birch, David L. 6-10, 5-19
Bish, Robert L. 6-10a, 6-11
Black, Guy 1-9
Blair, John P. 5-20
Blumestein, James F. 5-139
Bockman, Sheldon 3-9
Boggs, James 4-13
Bolan, Richard S. 5-21
Bollens, John C. 6-12, 6-13,
    6-14, 1-10
Bonjean, Charles M. 3-18
Booher, David E. 4-14
Booth, David A. 6-15, 1-12
Bosselman, Fred P. 5-10, 5-22,
    5-23
Bostick, C. Dent 5-18
Bowman, Lewis 5-11
Boyd, William L. 4-15, 5-24
Boyer, Brian D. 7-10
Boynton, Robert Paul 1-13
Bramhall, Billie 5-26
Brandwein, Robert 7-102
Branfman, Eric 5-27
Break, George F. 7-17
Bresnick, David 1-14
Bridgeland, William 7-18
Brilliant, Eleanor L. 7-19
Bromage, Arthur W. 1-15, 6-17
Browder, Glen 6-18
Brown, Andrew T. 2-6
Brown, F. Gerald 1-9, 1-16, 1-18,
    3-45a, 5-99a, 5-162a, 6-11a,
    6-18a, 6-50a, 6-72a, 6-74a,
    6-80a, 7-83a, 7-84, 7-109a
Browne, Edmond, Jr. 7-21
Browne, Robert S. 4-16
Browne, William P. 3-14
Bryant, Coralie 7-22
Burchell, Robert W. 4-119, 5-30,
    5-110, 5-142, 7-77
Byrnes, John W. 7-23

C

Caile, Charlene 6-19

Calaldo, E.C. 4-17
Caldwell, Lynton C. 5-31
California State Advisory Committee
    to the United States Commission on
    Civil Rights 4-18
Callies, David 5-23
Campbell, Alan K. 6-20, 7-24, 7-55
Cantor, Arnold 5-32
Caplovitz, David 4-19
Caputo, David A. 6-22, 7-26, 7-26a,
    7-32, 5-33
Caraley, Demetrios 7-27
Carmichael, Stokely 4-20
Caro, Robert A. 2-7
Carrol, Michael A. 7-28
Carver, Joan 6-21
Catanese, Anthony James 5-33a
Chamberlayne, Prue 4-21
Chapin, F. Stuart, Jr. 4-22, 4-23
Chinoy, Ely 6-44
Chisholm, Shirley 4-24
Cho, Yong .Hyo 4-25
Christmas, Walter 4-26
Christopher, Maurine 4-27
Clark, Dennis 4-28, 4-29
Clark, Kenneth B. 4-30
Clark, Terry N. 3-15, 3-16, 3-17,
    3-18, 3-60, 5-33b
Clark, Timothy B. 7-29
Clubb, Jerome M. 3-19
Cohen, David K. 7-30, 4-31
Cohen, Fay G. 4-32
Cohn, Benjamin 5-27
Cole, Richard L. 1-17, 6-22, 7-26a,
    7-31, 7-32
Colman, William G. 5-33c
Conant, Ralph W. 5-34
Connolly, Harold X. 6-23
Conot, Robert 7-33
Corman, James C. 7-35
Costello, Timothy 1-18
Costikyan, Edward N. 6-24, 6-25
Costonis, John J. 5-35, 5-36
Cottingham, Phoebe H. 4-34
Council on the Environment of New
    York City 5-37
Cow, Peter 5-38
Cox, Kevin R. 5-39
Crain, Robert L. 3-21
Crecine, John P. 4-1

Author Index

Author Index

Author Index

TITLE INDEX

This index is alphabetized letter by letter and references are to entry numbers. Included are books and titles of articles cited in the text. Titles of articles have been placed within quotation marks.

A

"Administrative Decentralization and Political Power" 2-24b

"Aid to State and Local Government" 7-108

All Black Town: Suburban Prototype or Rural Slum, The 4-109

Alternative Approaches to Governmental Reorganization in Metropolitan Areas 6-1

"Alternatives to Zoning; Covenants, Nuisance Rules, and Fines as Land Use Controls" 5-57

American Assembly, The States and the Urban Crisis 7-24

American County Government 6-13

American Federalism 7-69

American Odyssey 7-33

"American Urban Politics: Social Class, Political Structure and Public Goods" 3-70

America's Black Congressmen 4-27

America's Housing Problem: An Approach to Its Solution 5-159

"Applied Behavioral Science in Local Governments" 1-23

"Applied Behavior Science in Urban Administrative/Political Systems" 1-24

"Art of Giving Away Federal Dollars, The" 7-70

"Atlanta's Solution to the Race Problem" 4-128

"Attack on Snob Zoning, The" 5-8

At the Pleasure of the Mayor 2-31

"Attitudes of Blacks and Whites Toward City Services: Implications for Public Policy, The" 4-1

"Autonomy and Political Responsibility: The Enigmatic Verdict of a Cross-National Comparative Study of Community Dynamics" 3-49

B

"Barriers to Minority Employment: Case Studies of Selected Employers in Metropolitan Atlanta" 4-84

Barrio as an Internal Colony, The 4-8

"Battle to Open the Suburbs: New Attack on Zoning Laws" 6-7

C

D

E

F

G

Title Index

Q

R

Title Index

Z

SUBJECT INDEX

This index is alphabetized letter by letter. Numbers refer to entry numbers.

D

Subject Index

K

Kansas City, Missouri 2-6, 2-10a, 2-38
Kerner Commission 4-7

L

Labor unions
  job training 4-75
Leadership. See Political leadership
Lindsay, John V. 1-14, 1-36, 5-103
Local government
  census of 1-72
  citizen attitudes 3-21, 3-35, 3-101
  city politics 1-6, 2-13
  decentralization 1-50, 1-62, 1-80
  federal role in fragmentation 7-46
  fiscal crisis 7-88, 7-107, 7-108
  great cities 1-59
  major issues 7-52
  neighborhoods 1-65, 2-25
  political ethos 3-101
  political problems 2-13
  political theory 1-75
  policy planning 5-90
  state/local politics 7-4, 7-9, 7-44, 7-67
  state/local revenue sharing 7-5, 7-91
  structure 1-55, 6-71a
  system analysis 3-75
  See also Community politics; Governmental reform and reorganization; Public services; Urban government
London 1-62, 3-83
Los Angeles 1-4, 1-59, 4-4

M

Machine politics 2-56, 3-89
  Boss Ruef 2-3a
  Chicago 2-33
  council-manager government 1-22, 2-10a, 2-38
Curley, James Michael 2-39
Daley, Richard J. 2-33

Pendergasts 2-6, 2-10a, 2-38
.Management 1-7, 1-23, 1-60, 5-87
Mass media
  black community needs 4-120
  black press 4-125
  New York City 1-63
  press in city politics 1-6
  racism 4-62, 4-71
  urban decision making 3-65
  urban policy process 5-92
Mayors 1-42, 2-27, 2-28, 2-41
  and administrators 1-51
  big city 1-61
  black 2-28, 4-66, 4-89b
  and city managers 1-39, 1-40, 1-46, 1-53
  Gary, Indiana 2-28
  New York City 1-36, 1-40, 1-46, 1-53
  Oakland, California 2-41
  policy-making 1-23
  roles 1-23, 1-42, 1-61, 1-63
  state politics 2-33
  suburbia 1-40
  See also Lindsay, John V.
Metropolitan government, general 5-96, 6-34, 6-52
  annexation 6-56
  black perspective 4-85
  compared to decentralization 6-56
  comparisons 6-74, 6-87
  consolidation 6-19, 6-53, 6-93
  decision making 3-3
  federal policy 7-11
  Indianapolis, Indiana 6-93
  intergovernmental aspects 3-3
  Jacksonville 6-21, 6-55, 6-93
  local government reactions 6-51, 6-57
  Miami, Florida 6-82
  Nashville, Tennessee 6-15, 6-93
  opposition to consolidation 6-22, 6-54
  reform 6-34, 6-46, 6-52, 6-66, 6-75, 6-76, 6-86, 6-87
  suburban support for consolidation 6-57
  Tucson metropolitan area 6-57
  "two tier" government 1-43
  voter reaction 3-3, 3-59, 6-67, 6-78, 6-69, 6-81
Metropolitan Washington Council of

Subject Index

Subject Index